"This is a remarkable book that seeks to unite instead of divide. Encouraging readers to acknowledge evolution and a simultaneous belief in God and his scriptures is challenging. However, this book carefully and convincingly presents the demise of faith-based creationism and science-based atheism. It's a refreshing and light-hearted look at how the origin of our body in Africa and the origin of our spirit in Eden help us to understand who we are and where we came from."

—Dr. Alan Russell,
Director, McGowan Institute for Regenerative Medicine;
University Professor of Surgery;
and Executive Director of the Pittsburgh Tissue Engineering Initiative

"The Bible's story of creation is inconsistent with what we know today from scientific discoveries and achievements. However, Dr. Enick provides an insightful and rational, yet entertaining evaluation of the teachings of the Bible in the context of the evolution of the Earth and Universe. He elucidates that it is possible to maintain faith in God and accept the findings of the scientific community."

—Dr. Janice L. Panza,
Senior Applications Scientist, ChemImage; and Adjunct Assistant
Professor of Bioengineering, University of Pittsburgh

"Written in accessible language that is sprinkled with bits of light-hearted humor, Evolving in Eden is an important reminder that science and faith need not be in conflict. This book will speak to anyone who has ever wondered whether humans could possibly be both spiritual beings and an evolutionary success story."

—Jeremy Mohn,
Biology Instructor, Blue Valley Northwest High School,
Overland Park, KS

"Many people, religious and anti-religious, are convinced that sincere faith and scientific reason are mutually exclusive. This book is a powerful antidote to this divisive world-view. If you have ever been concerned about the intersection of science and faith, this book is for you. Best of all, the presentation is infused throughout with humor and graciousness, making the book a joy to read.

—*Dr. David Sholl,*
Professor of Chemical Engineering,
Carnegie Mellon University

"Dr. Enick presents the crucial and stimulating information needed to avoid being swept away by the onslaughts of secular evolutionists and their neo-creationist counterparts in their misguided struggle to hold sway over God's creation."

—*Rev. Michael Johnson,*
Pastor of Servanthood Ministries for Men

Evolving in Eden

Evolving in Eden

Why science and Genesis are both right about our origins

Bob Enick

Adameve Publishing

Evolving in Eden
Why science and Genesis are both right about our origins
Copyright © 2007 Bob Enick
Published by Adameve Publishing

Scripture taken from the *Holy Bible, New International Version.* Copyright © 1973, 1978, 1984 by International Bible Society. Used by permission of Zondervan. All rights reserved.

For further information, please contact:

600 Glenrock Drive
Bethel Park, PA 15102
enick@engr.pitt.edu

Book design by:

Arbor Books, Inc.
19 Spear Road, Suite 301
Ramsey, NJ 07446
www.arborbooks.com

Cover art and the single illustration by Randy Henderson.

Printed in the United States

Evolving in Eden
Why science and Genesis are both right about our origins
Bob Enick

1. Title   2. Author   3. Evolution & Religion/Bible & Science

Library of Congress Control Number: 2006905480
ISBN: 0-9787052-0-3

Dedication

This work is dedicated to my wonderful wife, Kathy, our five great kids, Liz, Lora, Grace, Nathan, and Zac, and our constantly chewing, chunky, chocolate lab Charlie. My original intent was to simply have my kids read this book before Charlie ate it!

My message is simple. You can believe in the inspiration of the Bible while acknowledging the findings of science concerning our origins, without surrendering your faith or your brain.

Table of Contents

Many feel that when it comes to science and religion, it is an either/or proposition. But could the Bible and science both be right, while the creationists and atheists are wrong?

There are numerous contradictory creationist explanations of our origins, yet each one claims to be based on scripture. Are any of them scientific theories? Are any of them even biblical?

Evolution means different things to different people; it is a factual history of life on Earth and a sound scientific theory of how life changed over time. But some have also used evolution less convincingly as a springboard for left-leaning philosophies and skeptical religious doctrines.

Maybe "In the beginning" corresponds to the Big Bang event that occurred 13.7 billion years ago! The biblical descriptions of a beginning of time and the creation of everything from nothing seem to correlate loosely with the scientific explanation of the origin of the universe.

of sea life? Were birds of Day Five flying before land animals of Day Six were crawling?

The creation of livestock, wild animals and crawling critters is ascribed to Day Six. What does science tell us about their origins?

What does it mean to be made in the image of God? What is it about us that is so similar to God and so distinct from all other forms of life?

What does it mean to be "human" from a scientific perspective? Is it the same as the biblical definition of "man"? What is the scientific explanation of our human origins?

God rested on the seventh day, and so should we. But the contention between creationists and evolutionists is about to reach its focal point after this brief break in the action.

Were the events in the Garden of Eden historical, allegorical, or a little bit of both? What difference does it make to the Christian message whether Adam and Eve were real people or symbolic figures? Is it critically important to the faith, or just to creationists?

Did you know that centuries ago, long before the birth of modern science, there were Hebrew scholars who believed that Adam was a human being born the old-fashioned way? They believed that Adam gained prominence because he was the first human to receive an eternal, spiritual nature.

If Adam was a real person, then he probably lived roughly 10,000 years ago, based on Bible genealogies and the skills demonstrated by him and his immediate family. Creationists may try to push his birthday back to 40,000 B.C or 150,000 B.C. or 5,000,000 B.C. in a vain attempt to prove that Adam and Eve were the first and only humans on Earth when God formed them by hand.

stuff. You may want to think twice before claiming that you have great spiritual insight into how or when God made anything.

The creation story seems to make the most sense if you realize that a hypothetical observer on the surface of the Earth gives the descriptions, rather that an angel in orbit around the planet.

Fossils are valuable tools for understanding the history of life on Earth because they identify the plant or animal's structure and they also indicate the time of death.

Darwin's grand idea—that natural selection is the process responsible for the changing forms of life—is explained in the words of several prominent evolutionists.

The scientific community doesn't like to advertise it, but there are plenty of brilliant, creative, articulate, famous researchers who think that believers are stupid, God is non-existent, and the Bible is baloney. Is it any wonder many Christians think evolutionists are evil and that evolution is a sham?

The Big Bang model of the universe provides a cohesive explanation for the history of our universe. But keep your eyes on String Theory, too, because it may be able to unify relativity and quantum mechanics while shedding new insights into the origin of the universe—or universes!

It's no secret that no one knows how life began. But there are plenty of folks trying to figure it out. You should give them five centuries to sort it out before declaring that the origin of life was supernatural. Here are as few of their ideas.

Did man and dinosaurs dwell together? Did dinosaurs eat people? Did people hunt dinosaurs? The Flintstones and Youth Earth Creationists would say "Yes, yes, yes!", but everyone else says "No, no, no!" Here's why.

Introduction

My wife and I are convinced that our five children are gifts from God, although the temptation to return our teenagers to their Maker has been overwhelming at times. Despite my appreciation of their spirituality, I am well aware that these carnivorous bio-machines are living, breathing expressions of their twisted little DNA. Nonetheless, the more I learn about the biology that guides their development, the more I value them as evidence of God's creativity. I feel the same way about the universe, Earth, and the life it supports. My impressions of how smart God is only deepen when scientists uncover the mechanisms that explain the origin and behavior of His creation. Why, then, is it so hard for many Christians to acknowledge the scientific discoveries that unveil the beginnings and transformations of God's creation? Why is there still so much stress between science and religion? The reasons are apparent to those who take their kids to public school from Monday through Friday and follow up with Sunday School over the weekend. At church, droves of Christian kids have met well-meaning believers who consider "evolution" to be "evilution", a devious form of atheism that lurks below a thin layer of unsubstantiated technical gibberish. On Monday mornings, some of their public school biology teachers have informed these same young people that Genesis is just another goofy creation legend that became obsolete when Darwin's great idea arrived on the scene. As a result, Christian doctrines describing a loving Creator and scientific discoveries substantiating the evolution of life have been presented to them as incompatible. It is no wonder that many high school and college kids divorce themselves from their faith or their intellect over these seemingly irreconcilable differences.

There is no need to join the creationist or atheist camps in order to understand our origins, though. Several paths are available to those who sense that science and the Bible may both be on the right track! The easiest way to patch things up between scientists and believers is to accept the well-documented findings of modern science and to believe in the spiritual truths of the Bible, while keeping in mind that the creation story is ancient mythology. The first three chapters of Genesis, from the creation of the heavens until Adam and Eve were booted out of the Garden of Eden, can be regarded as a spiritual treasure chest that contains neither historical nor scientific information. Many would also lump the next eight chapters of Genesis, all the way to the birth of Abraham, into the collection of myths. This perspective extinguishes those stomach-churning moments that occur when deeply held spiritual convictions concerning the creation story fly in the face of well-substantiated scientific findings. Many Christians have followed this strategy in good conscience, and I share some of their sentiments. I don't need scientists to confirm the Bible's inspiration, and I don't expect the Bible to provide detailed scientific explanations of natural processes.

I do not think that Genesis is *completely* mythological, though. I believe that some portions of the first chapters of the Bible contain inspired, casual glimpses of actual creation events and real people, and that's what sets this book apart from most other publications that encourage you to acknowledge the conclusions of modern science while retaining your faith in God. I don't think that there is enough technical substance in these scriptures to prove that science validates the Bible or vice versa, and there certainly is not any data in Genesis that can be used to develop scientific theories or historical timelines. I will try to persuade you, though, that the creation story may contain a few divinely inspired peeks at the Big Bang, the emergence of the continents from beneath the ocean waters, the clearing of Earth's atmosphere, and the capacity of our planet to produce life. I'll even point out several biblical clues that if Adam and Eve were actual people, they were *not* necessarily the first and only humans on Earth; they were preceded by and surrounded by humans of unspecified origin.

Speaking of Adam and Eve, their story is of particular importance because most people are far more interested in the origins of man than the beginnings of bananas. In fact, the historical authenticity of Adam and Eve is the *only* topic related to human evolution that many believers really care about. Some of the faithful insist that Adam and Eve were the first and only humans when they were made by God in present-day Iraq, and that all people who have ever lived descended from this odd couple. The fossil record indicates otherwise. The history of *Homo sapiens* extends back about 150,000—200,000 years to Africa. Three other species of humans, the big-browed *Homo erectus*, the bulky *Homo neanderthalensis* and the teeny tiny *Homo floresiensis*, were living during most of the same period, but these species became extinct forty thousand to ten thousand years ago. Many other extinct human and human-like species date back about five million years. The genetic record hidden in our DNA also points toward our ancient human heritage[1]. It traces our *Homo sapien* ancestry to a small population that in Africa over a hundred thousand years ago. These scientific results are far removed from the solitary couple in the Garden of Eden. The Adam and Eve of the Bible—regardless of when you think they might have lived—could not have been the sole biological ancestors of mankind. It is impossible; and that's a hard pill for many Bible-believers to swallow.

But is it necessary to then immediately conclude that Adam and Eve were mythical characters? Not really. It's the "literal" interpretation of Genesis needs to be re-examined. The mundane details of the lives of Adam and Eve after their eviction from the Garden of Eden and the numerous references to them in the rest of the Bible make it apparent (to me at least) that the inspired authors of the Bible did indeed consider these two to be real people rather than symbols of primitive humanity. But Genesis also provides a few hints that Adam and Eve were *not* necessarily the first and only humans. For example, there are several passages in Genesis indicating that Adam and Eve lived in the company of other people who were *not* their descendants. Although creationists like to invoke the Hillbilly Intermarriage Clause to explain how all of these folks were actually one big happy inbred family, the Bible simply presents them as Adam's neighbors. In fact, long before the birth of modern science, several ancient Hebrew scholars taught that Adam had human ancestors and was surrounded by humans that were unrelated to him.

But if Adam was not the first-and-only human being, then what made him so special in God's eyes? I believe that Adam was a spiritual pioneer, our spiritual representative before God, and the direct ancestor of Abraham. From this perspective, the science of human evolution can be readily acknowledged while maintaining a belief in the relatively recent advent of our spirituality and the actual existence of Adam and Eve. God interrupted the long history of humanity and miraculously breathed an eternal spirit into our being, thereby upgrading us to "man"; humans with an eternal, spiritual nature. Perhaps the intangible, undetectable, immutable spirit that allows us to know our Creator is the attribute that most dramatically distinguishes us from all other creatures. Maybe being made in the image of God simply means that we have an eternal spirit, and Adam was one of the first, if not *the* first, to get this upgrade!

Having a natural body that houses a supernatural spirit is not a new idea. Jesus taught that man had distinct spiritual and physical natures in one of the most prominent passages of the New Testament. When Jesus admonished Nicodemus, a prominent Pharisee, to be born again if he wanted to see God's kingdom, Nicodemus countered with a humorous touch of skepticism. *John 3:4 "How can a man be born when he is old?" Nicodemus asked. "Surely he cannot enter a second time into his mother's womb to be born!"* Jesus answered with a brief biology blurb that tied the origin of our body to our parents, but linked our spiritual origin to the heavenly Father. *John 3:6 Flesh gives birth to flesh, but the Spirit gives birth to spirit.* The Old Testament also teaches that we have two components. The book of Ecclesiastes invokes symbols of death and dying to remind us of our impending death of our body while affirming the eternal existence of our spirit, *Ecclesiastes 12:1,6-7 Remember your Creator in the days of your youth, before the days of trouble come and the years approach when you will say, "I find no pleasure in them"—...Remember him—before the silver cord is severed, or the golden bowl is broken; before the pitcher is shattered at the spring, or the wheel broken at the well, and the dust returns to the ground it came from, and the spirit returns to God who gave it.*

Bottom line? In some magnificent and mysterious manner, God may have set the stage for a universe (or perhaps universes[2]) to emerge that yielded a planet upon which life formed and humans eventually evolved by purely natural means over unimaginably long periods of time, after which He supernaturally blessed us with a spiritual nature in the not-so-distant past. If you can accept this perspective, if only for a few hours, then you can gain a deeper appreciation of who we are and how we got here from scientific and spiritual perspectives. Science enlightens us about the human body and how it came to be, while the Bible reveals the spiritual truths concerning our relationship with the Creator. You *can* believe in God and trust in the Bible while exploring the wonders of our evolving universe. You can even believe in the historical existence of Adam and Eve as spiritual pioneers while understanding the wondrous science of human evolution. Hopefully this book will help you to sort through these issues without losing your faith or your mind. If I'm right, then it is possible to retain a belief in the inspiration of Genesis and the existence of Adam and Eve while accepting the hard science that describes our origins. If I'm wrong, then those who acknowledge the achievements of science but regard the early chapters of Genesis as divinely inspired mythology have the advantage.

The main body of the text is designed to be a quick read, but the appendices are packed with information for those of you that love to obsess over details. Most scriptural passages are taken from the New International Version[3] (NIV) of the Bible. Recently published science books intended for the general public have been used as references because these books are easy to understand and provide references to peer-reviewed scientific journal articles packed with data that back up the scientific theories. This will allow you to further explore the topics surveyed in this book while sipping cappuccinos at a cozy local bookstore rather than wandering through a food-prohibiting university library in search of baffling journal articles.

References
1. James Shreeve, The Greatest Journey Ever Told—The Trail of Our DNA, National Geographic, March 2006, 60–69
2. Leonard Susskind, The Cosmic Landscape—String Theory and the Illusion of Intelligent Design, Little, Brown and Company, New York, NY, 2006
3. Scripture taken from the HOLY BIBLE, NEW INTERNATIONAL VERSION. Copyright © 1973, 1978, 1984 International Bible Society.

Chapter 1. Who's Right?

Who and Why vs. What, Where, When and How

The Bible and science provide fascinating explanations of our origins; you should enjoy both of them. The Bible yields a fleeting glimpse of what God made, while emphasizing His role as Creator, His ownership of the Earth, the pleasure He takes in creation, and the unique privilege that we have of being made in His image. Scientists, on the other hand, explain when the universe began, how Earth formed, how natural laws govern our surroundings, what forms of life have inhabited this planet and where they lived. The Bible tells us "Who" made everything and "why" He did it, along with a dash of "what" He made. Science serves up gobs of the "what", "where", "when" and "how" and "why" things originated and behave as they do[1]. God has given us a spiritual nature, and the church typically does an excellent job of explaining the power and glory of the Creator[2]. God has also given man the curiosity required to understand nature, and scientists do an outstanding job of explaining the workings of the universe. There is no need to compromise the Bible in order to appreciate science, and you don't have to dumb down science to appreciate God.

Two Wrongs Make Two Wrongs

The peaceful co-existence of science and religion is reassuring to many people, but it is completely unacceptable to those who fuel the creation vs. evolution debate: evolution-bashing creationists and faith-bashing scientists. These two groups are not representative of mainstream Christianity or the scientific community. Nonetheless, their combative disputes, which are almost as exciting as my daughters' battles over who-stole-whose underwear, grabs our attention during school board battles and legislative debates over what is taught in public school science classes. Let's take a quick look at some of the trademarks of these cantankerous creationists and antagonistic atheists.

Some think that anyone dumb enough to believe in a Creator is a creationist, but this classification is typically promoted only by the staunchest atheists. I like to think of a creationist as someone who claims that his particular rendering of Bible yields scientific facts and theories that define the origins, history, or behavior of stuff. For example, most creationists insist that the Bible forbids plants or animals from ever evolving from one species into another. When subjected to even the mildest level of scrutiny, however, each brand of creationism fails to fulfill the most basic requirement of a scientific hypothesis; it cannot be tested and confirmed, even in part, even indirectly. Creationism is a belief to be accepted rather than a set of ideas to be rigorously examined. Despite its shortcomings, creationism is fun! Scientists spend their lives digging and exploring and studying and calculating and figuring complicated things out, but creationists can kick back, relax and declare the same puzzling phenomena to be miracles.

In the other corner, we have a group of notable researchers who litter their remarkable research of nature with scathing atheistic barbs. Their scientific work is often rock solid, but these folks just can't resist throwing in a little socialism, atheism, communism, fascism, environmentalism, skepticism, Marxism, astigmatism, or rheumatism into the mix. They dismiss the Almighty as a delusion that helps intellectually challenged people confront death, pay taxes, obey authorities, win the lottery, handle the stress of disease, or account for the wonders of creation. These smug scientists are happy to enlighten all of us dopey believers that God, who Himself evolved from an impotent collection of little gods into a singular deity, exists only in the deep recesses of our brains alongside the Tooth Fairy. These skeptics simply use the tools of their trade to prove what they presuppose; God doesn't exist because He can't be detected. Although many Christians may not be sophisticated enough to sort out the details of microbiology or quantum physics, nearly all believers can smell an attack on their faith a mile away. Consequently, many of the faithful—whether boneheaded or brilliant—refuse to believe anything these intelligent, articulate, atheistic scientists have to say, even if their carefully documented studies on the origins of the universe, the planet, life, or humans are absolutely correct.

Left Behind

The constant bickering between creationist believers and atheistic scientists shouldn't stop you from exploring our origins. There are far more productive relationships between science and religion than can foster our minds and our faith[3]. How can we sort through the contentious issues related to disputes over where we came from? Confession is good for the soul, so let's start with the faults of the faithful!

Creationists may be right on with God, but they are left behind concerning science. I should know! As a teenager I was engaged in just about every form of creationism and acne eradication known to man. For example, I believed that the Earth was made in six days roughly six thousand years ago, but three years later I realized those six days could have been four billion years, but one year after that I thought that Earth was first made four billion years ago and then remade in six days only six thousand years ago! Pretty persuasive reasoning, eh? Perhaps if the church summons the courage to recognize the impotence of the muddled messages it has fostered about our origins, then unbelievers who doubt God's role as Creator and Lord of all creation may more readily believe the gospel. So before we start whining about skeptical professors and atheistic researchers that malign God, let's own up to the trouble the church has brought upon itself.

References
1. Alan H. Guth, The Inflationary Universe—The Quest for a New Theory of Cosmic Origins, Helix Books, Perseus Books, Reading MA, 1997, ix, preface by Alan Lightman
2. Appendix A
3. I. Barbour; When Science Meets Religion—Enemies, Strangers or Partners; Harper Collins, 2000, 11-38

Chapter 2. The Enemy is Us

Brilliant men and women who believed in God, such as Isaac Newton, Gregor Mendel and Lord Kelvin, have made their marks in science. These fine folks did it the right way, though. Newton didn't develop the laws of mechanics via an intensive study of the walls of Jericho, Mendel's study of genetics was not derived from the who-begat-who listing in the Book of Genesis, and Kelvin's development of the absolute temperature scale was not related to the Lake of Fire. These scientists proposed hypotheses, thought of ways to test their ideas, made careful observations, interpreted their results, concluded whether they had a sound finding, and presented their results in such a way that anyone—saint or sinner—could verify their discovery.

Many creationists, however, have forged all forms of pseudoscience simply by deducing scientific principles from scriptures containing simple observations of nature[1] in a manner akin to the proverbial squeezing of blood out of a rock. Many of the faithful, especially scientifically untrained church hierarchy, have made embarrassing claims that had absolutely no scientific basis and a questionable scriptural foundation. Remember these other golden oldies?

A Poor Track Record

Flat Earth Society

Several early church writers who lived between 200-600 A.D., including Cyril of Jerusalem and Saint John Chrysostom, ridiculed the notion of a round Earth based on their own deductions from scripture that Earth was flat. The Bible never purports that the planet is a slab, however. The scriptures only hint that Earth is suspended in space, *Job 26:7 He spreads out the northern skies over empty space; he suspends the earth over nothing.*, and that the horizon appears as a circle from our perspective, *Isaiah 40:22 He sits enthroned above the circle of the earth...* The ultimate victory over flat Earth proponents was an easy win for science and explorers, including devout Catholics such as Christopher Columbus.

Geocentric Universe

The sixteenth and seventeenth centuries were not much better for the church. The Catholic and Protestant churches agreed that the sun moved around the Earth, even though there was not a *single* verse in the Bible that substantiated their claim. The Bible only describes the sun's movements from the perspective of an observer on the surface of the planet (a frame of reference that will be critical to understanding the Genesis creation story). *Psalm 19:4-6 In the heavens he has pitched a tent for the sun, which is like a bridegroom coming forth from his pavilion, like a champion rejoicing to run his course. It rises at one end of the heavens and makes its circuit to the other; nothing is hidden from its heat.* Using these poetic verses, they deduced incorrect geocentric astronomical theories and disparaged those who, like Copernicus and Galileo, sought to explore God's universe without being harassed by religious censors.

Young Earth Geology

The church's science slump stretched right into the eighteenth century. The creation controversy blossomed when scientific findings began to contradict a popular interpretation of the creation of man, in which the Master Potter created Adam's body out of dirt and then literally breathed life into him. A timeline of man's history was derived from Bible genealogies, and it indicated that Adam was created in 4004 B.C. Because man was made on the sixth day, Earth itself was declared to be only five days older than Adam! Therefore God made the entire world roughly 6000 years ago. Motivated by a simple desire to find out how old Earth was, geologists and naturalists—many of whom were Christians—closely examined the evidence and determined that this planet was ancient. These findings were first reported before Darwin was born and were soundly in place before Darwin's book on evolution by natural selection was published, therefore these geologists could not have been part of a vast left-wing conspiracy to accommodate the extensive time demands of evolution! The argument over the planet's age continued through the eighteenth and nineteenth centuries, even though the evidence demonstrating its antiquity became overwhelming. The scientists won the battle of the ages long ago. Some die-hard creationists *still* maintain that Earth is a few thousand years old, even though recent discoveries and improvements in analytical techniques that occurred during the twentieth and twenty-first centuries have only served to reinforce Earth's incredibly old age[2].

These embarrassing moments of church-related pseudo-science left mid-nineteenth century Bible literalists with a weak legacy. They were ill-prepared for the evolution's direct assault on their doctrines.

Evilution

Although the origin of various life forms had been batted about for thousands of years, it was not until Charles Darwin and Alfred Wallace independently determined how species originated that evolution became a vivid threat to many believers[3]. (Wallace presented the mechanism behind evolution at the same time as Darwin, but Wallace rightly garnered less recognition because Darwin's work was formulated twenty years earlier, was based on far more empirical evidence, and was more thoroughly documented[4].) Darwin's landmark book, *On the Origin of Species by Means of Natural Selection, or the Preservation of Favoured Races in the Struggle for Life*, published in 1859, explained that contemporary life had descended from earlier, different forms of life over a long period of time through a process that he referred to as "descent with modification". Ultimately, all forms of life could trace their history to an ancient common ancestor. Darwin's grand idea vanquished any hopes for clinging to the notion that all plants and animals had a supernatural, recent, and instantaneous origin, therefore, it isn't surprising that many Christians viewed evolution as a personal affront on their beliefs. Darwin realized how offensive the thought of evolving from a lower form of life would be to the faithful, as expressed in this classic understatement from his later book, *The Descent of Man*, "The main conclusion arrived at in this work, namely that man is descended from some lowly organized life form will, I regret to think, be highly distasteful to many."[5] Darwin knew that when people find something to be disgusting, they tend to disbelieve it, regardless of the evidence. It's just like the moment when your children realize that their life began when Mom and Dad had a romp in the sack! Nothing is grosser to kids than the thought of their parents having sex, and it takes a bit of courage for them to overcome the repulsiveness of that image and acknowledge the true nature of their biological beginning.

The notion of man evolving from an animal was equally offensive to those who cherished the recent, instantaneous molding of man by God in the Garden of Eden. It still is! All that you have to do to get many Christians riled up is to spew out a little tidbit, like "Can you believe scientists think that we came from monkeys?" Not that evolution teaches that we came from monkeys, but saying that we did gets the blood pressure surging more quickly than explaining that all apes, including chimpanzees, orangutans, gibbons, and siamangs, shared a common ancestor with humans millions of years ago. In fact, a strong case can be made that—regardless of how uncomfortable it may make you feel—humans are apes. African apes at that, because genetic studies indicate that we are more closely related to chimpanzees and gorillas, than we are to Asian apes such as gibbons and orangutans[6]. We may even consider humans to be the third chimpanzee roaming the planet, the others being the common chimp and the pygmy chimp (a.k.a. bonobo)—our nearest genetic relatives[7]. Such comparisons with hairy beasts incense creationists because they insist that only humans are made in the image of God, who is usually depicted as a bearded, retired, white male of European descent. I was never impressed by the creationist outrage against those who noted the obvious similarities between humans and apes. I had a dopey college roommate with a 1.35 GPA who was so hairy that he left a ½"-thick carpet of black curls on the bathroom floor every time he showered; I am convinced that he was 99% gorilla. Even my own back resembles a shag rug! Anyway, many Christians felt that evolution diminished man's status from the finest example of God's careful craftsmanship to a big-brained fuzzy mammal produced by a slow, natural, impersonal, brutal, unguided, ungodly process.

Darwin was well aware that his book would offend those who, like his wife, maintained a literal interpretation of Genesis. Although Darwin did not write his book to become a Bible-basher, some Christians viewed his work as a malicious attack on scripture. This is a bit harsh, given Darwin's own muddled religious convictions, which wavered between agnosticism, theism, and deism[8]. Despite his shifting sentiments concerning the nature of the Almighty, Darwin's convictions about the role of God in the evolutionary process was unwavering; He was unnecessary. Consider his response to Alfred Wallace's remarks that God's divine will was quietly influencing the progress of evolution. Darwin reminded Wallace that together they had produced a "child"; the idea that natural selection was the mechanism that shaped the evolution of life. Darwin was not impressed by Wallace's injection of supernatural shenanigans into the evolution of man, saying, "I differ grievously from you…I hope you have not murdered too completely your own and my child."[9] Wallace never did shake his belief that an Overruling Intelligence was essential for nature itself to have produced matter, life, animals, or humans. But don't even think about adding him to a list of Bible-believing anti-Darwinists because Wallace coveted the sixth sense; he tried to see dead people![10].

Ironically, Darwin ended the first edition of his book by dropping a few crumbs to the religious right. He suggested that the Creator may have fashioned the first form of life and then let it evolve, saying "Thus from the war of nature, from famine and death, the most exalted object of which we are capable of conceiving, namely the production of higher animals, directly follows. There is a grandeur in this view of life, with its several powers, having been originally breathed by the Creator into a few forms or into one; and that, whilst this planet has gone cycling on according to the fixed laws of gravity, from so simple a beginning endless forms most beautiful and most wonderful have been, and are being evolved." Although the phrase "by the Creator" was deleted in later editions, which has led most to question the sincerity of its initial inclusion, Darwin prefaced subsequent editions with an exhortation[11] quoted from Francis Bacon's *Advancement of Learning,* "To conclude, therefore, let no man out of a weak conceit of sobriety, or ill-applied moderation, think or maintain that a man can search too far or be too well studied in the book of God's word, or in the book of God's works; divinity or philosophy; but rather let men endeavour an endless progress of proficience in both." Although that quote seems to indicate that Darwin retained a measure of respect for the God of the Bible and the Bible itself, he routinely associated the origin of God with the ascent of human culture, reason, imagination, curiosity and wonder rather than the actual existence of a supernatural being[12].

The Empire Strikes Back

Some nineteenth century Bible-believing Christians did not go berserk when Darwin's theory gained notoriety. B.B. Warfield, for example, did not view Darwin's naturalistic evolution as incompatible with God's role as Creator[13]. Many Christians, however, were sent reeling. They came to believe that a Christian could not be an evolutionist or acknowledge that Earth was ancient without compromising their faith or the integrity of the Bible, which remains a viewpoint promoted by many contemporary creationists[14]. Numerous doctrines, many of which were first developed during the first half of the nineteenth century by conservative Christian geologists who felt compelled to provide "Bible-based" reconciliations of the antiquity of the Earth with Genesis[15], were reformulated to "prove" that evolution was wrong.

These anti-evolution theologies continue to flourish within contemporary churches, bookstores and websites. Their core concepts are best illustrated by how they answer one simple question: *What did God know, and when did He know it?* Oops, that was the Watergate question! Let me try again. *How did God make stuff and when did He make it?* First, let us consider the multitude of answers that creationists give for the "when" part of the question.

Glory Daze

Remember the six "days" of creation in Genesis One? On each of six successive days, marked by morning and evening, God made something. He then rested on the seventh day. Methods of determining the length of these "days" could therefore provide a direct answer to the question of when God made stuff[16]. Let's take a look at a few of the more popular ideas concerning what these days were, keeping in mind that there are as many variations of these notions as there are shades of paint at your local hardware store.

Working the Day Shift

The six days were six days. Any questions? Many creationists holding this view think that they alone have the courage and faith to believe God's Word at face value. Consider the assertiveness of John MacArthur, an outstanding Bible teacher and preacher, who said, "In fact, it is virtually impossible to begin with a straightforward reading of Genesis and arrive at the opinion that the universe is older than a few thousand years"[17]. "Straightforward reading of Genesis"? Just ask MacArthur, or anyone else who thinks that the "literal" reading is straightforward, how there could be light on Day One before the sun or stars were made on Day Four; you'll get some of the most twisted, unbiblical answers that you can imagine, including the existence of mysterious, high-wattage, celestial, angelic light-bearers! "Virtually impossible" to disagree with the 6000 year-old planet conclusion? Wow! That's quite a claim to make for interpreting the exact meaning of one of the most disputed passages in the Bible, especially when scientists have known for two centuries that the Earth is incredibly ancient. Creationists holding this 144-hour perspective will tell you that this viewpoint has been the church's position since the first century, and to think otherwise is to betray the true faith of our Christian forefathers. They are wrong. It may have not been the most popular opinion, but Christians have been kicking around the possibility that the six days served as metaphors since the second century, including St. Augustine's sixteen hundred year-old reflections on this topic[18].

Moses was a Weekling

It has been proposed that the author of Genesis, whether Moses[19] or an earlier author[20], received daily revelations of creation updates from God. The six days of creation merely corresponded to the amount of time it took to record the information found in Genesis One. Therefore these six days had nothing to do with how long it took God to create anything!

God Drives a Fiat

Each day contained an announcement of God's creative intent, or fiat, followed by a comment of what subsequently unfolded over a long period of time[21]. God spoke out the commands for creation to come into being over six days, but the physical creation that began at the moment of the fiat could have taken billions of years to unfold. It is like a waitress shouting back six orders to the kitchen during six seconds, but the cook needing plenty of time to get them ready. Further, the meals may not emerge from the kitchen in the same order that they were placed.

God Drives a Spaceship

One remarkable aspect of relativity is that clocks of different folks can tick along at different strokes (yes, I have been influenced by years of reading Dr. Seuss books). For example, Earth-bound observers would wonder why an astronaut traveling at a velocity close to the speed of light—the universal speed limit—would be moving so sluggishly within his spaceship. Even the second hand on the astronaut's wristwatch would appear to be creeping along! Under such circumstances, the space traveler could accelerate his craft in such a manner as to make a galactic U-turn and return to our planet. Upon exiting his craft, he could be just six days older while six thousand years had transpired on Earth! Aha! Perhaps as God was creating the universe, He was on the Starship Enterprise, cruising about the universe at velocities just under the speed of light. Six days could have elapsed on God's wristwatch as He commanded creation to emerge while fourteen billion years elapsed in our corner of the universe![22]

God Needed Some Recreation

God might have taken billions of years to form the universe and Earth. Some unknown, unspecified process could have accounted for the appearance of early life forms. The fossil record could have been deposited over billions of years. There could have even been humans prior to Adam, but these guys were either mere animals or an evil race worthy of God's judgment. Either way, they were wiped out by a planetary flood, sometimes called Lucifer's flood, allegedly described in the second verse of the Bible, *Genesis 1:2 Now the earth was formless and empty, darkness was over the surface of the deep, and the Spirit of God was hovering over the waters.* God was then anxious to be back in the ruling-the-planet business, so He then re-made Earth and its contemporary life forms in six literal days[23-25].

God was Bored

The substance of Earth may have taken a long time to form, but God had to intervene recently during six 24-hour days to transform the planet from a stubborn state of lifeless chaos into a magnificent fertile planet[26]. It's as if God was about to fail His science project because life didn't form, so He snuck in a few miracles just before He handed it in to get a better grade. The six days of miraculous creation that yielded life could have therefore been preceded by billions of boring, lifeless years.

God Had a Long Day

The days of creation correspond to long, sequential periods of time that transpired during the development of this planet. Rather than describing the duration of creation in terms of billions or millions of years, which none of the Bible's early readers would grasp, God couched it in terms of a week, with each successive day referring to a sequential era[27] of unspecified duration[28]. There are indeed some biblical arguments for believing that the days of creation may refer to periods of time greater than 24 hours[29, 30]. The Hebrew grammatical gyrations used to promote this view are not very compelling, however. Despite claims to the contrary offered up by creationists[31], there were Hebrew words and phrases at the disposal of the author of Genesis that could have been used to describe very long periods of time[32].

God Was Framed

My favorite! God selected a simple literary framework, the week, for the story of creation. The exact chronology of events was not the emphasis of His text; therefore the days of Genesis One may be completely unrelated to the sequence or duration of creation events. Perhaps God preferred literary simplicity over scientific precision because He knew that the men who were inspired to write the scriptures had no understanding of timelines, biology, physics and geology. The most compelling indication that the creation week is a literary vehicle is found in the pattern of what was associated with each day. Kingdoms were established during Days One, Two and Three, while the kingdom "rulers" were made during Days Four, Five and Six. This parallelism is illustrated by the correlation of the kingdoms and rulers of *Light* in Days One and Four, the *Seas and Skies* in Days Two and Five, and *Land* in Days Three and Six[33].

Day	Kingdoms	Day	Rulers
1	Light	4	Sun, moon & stars
2	Sea and sky	5	Life in seas & birds in sky
3	Land and plant life	6	Animals and man on the land

Conrad Myers presented a similar framework, but he correlated it with three problems noted in the second verse of the Bible; Earth was dark, watery and formless. Days One, Two and Three describe the corrective measures taken to address these problems, while Days Four, Five and Six describe the respective populations[34].

Problem	Preparation	Population
Genesis 1:2	Days 1–3	Days 4–6
Darkness	1a creation of light (day)	4a creation of sun
	1b separation from darkness (night)	4b creation of moon, stars
Watery abyss	2a creation of firmament	5a creation of birds
	2b separation of waters above from waters below	5b creation of fish

Formless Earth	3a separation of earth from sea	6a creation of land animals
	3b creation of vegetation	6b creation of humans
"without *form* and *void*"	Formlessness is formed	Void is filled

I find the Problem-Preparation-Population framework far more persuasive, and much more fun to say three times fast, than the Kingdom-Ruler explanation, so I will refer to it often in the remainder of this book. Both of these tables indicate that the days of Genesis One may have been intelligently designed to provide an outline that favored prose over physics while affirming God's role as Creator.

How Did He Do That?

Let's move on to the second part of the creation question that creationists answer with scriptures in an effort to stifle science. *How* did God make stuff? There is a truckload of contradictory creationist teachings on *how* God created things, each of which is peppered with miracles[35,36]. I have taken the liberty to assign acronyms for the major creationist theories, following the lead of a prominent Christian broadcaster, Hank Hanegraaf, a.k.a. the "Bible Answer Man". I usually enjoy Hank's broadcast when driving home from work and I agree with him on just about every spiritual topic. When he takes up science-related matters, though, I can only listen for a minute before turning on the oldies station in an attempt to avert road rage. In his exposé of the lies of science entitled *The FACE that Demonstrates the FARCE of Evolution*, Hanegraaf correlates each letter to the alleged failings of evolution[37]. "F" is for Fossil Follies, "A" is for Ape-Men Fiction, Fraud and Fantasy, "C" is for the inability of Chance to account for complex life, and "E" is for the ability to use Empirical Science to prove that evolution is false. He throws in "R" for the Recapitulation Theory—a mistaken notion that claimed an embryo's development replayed its entire evolutionary history, which saw its demise in the early twentieth century[38]. The FARCE of evolution is meant to be an easy-to-remember-when-you-bump-into-a-raving-scientist slap-in-the-face of evolutionary science, and Hanegraaf even authored a pocket-sized version of his views on FARCE to make an assault on nearby evolutionists easier than ever[39]. It would be easy to follow Hank's lead and produce condescending acronyms for creationist ideas concerning how God created things, such as groups that may proudly declare, "**Intelligent design is our theory!**" I'll stick with acronyms that are a bit more cordial, though.

TOES—Tired Of Evolution and Science

TOES are satisfied knowing that God is their Creator. They don't have time or interest for any of these creation vs. evolution arguments. They don't care how God made anything. In fact, no self-respecting member of the TOES would lower himself to buy a book like this one! They think that this fuss is boring and irrelevant to their daily struggles. I don't blame them. Despite what creationist preachers say, it is easy to live a fulfilled life while remaining completely ignorant of the details of human origins; people have been doing it for millions—or is it thousands?—of years. The pleas offered up by scientists who insist that we cannot appreciate who we really are until we understand the biological origins of our species also ring hollow for the TOES. After all, when was the last time that you heard of a stocky high school linebacker bursting into tears upon discovering that he wasn't a direct descendant of the Neanderthals after all?

YEC—Young Earth Creationists

The YEC acronym is an old one that I take no credit for. This is a well-established group with a comprehensive set of clear-cut marching orders and doctrines. For example, Henry Morris and John Morris have authored a trilogy that explores the scriptural foundations of Young Earth Creationism[40], the scientific basis for creationism and the errors of modern science[41] and the corrupting influence of evolution on the social and religious fabric of society and the church[42]. Young Earth Creationists believe that the Earth was fashioned supernaturally during six consecutive days. Early YECs started out under the banner of a 6000-year old universe. Swamped with evidence that human civilization and several U.S. senators were older than that, many YECs now concede that the universe and Earth may actually be tens of thousands of years old.

YECs aren't too sure how God made things, but they are certain that He made them really, really, really fast! YECs believe that all species, including humans, were created supernaturally, suddenly, and recently. There was no death, disease or violence until Adam and Eve sinned. There wasn't time for any of those maddeningly slow geologic or biologic processes that scientists love so much; therefore Noah's flood is credited for shaping the planet's geology and seeding the fossil record[43], even though that "solution" provides believers with more problems than answers[44]. Once the dominant species of creationists, YECs are now going the way of the dinosaur 65 million years ago. Their refutations of modern science are so silly that most churches have quietly abandoned them.

YEOUCH—Young Earth, Old Universe Creation History

Given the mountain of evidence that galaxies can be billions of years old, YEOUCHs concede that God began his creative work eons ago. The raw materials of the universe and the dark, lifeless Earth may have also taken billions of years to form, but the supernatural intervention of God within a week was required to shake the planet out of its lifeless doldrums and establish a fertile planet. YEOUCHs are YECs, but with extra time before Day One[45].

CIA—Created with the Illusion of Age

Although the CIA realizes that the scientific evidence of an ancient universe and a somewhat younger yet still ancient Earth is extremely persuasive, they want to retain their belief in the 24-hour-per-day interpretation of Genesis One. Therefore they postulate that God created antiques. That's right, God makes things with the illusion of age. The Creator deceptively made new things look old in order to…uh…ah…um…hmmm…well, just because He wanted to, and that's that! For example, Earth is 6000 years old but it has the appearance of a 4.6 billion year old planet[46-48]. My Mom says that despite her appearance she isn't old, so I guess she's a member of the CIA too!

GATORS—Gaps and Theories of Re-creation Science

GATORS believe that there were two eras during which humans

were on Earth, separated by a gap of unspecified duration. God may have made things by some slow-poke process the first time around, but He rushed the second time He had to do it. The first humans, pre-Adamites, roamed an Earth populated by now-extinct plants and animals. Some even believe that Lucifer had a throne on Earth during this period of time, based on Old Testament passages such as Ezekiel 28:13-17. God wiped out this biosphere in a planetary flood that is described in the opening verses of the Bible and in the New Testament passage 2 Peter 3:5,6. He then supernaturally re-created the Earth in six days[49-51].

REDS—Reasons for Everyone to Doubt Scientists

Scientists typically present their findings in a professional manner that lacks spiritual bias. Scientific organizations usually avoid extracting spiritual conclusions from their work. Nevertheless, some very famous scientists have denigrated the Bible, mocked Christianity and attributed belief in God solely to brain chemistry or innate stupidity. Therefore Christians have justifiably mounted a vigorous defense of their faith against these atheists, and no one does it better than Philip Johnson in books such as *Darwin on Trial*, *Objections Sustained* and *Defeating Darwinism by Opening Minds*[52-54]. REDS remind their audience that atheistic evolutionists may hold amoral spiritual, philosophical, political and social views, and that these prejudices can permeate their science. Documented scientific errors and frauds, most notably the Piltdown man fossil found in 1912 that was exposed as a forgery about 40 years later[55], that blemish the history of science are repeatedly exhumed to illustrate the intentional and unintentional misrepresentations of scientists. REDS mount an admirable assault on the naturalistic philosophies and antichrist theology associated with some evolutionists, and I applaud their tenacity when defending the faith in the culture wars. But REDS cross the line when they attempt to persuade us that scientists are prejudiced against God and His church because they refuse to consider miracles as the cause of complex or unexplained biological or physical phenomena. Sorry, Phil, but on behalf of all of us who have a heartfelt desire to understand how galaxies, cancer cells, toilets, black holes, and our immune system function, I hope that scientists never throw up their hands and scream "It's a miracle!" when they are stumped.

Despite their harsh criticisms of evolution, REDS are downright evasive when it comes to offering up a scientific alternative. REDS never state how God made stuff! Why? They don't have the slightest idea of how He did it! REDS like Johnson are way too smart to get stuck in such an embarrassing predicament, so they promptly pass this hot potato to any nearby creationist, especially a GUIDE!

GUIDE—God Used Intelligent Design Extensively

Let's spend some time with the GUIDEs because they are quite popular right now. There are many variations of Intelligent Design, but most accept the Big Bang, the old Earth, some degree of evolution, and the spiritual nature of man. These folks are also known as *POETs*; those with a *Progressive Old Earth Theology*[56]. POET GUIDEs believe that God can use a blend of natural or supernatural methods to make things. They have no trouble acknowledging that once something has been fashioned its everyday workings can be explained by physics, chemistry and biology. There is a wide variation among POET GUIDEs when it comes to deciding just how much supernatural intervention was required to make the universe function. Nonetheless, all POET GUIDEs can identify at least one thing (e.g., the origin of life) that is really complicated or extremely unlikely and attribute its cause to the careful, supernatural manipulation of the Almighty God. Despite never having discovered anything at all, POET GUIDEs boldly state that scientists will never figure out a natural explanation for many of the universe's mysteries because God designed them supernaturally! Actually, most POET GUIDEs attribute the design to an unspecified intelligence rather than the God of the Bible in an unpersuasive effort to seem less spiritually biased. Such reasoning leaves the door open for secular intelligent designers, such as the riders of the Chariots of the Gods[57], the alien authors who left us the "Bible Code"[58], creatures who traverse the universe in order to make cute patterns in corn fields, and Darth Vader.

But is the central argument of the POET GUIDEs reasonable? They insist that if one cannot determine how natural phenomena resulted in the origin of an organism or some biological function, then it must have been supernaturally fashioned[59, 60]. Really? If Intelligent Design (ID) believers cannot figure out how some of the intricate marvels of life originated, there are explanations other than (a) the supernatural, such as (b) someone else already figured it out and they don't know it, (c) someone already figured it out and they won't admit it, (d) they aren't smart enough to figure it out, (e) no one else is smart enough to figure it out either, (f) it may take 100 years before someone develops the technical tools to figure it out, (g) it may take 100 years before someone smart enough to figure it out is born, (h) it may take 100 years before the evidence is found, (i) it may take 100 years before someone funds the research, (j) no one will ever figure it out because our brains are too puny, (k) the evidence that would allow someone to figure it out has been destroyed by natural forces, or (l) the general principles of how it happened are known even though the details are not. Sadly, GUIDEs simply won't accept the fact that none of these options rule out the existence of God. GUIDEs disagree, asserting that God had to flaunt his miracle-working power somewhere along the line if He really was a cool Creator.

Because the science of evolution is well substantiated and so frequently upgraded, Intelligent Design arguments against evolution are becoming less and less impressive. GUIDEs are an intelligent group, though, and they have wisely shifted their emphasis to mysteries that are grander in scale. They are far more persuasive while explaining that numerous constants of nature appear to be "fine-tuned" to values precisely suited to the emergence of intelligence on a hospitable planet. If something is fine-tuned, there would have to be a fine-tuner, and we all know Who that would be! To their credit, their favorite example is the best example, the "cosmological constant"; a parameter with a name so cool that it even sounds like God came up with it! Einstein actually introduced this term when he was convinced that the universe was static, because without this repulsive force all of those galaxies would be moving toward one another. When it subsequently became undeniably apparent that the universe was not at all static, but rather expanding, Einstein called the cosmological constant the greatest mistake of his life. But recent evidence shows that the expansion of the universe is accelerating, and a very, very small value of a cosmological constant provides the extra pull that is needed for the accelerating expansion. The cosmological constant accounts for the energy and associated repulsion (an anti-gravity of sorts) in the nothingness of a "vacuum" caused by virtual particles that briefly pop into and out of existence like crazy. (That's right, "nothing" is actually "something"!) The implications of this tiny cosmological constant are immense. It enables the universe to be hospitable for solar systems, planets and people.

What is so remarkable about the cosmological constant (also known as vacuum energy or dark energy) is its degree of fine-tuning[61]. Imagine having ten folks over for dinner, and asking them to write down a number between 0 and 10, but with 120 other digits after the decimal point. Four guests were then instructed to put a minus sign in front of their number, while the numbers of the other six guests remained positive. Before dinner, you begin to add the ten numbers, expecting the total to be something like

+3.6254039372515142739400487356485965836252738475653423121453638856537496873578202937353737 58999 4763564859569835414253748898

or

−2.8226649927718283542820040387362623773836256373836266272838394948764134133253536720299827 63843 98762154243623839927 62342563

or

+7.2477663456777662431425464890576455853326537965243658533285652635786746332125365899798656 36567 8990900986868875374752766432

But to your utter amazement, they sum to an incredibly small number; a number that is about 10^{120} times smaller than you thought it would be;

+0.00000000000000000000000000000000000000000000000000000000000000000000000000000000000000000 00000000000000000000000001.

That's a zero, followed by a decimal point, followed by 119 zeroes, followed by a 1, otherwise known as 10^{-120}. Therefore the sum that you expected was about 10^{120} times too big! Now if you had told your guests that there would be no meal unless they conspired to have their numbers sum up to 10^{-120}, or if you had forced them at gunpoint to make sure that the answer turned out to be so precisely small, then this result would not be a surprise. But if you didn't, who would blame you if you called the result a miracle? Likewise, if the best laws of physics predicted that the value of the cosmological constant should be really, really, tiny, then it would be no big deal. But the modern theories do *not* predict that it should

be small, so it *is* a really big deal! How far off are the scientific predictions? When the best theoretical estimates of the negative contributions of virtual neutrinos, electrons, muons, and quarks are
summed with the positive contributions of the virtual W-bosons,
Z-bosons, Higgs particles, photons, gravitons, and gluons, the modern theories of physics yield an answer that is 10^{120} times too big[61].

How important is it that the answer be as precise as it is[61]? If
the cosmological constant was ten to one hundred times bigger,
then the expansion of the early universe would have been so fast
that solar systems would have never formed. If there was a negative
sign in front of the cosmological constant and it was a bit bigger,
then the vacuum energy would have been attractive and caused the
collapse of the universe before you or I had the chance to appear.
There seems to be no reason that the cosmological constant is so
small, other than assuring our arrival! Is dumb luck responsible?
Only the staunchest atheist who was battered as a youth with a
stainless steel Bible would attribute this to luck. GUIDEs then provide the only other apparent alternative, God's carefully-calibrated-
clandestine-cosmological-constant-controller! Given the choice
between the divine and fortuitous, I would pick Father God over
Lady Luck in a heartbeat!

What the GUIDE doesn't know or won't admit, however, is
that there are other choices. The options that you should consider
while pondering the fine-tuned parameters of nature include (a)
the supernatural, (b) the parameters are actually constrained to the
"right" values and we haven't figured that out yet, (c) changes in
the value of one parameter may be compensated for by changes in
the values of other parameters thereby making the fine-tuning not
so fine after all, (d) better models of the universe that will be developed in the future may have fewer, if any, adjustable parameters, (e)
some of the parameters may be able to be varied more than we
think without the dire consequences that we imagine, (f) the values are bound to be at the correct value in one universe (ours) if
it is but one of an unimaginably large number of other universes
in the "multiverse"[62], or (g) dumb luck. Once again, Intelligent
Design advocates refuse to acknowledge that none of these options
impugn the integrity or sovereignty of God.

Unfortunately, GUIDEs give the impression that Christianity
cannot stand on scriptures and the person of Christ alone, as they

have for thousands of years, and foolishly attempt to include the temporary befuddlement of physicists as a pillar of the faith. Apparently God can only impress POET GUIDEs if He runs a magic show, or behaves like "a supernatural deity who was pulling the strings behind the scenes"[63], like those circus performers who keep those plates rotating on the top of narrow wooden rods by frantically running back and forth in a comical attempt to keep them all spinning! Despite the multitude of fine-tuned parameters in this universe in Appendix D, there are a host of other reasons, also found in Appendix D[64], not to place your faith in Intelligent Design. Consider the design flaws in all forms of life, including you! For example, think about puberty. Honestly, would you consider any teenager to be intelligently designed? Nonetheless, ID has triumphed over all of the other forms of creationism in recent years because of its sophisticated mix of cutting edge science, subtle supernatural suggestions, and an emotional appeal to believers that POET GUIDEs are worthy of our trust because they have PhDs and believe in God[65].

ENCHANT—Evolution Needs Constant Holy Assistance, Nudging, & Tweaking

Unlike your run-of-the-mill GUIDE, the ENCHANTed accept nearly all of the findings of evolutionary science, including human evolution. They also believe in a personal, loving God. Yet the ENCHANTed insist that God must have been supernaturally meddling about in the obscure details of evolution. Maybe He selected the mutations that would favor the eventual appearance of humans, or He started life, or He configured some of the biochemical cycles of animals, or He put the engines of photosynthesis into action. Even if His actions were so subtle that they may forever remain beyond the scope of scientific detection, God's miraculous intervention is deemed essential for evolution to work. The ENCHANTed just can't bring themselves to the point of accepting that God is allowed to use chance events and well-behaved laws of nature to get things done in His universe. They think that such unguided phenomena are inherently ungodly, but they never really explain how they know what God was or was not "allowed" to do when He made the universe. Last time I checked, God didn't need to get a building permit from creationists—or anyone else—to get things done.

The common thread of the YECs, YEOUCHs, CIA, GATORS, REDS, POET GUIDEs, and ENCHANTed believers is that supernatural events played an integral part in the making of planets, plants and people. The theological problem with these creationist ideas is that each one claims to be biblical, but they are all contradictory! The basic technical problem is that their claims are rooted in supernatural slight-of-hand and an insistence that they somehow know how to identify miraculously made objects. *Could they all be wrong?* Could it be that God let the universe, solar system, Earth, life and humans unfold via purely natural phenomena? Yes, according to the GRABBers and SCUMBAGs!

GRABB—God Retired After the Big Bang

GRABBers, otherwise known as deistic evolutionists, speculate that God created the universe 13.7 billion years ago, and then retired. Their deity is a lazy recluse who sips cappuccino at a Starbucks in the Andromeda Galaxy without regard for our pathetic little lives; especially those scrumptious sins that we indulge in. How convenient! GRABBers maintain that the origin of everything, including our delusions of eternal life, can ultimately be traced back to natural forces released at the Big Bang. Belief in a caring Heavenly Father is nothing more than the well-intentioned but misguided ramblings of our soft grey matter. Death is the ultimate end of our existence.

SCUMBAG—Scientists Constantly Unraveling Mysteries and Believing in Almighty God

These folks are my favorites! SCUMBAGs, more commonly referred to as "theistic evolutionists" or proponents of a "fully gifted creation" or an "evolving creation"[66], believe in a Creator, but they are usually not considered to be creationists because they accept the findings of science with open arms. SCUMBAGs believe in a personal God who is interested in our lives and provided a means of salvation, so they are theistic evolutionists. Unlike the Intelligent Design crowd, however, most SCUMBAGs think that God was free to refrain from tinkering with the evolution of the universe, the solar system or life. In fact, SCUMBAGs believe that God is so smart that He may somehow set the stage for a universe to emerge where life would eventually flourish on Earth *without* the need for constant miraculous meddling. Indeed, an unguided evolutionary process capable of producing such a rich diversity of life is considered to be one of His crowning achievements, rather than an indication that He does not exist. (The unguided emergence of our wondrous universe may be another!) Both atheists and creationists have a real problem with this type of god or God, respectively. They simply can't accept that the Intelligent Being could let a tiny planet in a vast universe produce life via the slow, painful, dangerous, and brutal mechanism of natural selection, yet show such an intense personal interest in our particular species that He would send His Son to Earth to save us from our sin. Darwin himself couldn't warm up to such a God, a conviction that was intensified by the death of one of his children. SCUMBAGs, however, think that it is perfectly acceptable for God to be intensely interested in an incredibly small part of the universe. After all, intelligent people like you do the same thing all the time! Every one of us has no problem ignoring 99.999999999999999999999999999% of the known universe as we merrily go about our daily regimen, yet we deem ourselves to be fairly smart mammals. We devote 96% of our thoughts to our bank account, stomach and libido, yet these three items are really tiny compared to the Milky Way! Most of us parents consider ourselves to be bright, yet we spend nearly all of our time and energy raising our own children while neglecting three billion other less fortunate kids on Earth. So what's the problem with a God who creates a vast universe via natural forces and then demonstrates an intense and miraculous love for a minute part of creation—humanity—13.7 billion years later? Is it really that hard to believe that God finds humans far more fascinating than interstellar dust and black holes? SCUMBAGs don't think so.

There are two species of SCUMBAGs[67], *Scumbagus liberalus* and *Scumbagus conservatos*. The liberals think that Genesis is a spiritual myth, while the conservatives believe that there is some ancient history in the early chapters of Genesis. All SCUMBAGs agree with chapters 38 and 39 of Job[68], however, where God tells his servant Job that He had given us no spiritual revelation of how or when He made anything at all.

Where I Stand

I am a conservative SCUMBAG who believes that God inspired the author of Genesis One to tell the story from the perspective of a hypothetical observer on the Earth's surface. I call him the Genesis Observer[69]. I readily accept that conclusions of the community of scientists concerning origins, regardless of their spiritual standing, as long as they have the evidence to back up their claims! I have no reason to deny or twist the well-documented consensus of the scientific community on any topic related to the natural universe, including human evolution.

I believe that there is more to modern man than molecules, though. The human body may indeed be the magnificent product of four billion years of evolution, but we also possess a spiritual nature. *The making of man in the image of God combined both the natural evolution of the human body and mind, followed by the miraculous impartation of an eternal spiritual nature.* The origins of *Homo sapiens* may stretch back to a population of several thousand living in Africa about 150,000 years ago, but I believe that man's spiritual roots are much younger and extend directly from the hand of God.

Give Me a Chance to Explain

I'm going to ask you to set aside the rhetoric of creationists and atheists for a few hours to consider that the scientific explanation of our bodies and the biblical insight into our spirit can readily reconciled while acknowledging the rigorous findings of science and respecting the Bible as the Word of God. I am not out to persuade you that the Bible confirms scientific facts and theories. Neither will I try to convince you that science has proven that the Bible is the Word of God. I will, however, make the case that there are a few descriptions of ancient creation events that seem to be remarkably consistent with our current scientific understanding of these events. Is this a comforting indication that the scriptures may indeed be inspired? Or am I bending the Bible in a vain attempt to conform it to the findings of science? I'll let you be the judge.

Before we dive into the Bible, though, let's examine the scientific frame of reference for understanding the history of life on Earth—evolution. What does evolution really mean?

References

1. Alan Hayward; Creation and Evolution—Rethinking the Evidence from Science and the Bible; Bethany House Publishers; Minneapolis, Minnesota ;1995; 69–81
2. Alan Hayward; Creation and Evolution—Rethinking the Evidence from Science and the Bible; Bethany House Publishers; Minneapolis, Minnesota; 1995; 72–74
3. Leslie Alan Horvitz; The Complete Idiot's Guide to Evolution; 2002; Alpha; Indianapolis Indiana; 13–118
4. H. James Birx; Introduction to: Charles Darwin, The Descent of Man, Great Minds Series, Prometheus Books, Amherst, NY, 1998, xv–xvi
5. Charles Darwin; The Descent of Man, Great Minds Series, Prometheus Books, Amherst, NY, 1998, 642
6. Richard Dawkins; A Devil's Chaplain—Reflections on Hope, Lies, Science and Love, Houghton Mifflin, 2003, 20–23
7. Jared Diamond; The Third Chimpanzee—The Evolution and Future of the Human Animal, HarperPerennial, 1993, New York, NY, 15–28
8. Kenneth Miller; Finding Darwin's God—A Scientist's Search for Common Ground Between God and Evolution; 1999, Cliff Street Books, Harper Collins; New York, NY, 285–292
9. William Fix; The Bone Peddlers, Macmillan Publishing Company, New York, NY, 1984, 213
10. Edward J. Larson; Evolution—The Remarkable History of a Scientific Theory, Modern Library, Random House Publishing, New York, 2004, 116–119
11. Charles Darwin; The Origin of Species—Complete and Fully Illustrated; 1998; Books; New York, NY; 6, 459–460
12. Charles Darwin; The Descent of Man, Great Minds Series, Prometheus Books, Amherst, NY, 1998, 636
13. B.B. Warfield; Evolution, Science and Scripture, Selected Writings; edited by Mark A. Noll and David L. Livingstone; Baker Books, Grand Rapids, MI; 2000
14. Henry M. Morris, John D. Morris; The Modern Creation Trilogy; Society and Creation—Volume Three; Master Books, 1996; Green Forest AZ; Chapter 6. Evolution and Compromising Christians; 181–196
15. Edward J. Larson; Evolution—The Remarkable History of a Scientific Theory, Modern Library, Random House Publishing, New York, 2004, 5–26
16. Alan Hayward; Creation and Evolution; Bethany House Publishers; 1995; 161–178
17. John MacArthur; The Battle for the Beginning, Creation, Evolution and the Bible, 2001, W Publishing Group, 62
18. Michael Ruse; The Evolution-Creation Struggle, Harvard University Press, Cambridge, MA, 2005, 10; Hugh Ross; A Matter of Days—Resolving a Creation Controversy, NavPress, Colorado Springs, CO, 2004, 41–49
19. J.H. Kurtz; Bible and Astronomy; (third German edition, 1857; as cited by B. Ramm in The Christian View of Science and Scripture; Paternoster, Exeter, 1964 edition, 150–154)
20. P.J. Wiseman; Clues to Creation in Genesis; Marshall, Morgan and Scott, London 1977
21. Hayward, Alan; Creation and Evolution; Bethany House Publishers; 1995; 168–178
22. G.L. Schroeder; The Science of God; Simon and Schuster; New York, NY; 1997; 41–71, 197–198
23. George Klingman; God Is; Gospel Advocate Co.; Nashville, TN; 1929
24. Milligan, Robert; Scheme of Redemption; Gospel Advocate Co.; Nashville, TN; 1972 printing
25. George W. DeHoff; Why We Believe the Bible; DeHoff Publications; Murfreesboro, TN; 1974; Paine, S. Hugh; Founded on the Floods—A Scientists Looks at Creation; Productions Plus; 1993, Walnut, CA; 60, 61, 116,117
26. R. Russell Bixler; Earth Fire & Sky; 1999; Treasure House, Shippensburg, PA; 65,66,121–127
27. Hugh Ross; The Genesis Question—Scientific Advances and the Accuracy of Genesis; Navpress 1998, Colorado Springs, CO; 29–58
28. Hugh Ross; The Genesis Question—Scientific Advances and the Accuracy of Genesis; Navpress 1998, Colorado Springs, CO; 29–67
29. Hugh Ross, A Matter of Days—Resolving a Creation Controversy, NavPress, Colorado Springs, CO, 2004, 59–84
30. Appendix B
31. Hugh Ross; The Genesis Question—Scientific Advances and the Accuracy of Genesis; Navpress 1998, Colorado Springs, CO; 29–58
32. Mark Perakh; Unintelligent Design, Prometheus Books, Amherst New York, 2004, 173–191
33. Hayward, Alan; Creation and Evolution; Bethany House Publishers; 1995; 176
34. Conrad Myers; The Meaning of Creation—Genesis and Modern Science, John Know Press, Atlanta, Georgia, 1984, 67–71
35. Ronald L. Numbers; The Creationists—The Evolution of Scientific Creationism, University of California Press, 1993
36. Robert T. Pennock; Tower of Babel—The Evidence Against the New Creationism, MIT Press, Massachusetts Institute of Technology, 2000
37. Hank Hanegraff; The FACE that Demonstrates the FARCE of Evolution; Word Publishing, Nashville, Tennessee; 1998; 33–107
38. Stephen Jay Gould; Ontogeny and Phylogeny; The Belknap Press of Harvard University Press; Cambridge, MA; 1977; 1
39. Hank Hanegraaf; Fatal Flaws—What Evolutionists Don't Want You to Know, W Publishing Group, A division of Thomas Nelson, Nashville, Tennessee, 2003
40. Henry M. Morris, John D. Morris; The Modern Creation Trilogy; Scripture and Creation—Vol. One; Master Books, 1996; Green Forest AZ

41. Henry M. Morris, John D. Morris; The Modern Creation Trilogy; Science and Creation—Vol. Two; Master Books, 1996; Green Forest AZ
42 Henry M. Morris, John D. Morris; The Modern Creation Trilogy; Society and Creation—Vol. Three; Master Books, 1996; Green Forest AZ
43. P. Nelson, J.P. Reynolds; Young Earth Creationism chapter; in Three Views on Creation and Evolution, J.P. Moreland and J.M. Reynolds, General Editors, 1999, Zondervan Publishing House, Grand Rapids Michigan
44. Appendix C
45. R. Russell Bixler; Earth Fire & Sky; 1999; Treasure House, Shippensburg, PA
46. Josh McDowell, Don Stewart; Answers to Tough Questions Skeptics Ask About the Christian Faith; San Bernadino, CA; Here's Life 1980; 102–103
47. Philip Henry Gosse; Omphalos—An Attempt to Untie the Geologic Knot, John Van Voorst, Paternoster Row, London, 1857, 290–297, 335, 341–351
48. Gary North; The Dominion Covenant—Genesis, Institute for Christian Economics, 1987, 254–255
49. George Klingman; God Is; Gospel Advocate Co.; Nashville, TN; 1929; 128
50. Milligan, Robert; Scheme of Redemption; Gospel Advocate Co.; Nashville, TN; 1972 printing; 23
51. DeHoff, George W.; Why We Believe the Bible; DeHoff Publications; Murfreesboro, TN; 1974; 27
52. Philip E. Johnson; Darwin on Trial, 2nd Edition, 1993; InterVarsity Press, Downers, Illinois
53. Philip E. Johnson; Objections Sustained; 1998; InterVarsity Press, Downers, Illinois
54. Philip E. Johnson, Defeating Darwinism by Opening Minds, 1997, InterVarsity Press, Downers, Illinois
55. Jonathan Wells, Icons of Evolution, Science or Myth, Why Much of What We Teach About Evolution is Wroing, Regnery Publishing, Washington D.C., 2000, 209–228
56. Newman, R.; Old Earth (Progressive) Creationism chapter; in Three Views on Creation and Evolution, J.P. Moreland and J.M. Reynolds, General Editors, 1999, Zondervan Publishing House, Grand Rapids Michigan
57. Erich von Daniken, Chariots of the Gods, Berkley Books, New York, 1999; first printing G.P. Putnam's Sons, 1970
58. Michael Drosnin, Bible Code II—The Countdown, Viking Books, 2002
59. The Creation Hypothesis—Scientific Evidence for an Intelligent Designer, J.P. Moreland, editor, InterVarsity Press, Downers Grove, Illinois, 1994
60. Mere Creation—Science, Faith & Intelligent Design, edited by William A. Dembski, InterVarsity Press, Downers Grove, IL, 1998
61. Leonard Susskind, The Cosmic Landscape—String Theory and the Illusion of Intelligent Design, Little, Brown and Company, New York, NY, 2006, 63–89
62. Leonard Susskind, The Cosmic Landscape—String Theory and the Illusion of Intelligent Design, Little, Brown and Company, New York, NY, 2006, 293—324
63. Lee Strobel, The Case for a Creator—A Journalist Investigates Scientific Evidence that Points Toward God, Zondervan, Grand Rapids, MI, 2004, 22
64. Appendix D
65. In Six Days—Why Fifty Scientists Choose to Believe in Creation, John F. Ashton, editor, MasterBooks, Green Forest AZ
66. H.J. Van Till; Theistic Evolution; in Three Views on Creation and Evolution, J.P. Moreland and J.M. Reynolds, General Editors, 1999, Zondervan Publishing House, Grand Rapids Michigan,161–218
67. Appendix E
68. Appendix F
69. Appendix G

Chapter 3. The E-word

The Four E's

Scientists frame their understanding of life within the "E" word: evolution. "Evolution" can mean different things to different people, and most of the squawking that surrounds the creation vs. evolution debate can sorted out if we recognize the common uses and abuses of this term. The first two meanings, the *history of life* and the *mechanism by which life changes*, are rock solid scientific principles that form the foundation of our understanding of life. Evolutionary science has enabled us to paint an incomplete yet exquisite picture of life during the last four billion years[1].

Evolution is the history of what type of life has inhabited the planet, *where* it resided, and when it was here. Evolutionary *history* can be considered a *fact* because the fossil record provides indisputable evidence numerous species have inhabited this planet over billions of years[2]. Although the fossil record is incomplete, patterns of ancestry between contemporary life and prehistoric life have been firmly established that ultimately point back to a tiny, ancient, common ancestor. Although the details of this family tree may not be clear, although new fossil finds may require revisions to be made to the lines of descent, and although it may be difficult to resolve whether some species reached a dead-end extinction or gave rise

to new species, it is a *fact* that the pattern of emerging life found in
the fossil record demonstrates a relationship between the past and
the present[3-5].

Evolution is a process that explains *how* life's transformations in
form, number, behavior, intelligence and diversity occurred[6, 7]. The
process of evolution can be considered a *theory*[8] that explains the
changes in the characteristics of populations of organisms from generation to generation[9], and Darwin's careful observations of nature
laid the foundation for this grand idea[10, 11]. The process of evolution is
substantiated by so much data that some scientists consider it to be a
fact or a law of nature even though many of its details have yet to be
resolved[12]. Nonetheless, most scientists still classify the current understanding of the process of evolution as a *theory*. I need to reinforce
what this term means, because creationists jump all over this "theory" designation, insisting that their own creationist "theory" should be
given an equal exposure in classrooms. What creationists don't know
or won't tell you is that when the term "theory" is used in a scientific context, it does not mean a good guess, a gut feeling, a hunch, a
revelation, wishful thinking, a biblical interpretation, a crazy idea, a
religious opinion, a secular opinion, a doctrine, or intuition. A scientific theory is a bit more reliable than your neighbor's theory on
Bigfoot's whereabouts, how LBJ killed JFK, or the final resting place
of the Roswell aliens. Just like the germ theory of disease, the atomic theory of matter, plate tectonic theory, and the theory of relativity,
the theory of evolution is a comprehensive model that provides a
well-substantiated explanation of the data. The theory of the process
of evolution, for example, explains the underlying mechanisms of
how organisms change, fits the observed historical data in the fossil
record, correlates the genetic evidence housed within DNA, matches present-day measurable changes in the characteristics of animals,
and integrates the findings from diverse fields of science ranging from
biology to paleontology to biochemistry to behavioral sciences to
genetics to anthropology. For nearly one and a half centuries, the theory of evolution has been relentlessly scrutinized, challenged and disputed, leading to a series of revisions, corrections, refinements and
improvements[13, 14]; a scrutiny far more aggressive than the obsolete
complaints lodged by modern-day creationists.

Let's take a look at Darwin's observations that formed the foundation for his theory of evolution. He noted that animals produce

so many offspring that if they all survived, they would quickly result in unimaginably large populations that could not be supported by this planet. Something prunes the explosive growth because we aren't knee-deep in roaches, toads or trout. Darwin also recognized that there was a tremendous variation of characteristics within a species, and that variations could be so dramatic that it could be difficult to tell if two organisms were variations of the same species or members of two different species. Further, he found that species endured an unceasing struggle for existence as they were subjected to a host of adversities, with nature itself selecting those most suited for survival and worthy of reproduction. Putting these observations together, he realized that this natural selection process not only kept the populations in check, but also changed the characteristics of the populations over time[15, 16].

Concise explanations of the theory of evolution have been written for the general public by many scientists and science authors. Appendix I[17] contains some of my favorites, authored by Steven Jay Gould, Niles Eldredge and David Quammen. Here is my take on how it works. Evolution is change brought about through cycles of mutation, variation and natural selection. Random mutations can occur during the reproduction process and these genetic alterations can lead to variations in the characteristics of the offspring. As the offspring struggle to survive in an environment of limited resources, they face competition for survival, with the stiffest competition coming from members of their own species because these peers desire the very same resources. Those most likely to survive the longest may have variations that make them more adept in their environment. They may be slightly faster, stronger, stealthier, or better insulated. They may have improved sight, hearing, or ability to slide or glide, or they may be better equipped to deal with dramatic changes in the environment. The organisms with variations conducive to survival may flourish, while their less fortunate and more poorly equipped peers perish early. This natural selection not only keeps the populations of organisms in check by weeding out the variations that are not advantageous, but also rewards the winners with the chance to reproduce—an appealing reward indeed—and pass on their advantages to the next generation. That explains how changes within a species (microevolution) occur, but how do new species appear (macroevolution)? When nature exerts forces, such as changes in the environment, on the population of a single species and splits it into two distinct populations, natural selection will act on each group. Eventually each population will accumulate enough variations such that two new species result. That's it. There is nothing complex or sinister about the theory of evolution. Darwin's great idea is simple and profound.

The *history* and the *process* of evolution are the foundations for the scientific understanding of life, and the overwhelming majority of the scientific community recognizes the validity of these tools. Yes, disputes over the details of evolution abound and many mysteries of evolution remain unsolved. But there is no controversy about the grand themes of the history or process of evolution in the scientific community, despite creationist attempts to misrepresent Intelligent Design as the "runner-up" that is ready to step in should Miss Evolution fall from grace.

Evolution has also been used by some scientists to formulate and validate *opinions* and *beliefs* that are unrelated to the history of life and the processes responsible for its transformations. Many popular scientific authors often delight in proclaiming their disdain for religion and have used the science of evolution as a springboard for publicizing their *social agendas, philosophies, politics* and *spiritual convictions.* Christians often take so much offense to these attacks of a few scientists on their faith that they view *all* scientists with suspicion, even if their scientific findings are irrefutable. These aspects of evolution are also referred to as "evolutionism".

Evolution has been used by some to shape social policies.

There is nothing wrong with evolutionists having opinions, beliefs, causes, and political affiliations. The problem, and it's an understandably big problem for Christians, is that the mental musings of famous evolutionists are usually presented either as facts or the only logical conclusions that a person with an IQ greater than 16 should reach. For example, some in positions of significant political power or social influence have cited evolution as an underlying basis of their radical policies, especially during the late 1800's and early 1900's[18]. Concepts associated with biological evolution of life were extracted from their proper context and twisted into political and social agendas. For example, the struggle for survival that produces winners and losers in the animal kingdom has been used to justify war, colonization, repression, racism, genocide, slavery, eugenics, Marxism, socialism, Nazism, communism, involuntary sterilization and NFL playoff games. Contemporary creationists have little difficulty in identifying those who wield evolution to promote social and political agendas, including abortion rights, homosexual unions, environmental extremism, promiscuity and drug use[19].

Evolution has been used by some to refute God, the Bible and Christianity.

Many scientists have been more than willing to batter the Bible, the church and Christianity with evolution. This is obviously not the case with all scientists. According to the website of the most prestigious scientific organization in the US, the American Association for the Advancement of Science, scientists should not be ripping on matters of faith. "Science does not take a position on an intelligent designer, which is a matter of religious faith, and is not testable scientifically. AAAS and other scientific groups do not want to create the impression that religion and science are inherently in conflict. They live together quite comfortably, including in the minds of many scientists. Science and religion ask different questions about the world. Many individual scientists are deeply religious. They see scientific investigation and religious faith as complementary components of a well-rounded life.[20]" Kenneth Miller[21], Niles Eldredge[22], and Carl Zimmer[23] are renowned evolutionists who carefully expose the scientific errors of creationism, yet do not use their findings to attack others' spiritual beliefs or infer that those who believe in God are fools. As Zimmer puts it, "God and evolution are not mutually exclusive."[24] In their book on brain science and the biology of belief, Newberg, D'Aquila and Rause concluded that the brain's ability to transcend the individual self is the basis for our religious compulsions, but they argue that this does not imply that religious teachings are untrue. In their words, "science and religion do not have to be incompatible: One need not be wrong for the other to be right."[25] Other authors cautiously avoid all mention of spiritual absolutes in their scientific work, which is fine with me! Nonetheless, it is easy to find stinging criticisms of faith in popular scientific literature at local bookstores, and believers are far

more familiar with the barbs of these prolific authors than they are
with the polite postings at the infrequently accessed AAAS website. A host of caustic quotes from some of these highly regarded
and influential evolutionists are provided in Appendix J[26]. Here are a
few particularly pointed ones from two very prestigious and brilliant scientists, Richard Dawkins and the late Stephen Jay Gould.
Richard Dawkins has declared that "The reason organized religion
merits outright hostility is that, unlike belief in Russell's teapot,
religion is a powerful, influential, tax-exempt and systematically
passed on to children too young to defend themselves."[27] Dawkins
also thinks that "Faith is such a successful brainwasher in its own
favour, especially a brainwasher of children, that it is hard to break
its hold. But what, after all, is faith? It is a state of mind that leads
people to believe something—it doesn't matter what—in the total
absence of supporting evidence. If there were good supporting evidence then faith would be superfluous, for the evidence would
compel us to believe it anyway."[28] Stephen Jay Gould said that "For
our favored and well tested theory, Darwinian natural selection,
offers no solace or support for these traditional hopes about human
necessity or cosmic importance."[29] Gould received some good press
for promoting the useful role of religion in society, but a careful
read of his works makes it clear that while Gould felt that religious
folks could do good things for society, the foundation of their faith
was, in his own words, "just a story we tell ourselves".[30]

These remarks, and many others like them found in Appendix
J, will quickly convince you that there are a many famous, intelligent,
influential, articulate, skeptical scientists who love to paint Christians
as a herd of stupid, boring, unsophisticated, medieval misfits that
refuse to acknowledge that the Bible is a pound of baloney—sliced
thin. Are these scientists brilliant? Of course! Are they smarter than
me? By far! Are they justified in their relentless criticisms of creationist errors? You bet! Are their studies of our ancestors' religious
customs fair game for scientific investigation? Certainly! Do they
have the right to be atheists or skeptics? Yes! But are they the final
arbiters of spiritual truth? I doubt it. Is their pompous insistence that
the Almighty God wasn't allowed to use an unguided evolutionary
process to establish life on Earth[31] based on irrefutable logic, theology or science? Of course not! Do the results of their investigations
of nature prove that the supernatural God does not exist? Hardly!

Their prohibitions on the methods a Creator may use to make life and their dismissals of His very existence consist of little more than decades-old refutations of creationist errors, centuries-old liberal criticisms of the Bible, routine atheistic talking points, one-sided presentations of scriptures that present only the "sophisticated" (i.e. ultra-liberal) theological perspective, and religious conclusions based on atheistic presuppositions. An entire field of Christian apologetics is available to defend the faith[32-34], but evolutionists rarely enjoin a legitimate debate over the scriptural, prophetic, historical, spiritual foundations of the Christian faith with serious theologians. They find it easier to tout their easy triumph over creationist nonsense as the demise of God Himself. (Sadly, some renowned Christian apologists, such as Norman Geisler, only make matters worse by spoiling their eloquent defense of the faith with creationist pseudo-science and erroneous scientific statements[35] in a futile attempt to disprove evolutionary science.) Fortunately, extracting the *philosophical* and *religious* spam from the immense body of scientific literature concerning the *history* and *process* of evolution is as easy as picking pepperoni off of a pizza. You can simply skip over these atheistic barbs or vigorously refute them. In either case, you must realize that the historical and mechanistic aspects of evolution presented by these investigators may be absolutely correct, regardless of how offensive you find their political, social, religious, sexual or spiritual leanings.

Open Your Bibles to Genesis One

Now that we have looked at one of the most important scientific principles related to our beginnings, evolution, we are ready to take a look at what the scriptures tell us about the origins of the universe, Earth, life and man. Let's walk through Genesis while we review the most recent understanding of our origins and see if it is possible to be a Christian who appreciates science, or whether we should, as the biologist William Provine suggested in a renowned remark, check our brains at the church house door[36]. It's my hope to persuade you that it really *is* possible for science and the Bible to be right about our origins. I believe that you *can* be a Bible-believing, God-fearing follower of Christ while acknowledging the scientific evidence for our origins without surrendering your faith or your brains. I even think that there *may* be a few divinely inspired glimpses of our evolving planet within the pages of Genesis.

References
1. Peter Andrews, John Barber, Michael Benton, Marianne Collins, Christine Janis, Ely Kish, Akio Morishima, J. John Sepkoski Jr., Christopher Stringer, Jean-Paul Tibbles; The Book of Life—An Illustrated History of Life on Earth, W.W. Norton and Company, general editor Stephen Jay Gould, New York, NY, 2001
2. Appendix H
3. Kenneth Miller; Finding Darwin's God—A Scientist's Search for Common Ground Between God and Evolution; 1999, Cliff Street Books, Harper Collins; New York, NY; 31-48
4. Niles Eldredge; The Triumph of Evolution and the Failure of Creationism; Henry Holt and Company; 2000; New York, NY; 24-61
5. Carl Zimmer; Evolution—The Triumph of an Idea, HarperCollins Publishers, 2001, Introduction by Stephen Jay Gould, x-xi
6. Kenneth Miller; Finding Darwin's God—A Scientist's Search for Common Ground Between God and Evolution; 1999, Cliff Street Books, Harper Collins; New York, NY; 43-53
7. Niles Eldredge; Niles; The Triumph of Evolution and the Failure of Creationism; Henry Holt and Company; 2000; New York, NY; 24-25, 62-90
8. Kenneth Miller; Finding Darwin's God—A Scientist's Search for Common Ground Between God and Evolution; 1999, Cliff Street Books, Harper Collins; New York, NY; 53-54
9. Leslie Alan Horvitz; The Complete Idiot's Guide to Evolution; 2002; Alpha; Indianapolis Indiana; 6
10. Kenneth Miller; Finding Darwin's God—A Scientist's Search for Common Ground Between God and Evolution; 1999, Cliff Street Books; Harper Collins; New York, NY, 7-9
11. Peter Andrews, John Barber, Michael Benton, Marianne Collins, Christine Janis, Ely Kish, Akio Morishima, J. John Sepkoski, Jr., Christopher Stringer, Jean-Paul Tibbles, The Book of Life—An Illustrated History of the Evolution of Life on Earth, general editor Stephen Jay Gould, W.W. Norton and Co., New York, NY,2001,28-29,32
12. Ernst Mayr; What Evolution Is, Basic Books, New York, NY, 2001, 275
13. Jeffery H.Schwartz; Sudden Origins—Fossils, Genes and the Emergence of Species, John Wiley and Sons, New York, NY, 1999, 1-13
14. Edward J. Larson; Evolution—The Remarkable History of a Scientific Theory, Modern Library, Random House Publishing, New York, 2004, 53-198
15. Leslie Alan Horvitz; The Complete Idiot's Guide to Evolution; 2002; Alpha; Indianapolis Indiana; 8
16. Kenneth Miller; Finding Darwin's God—A Scientist's Search for Common Ground Between God and Evolution; 1999, Cliff Street Books, Harper Collins; New York, NY, 6-10
17. Appendix I
18. Leslie Alan Horvitz; The Complete Idiot's Guide to Evolution; Alpha Books; 2002; Indianapolis, IN; 237-257
19. Henry M. Morris, John D. Morris; The Modern Creation Trilogy; Society and Creation—Vol. Three; Master Books, 1996; Green Forest AZ; 57-159
20. http://www.aaas.org/news/press_room/evolution/qanda.shtml
21. Kenneth Miller; Finding Darwin's God—A Scientist's Search for Common Ground Between God and Evolution; 1999, Cliff Street Books, Harper Collins; New York, NY
22. Niles Eldredge; The Triumph of Evolution and the Failure of Creationism, Henry Holt and Company, New York, first Owl Book edition, 2001, 8, 148-149
23. Carl Zimmer; Evolution—The Triumph of an Idea, Harper Collins Publishers, 2001, New York, NY, 313-344
24. Carl Zimmer; Evolution—The Triumph of an Idea, HarperCollins Publishers, 2001, New York, NY, 338
25. Andrew Newberg, Eugene D'Aquila, Vince Rause; Why God Won't Go Away—Brain Science and the Biology of Belief, The Ballantine Publishing Group, New York, NY, 2001, 173-174
26. Appendix J
27. Richard Dawkins; A Devil's Chaplain—Reflections on Hope, Lies, Science and Love, Houghton Mifflin, 2003, 117-118
28. Richard Dawkins; The Selfish Gene, Oxford University Press, 1989, New York, 330
29. Stephen Jay Gould, in the Introduction to; Carl Zimmer; Evolution—The Triumph of an Idea, Harper Collins Publishers, 2001, New York. xii
30. Kenneth Miller R. 170; Transcript of the program CBS Sunday Morning on Nov. 29, 1998. The interviewer was Rita Braver.
31. William Provine, Scientists Face It! Science and Religion Are Incompatible," The Scientist, 2, 1988
32. Josh McDowell; Evidence That Demands a Verdict—Vol. 1, Campus Crusade for Christ, 1973
33. Josh McDowell; The New Evidence That Demands a Verdict, Thomas Nelson Publishers, Nashville, 1999
34. Norman Geisler; Baker Encyclopedia of Christian Apologetics, Baker, Grand Rapids, Michigan, 1999
35. Norman Geisler, Peter Bocchino; Unshakable Foundations—Contemporary Answers to Crucial Questions about the Christian Faith, Bethany House, Minneapolis, Minnesota, 2001, 71-188
36. William Provine, Scientists Face It! Science and Religion Are Incompatible, The Scientist, 2, 1988

Chapter 4. Old News

Genesis 1:1 In the beginning God created the heavens and the earth.

Some think that "In the beginning" is simply a religious version of "Once upon a time", while others, including myself, view this as a simple statement saying that the universe had a starting point. Some believe that "heavens" refer to the atmosphere or to the invisible kingdom of God, while others, including myself, view the heavens as the sun, moon, stars and vastness of space. If "the heavens" do indeed refer to space, and if "the beginning" refers to a point in time (and those are two big "if"s), then let's see what the first verse of the Bible says about the origins of the universe.

Time began.

There was a beginning! Time itself has a birthday! Time began, but the Bible doesn't say when. History has not been marching along since eternity past, though, at least not in the universe that we occupy.

The universe began.

The sun, moon and stars in the sky were also created. In fact, everything that is has an origin. The entire contents of universe had a starting point.

Everything came from nothing.

Here's the kicker; the universe was established from scratch! The
Bible teaches that everything in the universe came from nothing—
or at least from something that was invisible! Here's how it is
phrased in the New Testament. *Hebrews 11:3 By faith we understand
that the universe was formed at God's command, so that what is seen was
not made out of what was visible.* Apparently, through a completely
unspecified process, God decided to make everything from nothing at all.

How does this line up with what scientists have learned about
the origins of time and space?

Our Universe is Not Eternally Old

In the early 1900s, scientists began to ponder the consequences of
light emanating from eternal, immobile stars—a commonly held
view of the universe at the time. Had their flames been burning
forever, though, the universe would be quite hot and the entire
night sky would be a sheet of white because stars and galaxies can
be found along every line of sight. But space is cold, our planet is
quite comfy, and our night sky is dark. The universe could not be
eternally old; it had a beginning[1].

The Universe is Old and Expanding, Not Young and Static

Could the stars in the heavens have been young and fixed in place?
If you look up at night, it certainly doesn't look like those little
twinkling things are moving around at all. In fact, the constellations
that I see as a 47-year old look just like they did when I was 12.
Heck, even the young Albert Einstein thought that the universe
was static! If all of the stars were young and fixed in place, then the
light from very distant stars would not have reached Earth yet,
enabling our night sky to be dark and the temperature on Earth
mild. This model even fit the young universe theology that envisioned God placing stars in their positions in space and turning
them all on at once 6000 years ago, just like a White House
Christmas Tree lighting ceremony!

Edwin Hubble's discoveries snuffed out the notion of a young
and static universe, though. His telescopic observations indicated

that the universe was filled with extremely faint galaxies so far away that their light must have been traveling for millions or billions of years prior to reaching Earth. Hubble also noted that, much like the low-pitched sound of an ambulance that has just passed by, the light waves from distant galaxies were stretched out to longer wavelengths at the red end of the spectrum. This effect was especially apparent for the most distant galaxies, meaning that they were moving away faster than the closer galaxies. As it turns out, it appears that *all* galaxies are moving away from ours, as if the universe was expanding in all directions! (This doesn't mean that we are at the center of the universe, though, because the same effect would be observed from any point in the known universe!)

This expansion also explained why the night sky was dark. The red shift from receding galaxies causes a smaller fraction of their radiation to fall in the visible range. To make matters darker, even if space is infinite, we can't detect galaxies that are so distant that there hasn't been enough time since the "beginning" for their light to make it to Earth!

Bottom line? The universe wasn't static at all; it was getting bigger, with the most distant galaxies receding quite rapidly[2]. The universe is just like a 47-year old male; old and expanding! Now if the universe is expanding in all directions as time marches forward, then models of the universe should show a contraction as we go back into time. Using Einstein's theory of relativity, it has been determined that about 14 billion years ago, space and time converged at a single point[3]. That's right; the entire observable universe began as an outburst that was smaller than a single atom, and this intense burst of unfathomable energy is still driving the universe's expansion today. The Big Bang, the Mother of All Fireworks, marked the beginning of time and space about 14 billion years ago.

Background Check

Need some proof that the universe is really that old and was smaller than a gnat when it began? Remnants of the Big Bang have actually been detected across the entire cosmos[4]. In 1948, George Gamow and Ralph Afner *predicted* that radiation from the early, hot period of the universe's youth, some 380,000 years after the Big Bang when the universe first became transparent to the passage of photons[5, 6] should still be detectable in deep space. This swarm of photons has aged for billions of years, losing energy along the way, causing them to shift from their infant state of gamma rays and X-rays to the microwave portion of the spectrum. Two Bell Lab scientists, Arno Penzias and Robert Wilson, stumbled upon this cosmic microwave radiation in 1964. In 1965 their experimental results were published along with a paper by a group of Princeton physicists that tied the background radio noise to the Big Bang event. This experimental validation of the background radiation not only affirmed the Big Bang as the premier model of the universe, but it dealt a death blow to competing models of the universe's origin. More accurate measurements of the radiation over the next several decades, culminating in the data obtained with the COBE satellite that was presented in early 1990, have reaffirmed these results. The detection of the cosmic background radiation, which indicates that our expanding universe is now at a quite cold 2.73 K—just a few degrees above absolute zero[7]—was an astounding verification of Big Bang cosmology. This cosmic microwave radiation is still detectable today and, like gunpowder residue, serves as an indisputable reminder of the universe's explosive origin[8, 9] about 14 billion years ago! Refinements of the Big Bang model are found in Appendix K[10].

Silly String

Is the Big Bang the best model of the cosmos? At the present time, most would say "Yes". Is it a perfect model? No! The Achilles' heel of Big Bang cosmology is no secret; it is not capable of reconciling the traditional formulations of general relativity, which precisely models the large scale behavior of our massive universe, with quantum mechanics, which describes the tempestuous nature of matter at the sub-atomic scale. In most situations this isn't a problem with physicists because they usually study either really massive things like galaxies *or* really small things like electrons, and therefore they only need to use general relativity or quantum mechanics. At the moment of creation of the universe, however, *both* models need to be called on because the universe was both massive *and* small. General relativity and quantum mechanics simply cannot be reconciled at this extreme condition, though, which means that they cannot both be right in their conventional formulation at these conditions. The Big

Bang model of the universe is also a bit disconcerting, even to these wacked out physicists, when they ponder the mathematical implication that the universe originated from an *infinitely* small point of infinite temperature and infinite density. Are there other models under consideration that address these problems? Yes! "Superstring theory", or "string theory" for short[10], is being enthusiastically kicked around by cosmologists. Brian Greene has authored two outstanding books on this topic for the general public[11,12]; they're both worth every penny! In string theory, the building blocks of the universe are smaller than molecules, smaller than the atoms that compose molecules, smaller than the protons neutrons and electrons that compose atoms, and even much, much smaller than the quarks that constitute protons and neutrons. The fundamental, indivisible, ultimate building blocks of nature may be incredibly small, one-dimensional, vibrating, oscillating loops that have been dubbed—you guessed it—"strings". String theory has some remarkable attributes for those of us who are used to living and thinking in three dimensions of space—height, width and depth—and the fourth dimension of time, such as the existence of six extra space dimensions that are curled up upon themselves! The promise of this symphony of strings is that it paves the way for the reconciliation of general relativity and quantum mechanics. As an extra added bonus, it appears to shed some insight into the moment of creation. Rather than erupting from an *infinitely* small, hot and dense point, the embryonic universe of string theory is an unimaginably small, yet *finite*, kernel. And just to make things even more interesting, or baffling, this tiny upstart on a universe may have had a pre-history! It may have actually emerged from an earlier universe[13,14]! String theory—while promising—remains in its infancy with regards to the devilish details of deriving its exact mathematical formulation and then figuring out how to completely solve these equations. For now, partial solutions to approximations of the exact equations will have to do!

The elegant universe envisioned by Brian Greene is not without its detractors. Leonard Susskind agrees that String Theory is the best hope for unifying gravity and quantum mechanics, but recoils at the notion of a unique, elegant universe[15]. In the last few years, string theorists' dreams of finding a singular solution were replaced by the nightmare of an incredibly large number of possible solutions. Yet this flaw may ultimately reveal the strength of string theory; there may be an unimaginable large number of universes, each governed by completely distinct laws of nature, at least one of which—ours—is fertile. Experimental verification of these little strings and other universes may remain beyond the reach of our most sophisticated current technology for a good long while, but I advise that you not bet your faith that it will forever remain a mystery. Even if string theory eventually triumphs as the ultimate model of the universe, however, it will *not* alter the current assessments of the age of the universe. *Whether banged out all alone or strung out with bazillions of others, the universe that we live in is about 14 billion years old.*

Burn Out

There are a number of other tools for providing independent assessments of the age of the universe[16], such as the appearance of stars and the abundance of radioactive elements.

The intensity and color of light from burning objects can tell you something about their age. My pathetic short stack of logs purchased at the neighborhood Seven Eleven will be a roaring orange flame about 20 minutes after ignition and nothing more than a warm, dusty mess after two hours. Therefore it is possible to date the age of a wood fire by observing the colors and intensity of its flames. The same can be said of charcoal grills and stars. In the mid-20th century, astronomers developed a tool for determining the age of burning stars based on their colors and luminosity. In essence, this model predicted the appearance of stars as they matured. By varying the age of the star in the calculations, they were able to accurately predict the color and luminosity of all known types of stars and star clusters in the night sky. The longest time needed to match the model with experimental measurements of stellar color and luminosity was roughly 17 billion years, give or take a few billion years. This technique was recently used to provide a more precise estimate of the age of the universe as 13-14 billion years based on Hubble telescope measurements of light from the dimmest objects in the universe[17].

Get a Life

The earliest supernova must have occurred after the universe began, therefore if we can date these incredible explosions we can obtain a conservative estimate the age of the universe. Radioactive elements heavier than iron were generated in these distant and ancient supernovae[18]. Therefore if we can figure out how long these elements have been around, then we can arrive at a conservative age of the universe. Radioactive elements decay at a rate that is characterized by their half-life; the amount of time required for half of the atoms to decay into more stable elements. After one half-life, 50% of the original element is still there. After two half-lives, one half of one half, or 25%, remains. Half of a half of a half, or 12.5%, is left after three half-lives. About 0.0000000001% remains after 40 half-lives; an essentially undetectable amount. How does this help us figure out when the earliest supernova occurred? If the radioactive version of an element known to have formed in stellar furnaces cannot be detected, then a period of time at roughly 40 times greater than its half-life has elapsed since it originated. This is the case for neptunium[237], with a half-life of 2.25 million years, which must have formed in supernovae along with more slowly decaying (and still detectable) radioactive elements thorium[232], uranium[238], and uranium[235]. This single observation tells us that the universe is more than (40*2.25 million), or 90 million years old[19]. There are two unsatisfying aspects of this result. First, conspiracy theorists out there may tell you that there was never any neptunium around in the first place! Second, it would be better to get an estimate of the age of the universe rather than only knowing that the answer is greater than 90 million years. Fortunately the age of the universe can be estimated by measuring the relative amounts of the more slowly decaying, and still detectable, elements in the heavens. The ages of the oldest supernovae determined with this technique have fallen in the 10-20 billion year range.

Could You Be A Bit More Precise?

There is *no doubt* that the universe began a very long time ago. Numerous assumptions are used to obtain these results, so in past decades there was some uncertainty as to whether the Big Bang occurred 9 or 12 or 17 or 14 or 15 or 19 billion years ago. Unfortunately for Young Earth Creationists, this level of uncertainty does not mean that the Big Bang occurred 6,000-60,000 years ago. It would be like expecting your Thanksgiving turkey to be ready to eat after baking it for four seconds rather than four hours because Martha Stewart made some inaccurate assumptions about the size of your oven. Recent advances have enabled a more precise age of the universe to be established. For example, results based on data from NASA's Wilkinson Microwave Anisotropy Probe have shown that the Big Bang occurred 13.7 billion years ago, give or take one hundred million years[20, 21].

The Solar System

What about our little corner of the universe? The solar system cannot be older than the universe in which it resides, but it can be much younger. Just how old is the solar system? 6000 years old? I don't think so!

My Sun's Mid-Life Crisis

The tools used to determine the age of distant stars can be applied to our local star, the sun. Results based on its color, luminosity, structure, and composition have placed the sun's age about 4.6 billion years, making it a middle-aged member of the universe[22].

Meteor Shower

We have some hard evidence from the smaller, colder, less intimidating members of the solar system. For example, iron meteors can survive the brutal entrance into our atmosphere and plow into the Earth's surface, thereby earning the promotion to meteorite. They can be cut and polished, revealing large crystals of iron. The size of these crystals indicates that some had been cooling at incredibly slow rates, as low as about $1°C$ per *million* years, while traveling through space. Radioactive techniques can also be used to date the age of meteorites, and the oldest ones are roughly 4.6 billion years old[23, 24].

Mars Attacks

Little chunks of Mars have even made it to Earth. Violent asteroid impacts there resulted in the ejection of Martian fragments into space, and a few found their way to Earth. These rocks contain trapped gases with a composition that can be correlated to the measurements of Mars' atmosphere from the Viking Lander in 1976. One of these Martian red rocks sparked a controversy because some linked its microscopic features to evidence of primitive life forms. There has been no dispute concerning the age of Mars based on these meteorites, though. For example, the rock designated ALH 84001, which was recovered in Antarctica, has an igneous age of about four and a half billion years[25].

Old as Dirt

Earth must be older than the oldest object we can find on its surface. How about an Old Maid? Our warranty expires at about 120 years and our memory goes long before that, so people cannot be used to date the origin of the planet. Fortunately, plenty of things that can be used to date the Earth[26] are older than your Aunt Gertrude. The oldest living things are trees, and their age can be estimated from a count of the annual rings in core samples, which are long, cylindrical samples removed from the tree trunk. The oldest living bristlecone pine alive today, named Methuselah, is about 4,800 years old. Methuselah was in second place for most of its life, though. Because a coring tool broke, a bristlecone pine named Prometheus was cut down (rather than cored) in 1964 in order to determine its age, which was about as smart as burning a winning Powerball lottery ticket to verify that it was made of paper. An analysis of the brutally butchered Prometheus revealed that it was 4,900 years old! Dead trees in close proximity to living trees can take us ever further back in time. By realizing that unusual ring patterns (markers of an unusual multiple-year weather pattern) in the relatively young portion of living tree trunks must have formed at the same time as the same patterns in the relatively old portion of nearby dead tree trunks, combined tree ring records can take us back 12,000 years. Inanimate objects can take us back even farther. Counting the alternating layers of dark winter clays and light summer silts in lakes that freeze over every winter captures 10,000—20,000 years of history. Seasonal variations of air constituents trapped in layers of snow found in Greenland indicate that 250,000 years have transpired since the ice pack began to form, while variations in oxygen isotopes found in deep sea sediments caused by climat-ic changes associated with our planet's orbit and axis can be used to establish 800,000 years of history. If Earth is older than a million years, though, something that slowly changes with time and is more resilient than people, trees, icepacks, or deep sea sediments must be identified to date the origin of our planet.

Rocks! There are no older or more rugged inhabitants of this terrestrial ball than igneous rocks[27]. There are numerous radioactive elements with half-lives ranging up to 6 million billion years that can be used to date minerals. Radioactive elements with a half-life less than 80 million years are unaccounted for (with the exception of radioactive elements whose supply is being replenished by the decay of other elements), while every single radioactive element with a longer half-life can still be detected[28]. Remembering that the radioactivity of an element becomes essentially undetectable after 30 or 40 half-lives have expired, we can determine that Earth is at least several billion years old. As it turns out, the age of our planet can be determined much more accurately based on levels of radioactive elements that are still detectable. There is a clever way to date rocks obtained from a specific location that does not even require an estimate of the amount of radioactive material that was in the rock when it originally formed[29]. This technique has been used to date rocks from around the world, and each continent has yielded three billion year old samples. Rocks that are about 4 bil-lion years old have been found in northwest Canada. It took about 0.5 billion years for the Earth to cool down enough for these rocks to be born via solidification in the first place, therefore our plan-et's age is 4.5—4.6 billion years[30,31].

Moonies

Radioactive dating of moon rocks brought home by the Apollo prospectors indicates that the moon is about four and a half billion years old; 4.3 billion year old rocks plus 0.2 billion years before that required for the moon to cool down enough for rocks to form[32]. Another clue provides an insight into the age of the moon; it is covered with several inches of dust. Unlike Earth, there is no atmosphere to heat and vaporize these tiny particles as they approach the moon's surface. Our astronauts have tromped on the moon (although some still insist they were actually in southwest Utah) and there are about 2 ½ inches of powder on the ground. Direct satellite measurements of dust inflow to our planet have been used to estimate that roughly 11,000 tons of dust impact the moon each year, which would lead to about 1 ½ inches in four and a half billion years. Other sources of dust, such as the disintegration of impacting meteorites, and forces responsible for sweeping dust off of the moon, such as the impact of meteorites blasting older dust into space, can be accounted for. When all of these contributions are considered, the results indicate that about 4 billion years would be required for several inches of dust to accumulate[33]. Ironically, Young Earth Creationists of decades past used an early, inaccurate, scientific estimate of the dust impact rate that indicated that the moon was only 6 million years old and then "corrected" it to attain the presumed age of 10,000 years. Although scientists have long since exposed the errors of this claim[34] and most creationists now steer clear of the topic, some creationist publications still use moon dust as evidence of a recent creation[35].

It Looks Like A Duck, and Walks Like a Duck and Quacks Like a Duck...

What do the sun, meteors, Mars, the moon and Earth have in common? They are old; billions of years old. Each has about the same age, indicating that they all formed at about the same time 4.6 billion years ago. Although younger than our 13.7 billion year old universe, our solar system is still quite ancient. These results are facts, not beliefs or opinions. There's absolutely no denying it.

Well, there actually still is some denying it! Consider the conclusion of John MacArthur, whose recent book attempted to settle this age-of-the-Earth issue once and for all. MacArthur takes aim at evolutionists, cosmologists and astronomers, especially a Christian astronomer named Hugh Ross. Ross is a persuasive and relentless Intelligent Design advocate for an ancient Earth and universe who is also a relentless critic of Young Earth Creationists like MacArthur. MacArthur recently made the following assertion[36], "For example, the big bang theory itself is still highly controversial, even among Ross's fellow astronomers. It is only the latest in the long line of "scientific" explanations of how the universe came to be. Big bang cosmology itself is in a constant state of flux. (For example, scientists once believed that the entire universe emerged when an unimaginably enormous mass of matter exploded, but the theory currently in vogue is that all the matter of the universe emerged from a particle that was infinitesimally small.) Yet despite all the uncertainty surrounding the Big Bang, Hugh Ross regards it as an "unshakable established" fact...". Unfortunately, John MacArthur thinks that what he mistakenly asserts, cannot understand, or does not like about science is either unbiblical or untrue. He tries to equate his own confusion about the continued improvements and refinements of the Big Bang model with mass confusion of the scientific community. If MacArthur is right about the age of our planet as deduced from a few scriptures, then all other biblical scholars with different interpretations of Genesis are wrong, relativity is wrong, the Big Bang is wrong, inflationary expansion is wrong, cosmic background radiation is wrong, and radiometric dating is wrong. If MacArthur is right, then Albert Einstein, Stephen Hawking and Edwin Hubble would have to be wrong about their discoveries. In fact, entire branches of science would be wrong. Cosmology, astronomy, biology, paleontology, anthropology, archeology, and geology would crumble before MacArthur, even though he has never presented a single piece of scientific evidence—not one—to support his ideas. John MacArthur is either the most prolific scientific genius of all time, or he is absolutely clueless in Cleveland concerning cosmology. Final answer? John is a fine Christian, a remarkable preacher, a gifted Bible teacher, and probably a better man than me, but he is not a scientist and shouldn't pretend that he is. The same goes for every other famous Bible preacher and teacher who substitutes religious opinions for indisputable scientific evidence because they are offended by the atheism of a few arrogant researchers who think Bible-believers are morons!

So Far, So Good

There is a prolific amount of incontrovertible evidence that time and space were birthed out of nothing some 13.7 billion years ago, and that Earth is 4.6 billion years old. God's Word starts with a simple declaration that the heavens and Earth had a beginning, and that everything that is seen was made from nothing. The Psalms confirm His role in creation of the universe. *Psalm 33:6 By the word of the*

LORD were the heavens made, their starry host by the breath of his mouth. Jeremiah also uses imagery to describe God's creative acts. *Jeremiah 32:17 Ah, Sovereign LORD, you have made the heavens and the earth by your great power and outstretched arm. Nothing is too hard for you.* Perhaps the Big Bang is the manifestation of God's will. Maybe God said "Bang!" and started things out with a supernatural flourish. I won't bet on it, though. The Big Bang event may be rooted in an even more mysterious, yet natural, phenomenon of God's creation that scientists have yet to grasp.

After one verse, there is no conflict between the Bible and science. The Bible tells us *Who* did it and *why* He did it, science tells us *when* and *how* it happened. Accepting the fact that Earth is really old is a not a rejection of the Bible[37].

References
1. Stephen Hawking; The Universe in a Nutshell, Bantam Books, New York, NY, 2001, 69-72
2. Stephen Hawking; The Universe in a Nutshell, Bantam Books, New York, NY, 2001, 72-79
3. Stephen Hawking; The Universe in a Nutshell, Bantam Books, New York, NY, 2001, 31-65,76
4. Alan H. Guth; The Inflationary Universe, Addison-Wesley, Reading, Massachusetts, 1997, 57-83
5. Alan H. Guth; The Inflationary Universe, Addison-Wesley, Reading, Massachusetts, 1997, 85-104
6. Neil deGrasse Tyson, Donald Goldsmith; Origins—Fourteen Billion Years of Cosmic Evolution, W. W. Norton & Company, New York, NY, 2004, 53-63
7. Neil deGrasse Tyson and Donald Goldsmith, Origins—Fourteen Billion Years of Cosmic Evolution, W. W. Norton & Company, New York, NY, 2004, 25-29
8. Stephen Hawking; The Universe in a Nutshell, Bantam Books, New York, NY, 2001, 78
9. Alan H. Guth; The Inflationary Universe, Addison-Wesley, Reading, Massachusetts, 1997, 57-83
10. Appendix K
11. Brian Greene; The Elegant Universe; Superstrings, Hidden Dimensions and the Quest for the Ultimate Theory, Vintage Books, New York, NY, March 2000
12. Brian Greene; The Fabric of the Cosmos; Space, Time and the Texture of Reality, Vintage Books, New York, NY, 2004
13. Gabriele Veneziano; The Myth of the Beginning of Time, Scientific American, May 2004, 54-65
14. Maurizio Gasperini, Gabriele Veneziano; The Pre-Big Bang Scenario in String Cosmology, Physics Reports 373 (1-2) 1-212, January 2003
15. Leonard Susskind, The Cosmic Landscape—String Theory and the Illusion of Intelligent Design, Little, Brown and Company, New York, NY, 2006, 122-130
16. Hugh Ross; The Fingerprint of God—Recent Scientific Discoveries Reveal the Unmistakable Identity of the Creator, Whitaker House, New Kensington PA, 1989, 79-96; Hugh Ross; Creation and Time—A Biblical and Scientific Perspective on the Creation-Date Controversy; NavPress Publishing Group, Colorado Springs, CO, 1994, 91-102
17. Richard Stenger; Hubble data: Universe's age in galactic embers, www.cnn.com/2002/TECH/04/24/hubble.age/index.html]
18. Hugh Ross; The Fingerprint of God—Recent Scientific Discoveries Reveal the Unmistakable Identity of the Creator, Whitaker House, New Kensington PA, 1989, 79-96
19. Hugh Ross; The Fingerprint of God—Recent Scientific Discoveries Reveal the Unmistakable Identity of the Creator, Whitaker House, New Kensington PA, 1989, 89
20. Science, 19 December 2003, Breakthrough of the Year, Illuminating the Dark Universe, 2038-2039
21. Discover, The Year in Science, 100 Top Science Stories of 2003, No. 2. Probe Reveals Age, Composition and Shape of the Universe, January 2004, 37
22. Mark A. Garlick; The Story of the Solar System, Cambridge University Press, New York, 2002, 42-43
23. V.F. Buchwald; Handbook of Iron Meteorites, Volume 1, University California Press, 1976, 137-139
24. Heinrich D. Holland; The Chemical Evolution of the Atmosphere and Oceans, Princeton University Press, 1984, 3-12
25. L.E. Nyquist, B.M. Bansal, H. Wiesmann, C.-Y. Shih; "Martians" young and old: Zagami and ALH84001 (abstract)1995 Lunar Planet. Sci. XXVI, 1065-1066
26. Robert H. Dott, Jr., Roger Batten; Evolution of the Earth, Fourth Edition, 1981, McGrawHill Book Company, New York, 89
27. Robert H. Dott, Jr., Roger Batten; Evolution of the Earth, Fourth Edition, 1981, McGrawHill Book Company, New York, 87-99
28. Kenneth Miller; Finding Darwin's God—A Scientist's Search for Common Ground Between God and Evolution; 1999, Cliff Street Books, Harper Collins; New York, NY; 69-72]
29. Kenneth Miller; Finding Darwin's God—A Scientist's Search for Common Ground Between God and Evolution; 1999, Cliff Street Books, Harper Collins; New York, NY; 66-76
30. Michael Zeilik; Astronomy—The Evolving Universe, Ninth Edition, Cambridge University Press, Cambridge, UK, 2002, 153
31. Mark A. Garlick; The Story of the Solar System, Cambridge University Press, New York, 2002, 42-43, 68
32. Mark A. Garlick, The Story of the Solar System, Cambridge University Press, New York, 2002, 68
33. Hugh Ross; Creation and Time—A Biblical and Scientific Perspective on the Creation-Date Controversy, Navpress Publishing Group, Colorado Springs, 1994, 105-106
34. Robert T. Pennock; Tower of Babel—The Evidence Against the New Creationism, MIT Press, Massachusetts Institute of Technology, 2000, 221-224
35. Richard B. Bliss; Origins—Creation or Evolution, Master Books, Green River, Arizona, 1996 (1st printing 1988), 68
36. John MacArthur; The Battle for the Beginning—Creation, Evolution and the Bible, 2001, W Publishing Group, 58
37. David Snoke, A Biblical Case for an Old Earth, Interdisciplinary Research Institute, Hatfield PA, 1998

Chapter 5. Old Blackwater

Genesis 1:2 Now the earth was formless and empty, darkness was over the surface of the deep, and the Spirit of God was hovering over the waters...

This description reveals three traits of our newly formed planet.

Earth was without form and empty.

Unformed and unfilled? What was the Genesis Observer referring to? Water? Beer? What was missing at the time that this description of Earth was given? Probably the things created during the approaching six days of creation; life and the conditions required for life to thrive.

Earth was dark.

The surface of the waters was not illuminated by the sun. The Genesis Observer was on a planet shrouded by a dreary, foggy, dark, rainy atmosphere that completely blocked the sunlight. This dismal condition will become more evident as we study the events associated with the six days of creation, half of which describe the changes in the Earth's atmosphere.

Earth was wet.

The Genesis Observer was sailing in waters of unspecified breadth and depth. The surface of the young Earth apparently retained a dark ocean of liquid water. What does science have to say about Earth's appearance as it formed?

Earth Birth

Nine billion years after the Big Bang, a vast cloud of interstellar dust, the scattered remains of dead stars, was suspended within the Milky Way. An unknown disturbance, perhaps the gravity of a star or the energy of a supernova, may have provided enough of a jolt to start the shrinkage of this cloud under the force of gravity[1]. This contraction was the first sign of labor; a newborn solar system was beginning to take shape about five billion years ago. The best model of the solar system's genesis is the nebular hypothesis, which envisions a large interstellar cloud of particles and gases (the nebula) that flattened out as it spun around, like a cosmic pizza. The solar nebula yielded the sun at its center, surrounded by a disk of gases and particles composed of minerals, metal and ice. The events leading to the formation of planets began when molecules in this dusty disk condensed and formed tiny particles. Electrostatic forces caused these little bits of iron and rock to stick together when they bumped into one another, yielding pebble-sized particles. Even larger boulders formed as this agglomeration continued, eventually yielding mountain-sized masses. These planetesimals were still able to retain chunks that they bumped into, but they were also large enough to exert a substantial gravitation force that reeled in nearby boulders, enabling them to grow to hundreds—and then thousands—of kilometers in size. Ten million years after the solar system began to form, some of these planetesimals had merged into a large terrestrial protoplanet roughly half the size of today's Earth. After 100 million years, the gravity of the protoplanet had swept a clear path as it revolved around the sun, enabling it to attain its current size. Earth was born[2].

During this gradual growth, Earth's constituents were compacted by gravity into a dense sphere. This fusion generated heat, which was supplemented by heat from the radioactive decay of unstable elements within the planet's interior. The original components of the atmosphere, including hydrogen and helium from the solar nebula, were so light that gravity could not retain them, and they were pushed away from the planet by solar radiation. Therefore the new-born planet was a vacuous, hot ball of molten rock with an unimpeded view of the sun[3,4].

Getting Mooned

Most of the planetary satellites in our solar system were formed from materials swirling about the protoplanets. Our satellite is unusual, though. It was adopted. Roughly 4.5 billion years ago, it appears that the Earth got mooned! A huge object, roughly the size of Mars, grazed our planet. This space invader struck a glancing blow at a relative speed of 25,000 miles per hour, sending a massive amount of matter into Earth's orbit along with the remains of the intruder. These ejected fragments from this giant impact were eventually drawn together by gravity and aggregated into one large satellite. Our moon may have been birthed by this Big Bump[5-7]!

Passing Gas

About 4.5 billion years ago, the Earth cooled and segregated into a metal-rich core at its center surrounded by a less dense mantle and a relatively light crust, and oceans began to emerge along with a heavier atmosphere[8]. Although the Earth's initial atmosphere of light gases had been lost, a new atmosphere was being generated from the materials within the Earth itself. A volcanic out-gassing of heavier gases, such as carbon dioxide, carbon monoxide, sulfur dioxide, methane, water, ammonia and nitrogen, coupled with the production of helium and argon as byproducts of radioactive decay of heavier elements, began to cover Earth's surface. This "big burp" lasted several hundred million years and spewed out enough vapor to establish Earth's second atmosphere[9-11].

Getting Stoned

Comets and asteroids assaulted the Earth for several hundred million years after it formed[12,13], with the most intense bombardment occurring more than four billion years ago. These extraterrestrial objects were composed of ice, rocks, gases and carbon. Their violent impacts on the Earth's surface released more water and gases, enhancing the rate of the atmosphere's formation. The combination of volcanic out-gassing and impacts of comets, meteors and asteroids yielded an atmosphere rich in water, carbon dioxide and nitrogen that shrouded the Earth, causing a greenhouse effect that kept the planet's surface immersed in a steamy blanket.

Waterworld

As Earth's surface cooled, the steam in the atmosphere began to condense and the planet experienced torrential rainfalls that yielded oceans of liquid water on the planet's surface. There is evidence that large bodies of water were formed more than four billion years ago[14, 15], although the relentless bombardment of comets and meteors would disrupt, heat and even vaporize these early oceans.

Vacancy

There is currently no evidence that life existed more than four billion years ago. Although the planet's atmosphere and ocean had begun to evolve, life apparently had not. Perhaps the environment was too harsh for the tree of life to take root.

A Good Match

Despite the lack of mechanistic details or historical timelines in the Bible, Genesis 1:2 provides several observations that *may* be consistent with Earth's characteristics about four billion years ago; our planet was cool enough for an ocean of water to form, the surface of the waters would have been darkened by the intense cloud cover and rainfall, and the ocean was barren of life. But if the first verses of the Bible provide a window with a view of the early Earth, then why does Genesis start with a description that seems to match conditions 4.0 billion years ago? Is the Bible's description of the young Earth divinely inspired, or am I just a Monday morning quarterback forcing the scriptures to fit the findings of science? Why didn't the Bible start with a description of interstellar dust, or planetesimals, or a protoplanet? Why not begin with the bright, hot, dry, molten, lifeless Earth 4.6 billion years ago? Why not initiate Genesis with a recount of the Big Bump 4.5 billion years ago? How about the steamy, cloudy, lifeless

Earth that may not have yet retained an ocean about 4.4 billion years ago, or the Big Burp 4.3 billion years ago? I think that God selected the overcast, watery, lifeless surface of the Earth about four billion years ago as the starting point for the Genesis story because life was about to debut. Genesis One emphasizes life, making this stage of the Earth's development an appropriate starting point. What makes me even more suspicious that life's first appearance was imminent in the first half of Genesis 1:2? The second half of Genesis 1:2! That's next.

References
1. Mark A. Garlick; The Story of the Solar System, Cambridge University Press, New York, 2002, 24-27, 34-36
2. Mark A. Garlick; The Story of the Solar System, Cambridge University Press, New York, 2002, 34-36
3. Mark A. Garlick; The Story of the Solar System, Cambridge University Press, New York, 2002, 24-39, 70
4. Michael Zeilik; Astronomy—The Evolving Universe, Ninth Edition, Cambridge University Press, 2002, 161-163
5. Mark A. Garlick; The Story of the Solar System, Cambridge University Press, New York, 2002, 67-68
6. Michael Zeilik; Astronomy—The Evolving Universe, Ninth Edition, Cambridge University Press, 2002, 248
7. Ron Redfern; Origins—The Evolution of Continents, Oceans and Life, University of Oklahoma Press, 2001, 40-41
8. Heinrich D. Holland; The Chemical Evolution of the Atmosphere and Oceans, Princeton University Press, 1984
9. Jon Erickson; Plate Tectonics—Unraveling the Mysteries of the Earth, Revised Edition 2001, Checkmark Books, New York, 182-190
10. Mark A. Garlick; The Story of the Solar System, Cambridge University Press, New York, 2002, 38-39
11. Michael Zeilik; Astronomy—The Evolving Universe, Ninth Edition, Cambridge University Press, 2002, 151-164
12. Jon Erickson; Plate Tectonics—Unraveling the Mysteries of the Earth, Revised Edition 2001, Checkmark Books, New York, 183
13. Mark A. Garlick; The Story of the Solar System, Cambridge University Press, New York, 2002, 36
14. Heinrich D. Holland; The Chemical Evolution of the Atmosphere and Oceans, Princeton University Press, 1984, 64-88, 110
15. Jon Erickson; Plate Tectonics—Unraveling the Mysteries of the Earth, Revised Edition 2001, Checkmark Books, New York, 184

Chapter 6. Is It Soup Yet?

Genesis 1:2...and the Spirit of God was hovering over the waters.

Hovercraft

The Spirit of God was hovering over the waters of the Earth's earliest waters. Hovering? Why would He be doing that? This same "hovering" term was used later in the Old Testament to describe a bird protecting the young life in its nest. *Deuteronomy 32:11 like an eagle that stirs up its nest and hovers over its young,* Does this imagery apply to God as well? Was God protecting the youngest forms of life while hovering over the ocean? Did God decide that this seemingly insignificant planet in His vast universe was well suited, perhaps uniquely suited, for a grand experiment? Was God awaiting the first appearance of life that was emerging via natural means? Maybe He was supernaturally formulating life because it was too complex to occur naturally. Or did He divinely protect the early life that had already formed on its own? Perhaps a natural process responsible for life's genesis was being divinely turbocharged to ensure success.

Maybe I am crazy and this verse has nothing to do with the origin of life; perhaps God was just hanging out. But even if this verse hints that life was starting in the ocean waters, it tells us absolutely nothing about *how* or *when* it happened; it only confirms that God was there when it did. After all, the Bible does not teach us about bacteria or their predecessors, so why would anyone expect biochemical details about life's origin to leap off of the page? There is no biblical basis for demanding a supernatural jump-start for life on Earth; the origin of life via a natural mechanism may have been God's intent from the beginning. Personally, I find such a scenario to be a far more impressive display of God's intelligence than imagining Him "influencing" or "guiding" or "intelligently designing" creation by sneaking in a miracle when no one was looking in order to get those pesky little microorganisms to form. Why is it so difficult to acknowledge that Big-Banging a universe in which life could evolve via natural mechanisms on a beautiful blue planet could have been a stroke of divine genius? Is our faith so weak and our intellect so dim that when some arrogant unbelievers suggest that "natural" phenomena are "atheistic" phenomena, we react by concluding that only "supernatural" acts can be "godly"?

Something's Fishy

Creationists shudder at the thought of a natural vehicle delivering life to this planet. In an attempt to defend God's honor and retain His membership in the Magical Creator Union, they insist that mind-boggling supernatural acts must have initiated life because that is how they think any decent Creator creates complicated creatures. (Am I the only one who thinks that's the same as saying that God is too stupid to have made a planet where life could evolve naturally?) Can God make animals appear suddenly? Sure! Jesus gave thanks for five loaves and two fish, multiplied them and fed thousands[1]. The multiplication of the fish was a timely method of demonstrating Jesus' deity while feeding a hungry throng, but this passage never states that supernatural acts are the only way, the best way, the most efficient way, or even the most impressive way for God to make fish. There is nothing ungodly about anything God does, even if He lets nature—the nature that He created—do it for Him.

No Comment

The Bible does not restrict the creation of life to supernatural intervention, nor does it define the chemistry that bridged inanimate chemicals and the microscopic pioneers of life. The only revelation that God gives concerning the creation of life is that it happened under His watch. Creationist complaints to the otherwise have no biblical basis. Rather, they reflect a desire to disprove Darwin, defy evolution, debunk modern science, and destroy the evil influences of atheism[2].

If the foundation of your faith is science's inability to ascertain life's origin, you have a serious problem in your basement. Let the scientists try to figure it out. Their progress should have no impact on your relationship with God or your confidence in the Bible because the origins of microscopic life are not discussed in Genesis.

What can scientists tell us about the origin of life, anyway?

Made from Scratch

Not as much as they would like to! No one knows how life began[3] and there is no secret society trying to convince you otherwise. But make no mistake about it; scientists are still trying to figure it out for a host of reasons. First, it is probably the greatest scientific discovery that could ever be made. Second, figuring out how those little buggers formed on Earth would help us to more accurately estimate how likely it is that life exists on other planets. Third, unlike creating a universe or a solar system or a continent, forming life appears to be an experiment that can be performed in small vessels under laboratory conditions that mimic the early Earth. Lastly, the fame associated with figuring how life began on Earth would be prolific; it would no doubt land a picture of the lucky geek on the Life cereal box. (Get it?…forming life…Life cereal…never mind.)

People have pondered this problem for a long time. Darwin recognized the magnitude of difficulty of the origin-of-life problem, hinting in the first edition of *The Origin of Species* that the Almighty may have gotten the ball rolling. Most scientists have not shared these sentiments, and neither did later editions of Darwin's book. In fact Darwin wrote a letter in which he mused about the origin of life in a warm, primordial pool that had the appropriate ingredients. A century and a half later, scientists still cannot create life from scratch in the lab or explain how it started on Earth, and there is no consensus that they will ever be able to do so. They have made great strides in the study of life's origin, however, utilizing the characteristics of contemporary life, the history of life in the fossil record, surveys of the chemical composition of the cosmos, identification of organic compounds contained within comets and meteors that crashed into the Earth, and the study of chemical reactions that can turn simple compounds into the small building blocks of life[4]. Let's consider some of the probable characteristics of early life forms.

Young Life

Early life was simpler than bacteria.

The most ancient fossils are not ducks, turtles, bullfrogs, birds, or trees. The oldest fossilized life corresponds to lowly little bacteria. These little beasties are incredibly complex but are undeniably the simplest form of life on the planet. They have a single cell that lacks a nucleus and their DNA consists of a single strand of genetic code, rather than two copies of genes found in the chromosomes of more complex life[5]. Scientists do *not* think that ancient bacteria suddenly self-assembled from inanimate materials in one incredibly lucky step. There were ancestors to these bacteria, but their identity may be impossible to extract from the fossil record. Geologic forces have recycled most of the rocks formed during the early period of Earth's history, and clues concerning the identity of the living and non-living precursors to the most ancient bacteria and the processes that established life may never be found[6]. (Of course, most creationists counter that there is no evidence of their predecessors because there were no predecessors!)

Early life faced a rough start.

The path leading from inanimate matter to our microscopic common ancestor was not an easy one[7, 8]. This most recent common ancestor had its own history that probably began with the basic chemical building blocks of life. Life may have even originated more than once, but may have been pummeled or vaporized into extinction by meteors and comets more than four billion years ago. Eventually, species may have then formed whose descendents were able to endure as the ocean's environment became more hospitable. Life may have then reproduced while being subjected to extinctions and the manifestations of new forms, leading to the last common ancestor of all contemporary life[9].

Early life began slightly less than 4 billion years ago.

Geochemists have detected carbon in several isotopic forms—an indirect signature of life—in rocks about 3.8 billion years old[10]. Photosynthetic life tends to accumulate a bit more carbon 12 than carbon 13, therefore ancient rocks that are enriched in carbon 12 may have formed in the presence of photosynthetic life[11]. The oldest direct indications of life, bacteria fossils, have been found in sedimentary rocks about 3.5—3.6 billion years old.

Early life appeared "rapidly".

It appears that several hundred million years after oceans began to form and just after the intense bombardment of the oceans by comets and meteors had subsided, single-celled organisms were thriving[12]. On a geologic time scale, life formed very quickly on this planet after pools of liquid water were available.

Early life could have thrived at seemingly "sterile" conditions.

Did you ever notice how life thrives in the most disgusting places? Like that disgusting green or yellow slimy gunk in your refrigerator, behind your toilet, under your toenails, in your sneakers or beneath rocks? Life is tenacious, and the relatively recent discovery of single-celled life forms that thrive in extreme environments sheds light on just how rugged single-celled life forms can be[13]. During the last third of the twentieth century, the existence of organisms that thrive under conditions we have previously considered as sterile has revolutionized our understanding of life while possibly opening a window on the origin of life. These organisms are called "extremophiles". They are the senseless teenagers of single-celled life—hanging out in dangerous places and reproducing like mad. They can be found near thermal vents on the ocean floor where ice-cold water is greeted by searing hot lava under crushing pressures in complete darkness. They live in the pores of solid rock at great depths below the Earth's surface. They can be found thriving in glaciers. They can endure chemicals that kill other forms of life, and most do not need oxygen to survive. This implies that this planet's pioneer life forms could have originated under equally extreme conditions and may be more closely related to the extremophiles than any other contemporary form of microscopic life. Maybe the visions of life beginning in warm waters near a beautiful beach on a crisp summer day are completely off the mark. Life may have started under the nastiest of imaginable conditions.

Early life produced energy to power its functions.

Every living organism has the capability to produce energy to power its functions. There are only a few closely related metabolisms that perform this transformation, and the earliest life undoubtedly had the same capacity[14]. Most scientists favor the notion that the first life fed off of compounds found in the primordial soup, while others propose that the first life forms were photosynthetic microbes capable of taking in carbon dioxide and water to generate organic compounds[15].

Early life contained ingredients common to all life.

Living systems are composed of chemicals, and the earliest life was probably composed of the same ingredients. Most scientists are inclined to think that even the complex, long-chain molecules of life such as RNA evolved naturally from the linkage of smaller molecular building blocks, which in turn had formed via reactions of even smaller molecules and elements. A quick look at these common elements, compounds, building blocks and long chain molecules of life can provide clues about the origin of life.

Let's Get Started

Organic Chemistry 1

The chemistry of life is well-documented in numerous books written for general audiences, including *The Human Genome*[16], *Instant Biology*[17], *The Cartoon Guide to Genetics*[18] and *DNA—The Secret of Life*[19]. A tremendous amount of information has been accumulated that provides tantalizing clues about the natural genesis of life. Most scientists believe that life originated in some manner from this Earth-bound mix of water, gases, chemicals, rocks, minerals and energy[20].

Space Invaders

There are some who feel that the crock pot of the early ocean could not have produced complex bacterial life as quickly as it emerged on Earth. They think that life was imported. We're not talking about organic chemicals that fell (and continue to fall) to Earth within comets and meteors, but tiny little fully functional one-celled astronauts. Perhaps our origins can be traced to a resilient little alien germ that was minding its own business when a tremendous meteor impact on its home planet sent it into outer space and directed it toward Earth. Such an organism may have had a very slow and rugged metabolism that enabled it to survive the travails of extended space travel and stresses of entering the atmos-phere and impacting into the ocean. Freed from its rock-like space capsule into an empty ocean, it began to reproduce and evolve. Although such a story may explain the sudden emergence of life on our planet, it poses other fundamental problems. How did the extraterrestrial life form in the first place on its home planet, and did it earn frequent flier miles?

Aliens

"Directed panspermia" explains away these interstellar transport dif-ficulties in a very sensible manner. It's a well known that animals can carry seeds from one place to another in their hair, feathers or drop-pings. Species have been transported from one continent to anoth-er on the clothes and ships of sailors in a similar manner. Even Steven King got mileage out of this phenomenon in his novel *Arachnophobia*, where these nasty spiders from…well, I'll let you buy the book or rent the movie to find out more. Perhaps this is how life began on Earth! Aliens did it! Maybe they accidentally left bac-teria behind when they didn't clean up after their picnic, or pur-posely planted some scum as an experiment. Teenage aliens on a galactic joy ride may have impregnated the planet during a low-fly-ing UFO prank. Perhaps all of us are the product of government-sponsored research on the planet Vidarspackal. But who made the aliens? Did they evolve or did God create them instantly? In what type of Vidarspackalien spaceship did they traverse the vast universe? Were the Vidarspackaliens themselves the evolutionary product of directed panspermia emanating from the Spangorian galaxy? These ideas are intriguing, but this solution requires not only the origin of life on another planet, but also the evolution of intelligent life on that other planet, the construction of interstellar spaceships, and the well-timed arrival of alien biochemists at the infant Earth. I'm not buying it. Until those Roswell corpses are recovered with packets of Extraterrestrial Bacteria Blast in their back pockets and smashed warp drives in their crashed craft, I expect that most scientists will continue to hypothesize that life on Earth is a domestic product[21].

Good Luck and God Bless

It is no secret that no one knows how life began on Earth. Scientists are acutely aware of the difficulties that confront them as they explore life's origin. *Life's Origin*, a recent book that summarized the state-of-the-art understanding of life's beginnings, contains more frank assessments of the excruciating problems that perplex scientists than any creationist tract could even hope to conjure up[22]. *Rare Earth*, a fascinating book that argues for the common occurrence of microbial life but the rare appearance of animal life in the universe, carefully establishes the solar, planetary, geologic, atmospheric, and oceanic conditions required for life and a summary of ideas on life's origin, while acknowledging that there are still "more questions than answers about life's origin on Earth."[23]. Nevertheless, scientists exude so much intellectual curiosity that they can't stop trying, and they have made enough progress to justify their continued study. They have only started to attack the problem aggressively during the last 50 years, so you should give them at least a couple hundred more before criticizing their lack of progress. Martino Rizzotti, for example, has encouraged others to address the mind-bending problems of life's early evolution, including origins of the cell, the protein complex, the flagellum, the membrane and the nucleus[24]. Lynn Margulis and Michael F. Dolan have written an elegant text on the evolution of early life from Earth, covering the origin of life, the origin of cells, the origin of sex, and the origins of metabolisms[25]. These scientists have framed the problems and offered hypotheses concerning the origin and early evolution of life on Earth that encourage exploration, investigation and debate. Why should Christians be disconcerted by such well-organized zeal? Given the poor track record of church-based science, why would creationists ask Christians to bet their faith on the continued inability of scientists to solve a biochemistry problem? What threat do these scientists really pose to our faith? Consider the boundless optimism Jack Szostak of Harvard Medical School whose goal is to create a self-replicating RNA that can evolve before his eyes[26] and to ascertain how life began, while my personal goal remains getting my teenage girls out of college, out of my house, and into a marriage where they can replicate at their husbands' expense. What of Carl Woese[27], who conjectures that bacteria were preceded not by a simple, distinct, enduring organism, but rather by multiple temporary teams of genes[28]? If the origin of life was indeed an intelligently designed supernatural event, then investigators like Szostak and Benner and Woese will be a very frustrated group worthy of our compassion rather than criticism! But if the natural causes of the origin of life are one day revealed, it would be yet another well-deserved nail in the coffin of the creationism. God, however, would not be fazed. The integrity of the Bible would also remain unaltered because it says nothing, absolutely nothing, about the processes that accounted for the origin of microscopic life. We are now two verses into the Bible, and there is still no need to panic over the conflict between science and the Bible. There isn't one.

References
1. Matthew 14:14-21
2. L.R. Croft; How Life Began, Evangelical Press, Darlington England, 1988, 156
3. Ernst Mayr; What Evolution Is, Basic Books, New York, NY, 2001, 43
4. Life's Origin—The Beginnings of Biological Evolution, edited by J. William Schopf, University of California Press, Berkeley, California, 2002
5. Niles Eldredge; The Triumph of Evolution and the Failure of Creationism, Henry Holt and Company, New York, first Owl Book edition, 2001, 35-37
6. Life's Origin—The Beginnings of Biological Evolution, edited by J. William Schopf, University of California Press, Berkeley, California, 2002, 1-2
7. J. William Schopf; "When Did Life Begin?" in Life's Origin—The Beginnings of Biological Evolution, edited by J. William Schopf, University of California Press, Berkeley, California, 2002, 160-164
8. Peter Andrews, John Barber, Michael Benton, Marianne Collins, Christine Janis, Ely Kish, Akio Morishima, J. John Sepkoski, Jr., Christopher Stringer, Jean-Paul Tibbles; The Book of Life—An Illustrated History of the Evolution of Life on Earth, general editor Stephen Jay Gould, W.W. Norton and Co., New York, NY, 2001, 30-31
9. Rizzotti, M.; Early Evolution—From the Appearance of the First Cell to the First Modern Organism; Birkhauser, 2000, Basil, Switzerland, 49-50
10. Niles Eldredge; The Triumph of evolution and the Failure of Creationism, Henry Holt and Company, New York, first Owl Book edition, 2001, 35-37
11. Richard G. Colling; Random Designer—Created from Chaos to Connect with the Creator, Browning Press, Bourbonnais, Illinois, 2004, 97
12. J. William Schopf, "When Did Life Begin?" in Life's Origin—The Beginnings of Biological Evolution, edited by J. William Schopf, University of California Press, Berkeley, California, 2002, 158-179
13. Peter D. Ward, Donald Brownlee, Rare Earth—Why Complex Life Is Uncommon in the Universe, Copernicus, Springer-Verlag New York Inc., New York, NY, 2000, xiii-xxiv, 1-13
14. J. William Schopf, "When Did Life Begin?" in Life's Origin—The Beginnings of Biological Evolution, edited by J. William Schopf, University of California Press, Berkeley, California, 2002, 160
15. Stanley L. Miller, Antonio Lazcano; "Formation of the Building Blocks of Life," in Life's Origin—The Beginnings of Biological Evolution, edited by J. William Schopf, University of California Press, Berkeley, California, 2002, 81-84, 105-107
16. Jeremy Cherfas; The Human Genome—A Beginner's Guide to the Code of Life, Doring Kindersly, London, 2002
17. Boyce Rensberger, Instant Biology—From Single Cells to Human Beings, and Beyond, Fawcett Columbine, New York, 1996
18. Larry Gonick, Mark Wheelis; The Cartoon Guide to Genetics, Harper Perennial, New York, 1991
19. James D. Watson with Andrew Berry; DNA—The Secret of Life, Alfred A. Knopf, New York, 2003
20. Appendix L
21. Appendix L
22. Life's Origin—The Beginnings of Biological Evolution, edited by J. William Schopf, University of California Press, Berkeley, California, 2002
23. Peter D. Ward, Donald Brownlee, Rare Earth—Why Complex Life Is Uncommon in the Universe, Copernicus, Springer-Verlag New York, Inc., New York, NY, 2000, 61
24. Rizzotti, M.; Early Evolution—From the Appearance of the First Cell to the First Modern Organism; Birkhauser, 2000, Basil, Switzerland
25. Lynn Margulis, Michael F. Dolan; Early Life—Evolution on the PreCambrian Earth, Second Edition, 2002, Jones and Bartlett Publishers, Sudbury, MA
26. Carl Zimmer, What Came Before DNA?, Discover, June 2004, 34-41
27. Matt Ridley, Genome—The Autobiography of a Species in 23 Chapters, Harper Perennial, 1999,19-21
28. Carl Woese, The Universal Ancestor, Proceedings of the National Academy of Sciences of the USA, 1998, 95:6854-6859

Chapter 7. Day One: Who Turned On the Lights?

God had already created the heavens and Earth and His Spirit was hovering over bodies of water that were shrouded by clouds. Torrential rainstorms were flooding the Earth. This fog was so dense that the surface of the planet was dark and the Genesis Observer could only see blackness. And then things started to lighten up!

Genesis 1:3-5 And God said, "Let there be light," and there was light. God saw that the light was good, and he separated the light from the darkness. God called the light "day," and the darkness he called "night." And there was evening, and there was morning—the first day.

Lighten Up

Sunlight penetrated the dense clouds and fog and reached the surface of the Earth's ocean waters.

The Earth's thick, dank atmospheric cover was finally penetrated by light from the sun. Hours and hours of faint light were followed by hours of darkness. It was possible to differentiate morning and evening even though the sun, moon and stars could not be seen from Earth's surface because of the dense cloud cover. Perhaps that is why the creation of light and the observation of day and night were reported on Day One, even though the sun, moon and stars were not described until Day Four. It is more likely, though, that the creation of light may have been described on Day One in order to fit the literary pattern that would associate it with light-emitting objects on Day Four that would solve the problem of darkness on the planet.

Problem	Preparation	Population
Genesis 1:2	Days 1-3	Days 4-6
Darkness	**1a creation of light (day)**	4a creation of sun
	1b separation from darkness (night)	4b creation of moon, stars
Watery abyss	2a creation of firmament	5a creation of birds
	2b separation of waters above from waters below	5b creation of fish
Formless Earth	3a separation of earth from sea	6a creation of land animals
	3b creation of vegetation	6b creation of humans
"without *form* and *void*"	Formlessness is formed	Void is filled

What have scientists learned about our early atmosphere and the appearance of light?

A Breath of Fresh Air

The atmosphere has been changing since the Earth formed 4.6 billion years ago. The primitive atmosphere of hydrogen and helium was so light that the Earth's gravity could not retain it. The Earth's second atmosphere, which was derived from heavier gases expelled from the Earth itself, was so hot that the water could not readily condense and a heavy cloud cover—similar to the one that still envelopes Venus[1]—blanketed the planet. Earth cooled, though, and about 4.4 billion years ago the water vapor began to condense, causing the torrential rainfalls. These rainfalls continued to deluge the Earth's surface and swell the oceans while the Earth's water supply was being supplemented by water released during comet impacts that continued for several hundred million years. The atmosphere continued to be depleted of its water content[2] and roughly four billion years ago, sunlight was able to penetrate the cloud cover and reach the planet's surface.

The Genesis Observer's report from the surface of the Earth on Day One is the simple observation of light making it through the cloud cover as the Earth's second atmosphere began to dissipate. All remains well between science and the Bible.

References
1. Jon Erickson; Plate Tectonics—Unraveling the Mysteries of the Earth, Revised Edition 2001, Checkmark Books, New York, 184-185
2. Mark A. Garlick, The Story of the Solar System, Cambridge University Press, New York, 2002, 70-71

Chapter 8. Day Two: Sky High

Genesis 1:6-7 And God said, "Let there be an expanse between the waters to separate water from water." So God made the expanse and separated the water under the expanse from the water above it. And it was so. God called the expanse "sky." And there was evening, and there was morning—the second day.

Sky High

During Day Two, a clear atmosphere emerged along Earth's surface, separating the water in the dense cloud cover above from the ocean waters below. The Genesis Observer now had an extended range of visibility that allowed him to clearly see the surface of the burgeoning ocean and the clouds in the heavens. At the end of the day, there was water in the ocean, water in the clouds, and a clear layer of air between them. It appears that the Earth's dense fog blanket was being transformed into oceans of water below a sky filled with billowing clouds.

Problem	Preparation	Population
Genesis 1:2	Days 1-3	Days 4-6
Darkness	1a creation of light (day)	4a creation of sun
	1b separation from darkness (night)	4b creation of moon, stars
Watery abyss	2a creation of firmament	5a creation of birds
	2b separation of waters above from waters below	5b creation of fish
Formless Earth	3a separation of earth from sea	6a creation of land animals
	3b creation of vegetation	6b creation of humans
"without *form* and *void*"	Formlessness is formed	Void is filled

What can science tell us about the changes in the Earth's atmosphere that occurred after light had penetrated through the clouds and the ocean "waters" had begun to collect?

Let's Clear the Air

Let's look at some of the changes in the atmosphere that were probably transpiring 3.7—4.0 billion years ago.

Ashes, Ashes, We All Fall Down

Nasty soot that was belched out of volcanoes darkened the skies of the young Earth. Volcanic activity decreased with time, however, as the radioactive material in our planet's interior was slowly depleted. As the frequency of volcanic eruptions lessened, the pull of gravity and the flush of rain and snow combined to clear this dust from the air.

Deep Impact

The Earth and the moon were subject to a several hundred million year-long assault of comets, asteroids and meteors. Unlike Earth, the moon's surface is sedentary and lacks the wind or water required to erode its features. As a result, the remnants of this assault are still clearly seen on the moon's pockmarked surface. Although the comets added to the supply of Earth's water that would ultimately harbor life, their impacts could have frustrated the origin of life by churning, heating, boiling, and vaporizing the young bodies of liquid water[1]. These crashes lessened as the solar system became depleted of the majority of these rouge interplanetary wanderers. Their reign of intense terror ended about 3.9 billion years ago[2-4], although the less frequent impacts since then have had global implications on Earth's biosphere[5].

Raindrops Keep Fallin' on My Head

The changes that occurred in Earth's atmosphere were directly related to the evolution of the oceans[6,7]. The rain was unrelenting, and an unimpeded storm flooded Earth's surface. The pools of liquid water that had begun to form more than four billion years ago had covered most of Earth's surface within several hundred million years[8], during which time the atmosphere probably remained steamy[9]. Because the continent-building epoch had not yet started, the entire surface of Earth may have even been covered with water, with the exception of a spattering of volcanic islands[10-12].

A Small Greenhouse

Earth's early atmosphere contained roughly a thousand times as much carbon dioxide as it does today. Some of the carbon dioxide dissolved in water droplets of the clouds, and a portion of the dissolved gas reacted with water to form carbonic acid. The resultant acid rain reacted with rocks on the emerging continents and slowly formed stable carbonate minerals such as limestone and dolomite. These processes steadily depleted the atmosphere of carbon dioxide. The cycle continues today, as the movements of the planet's plates plunge carbonate minerals on the ocean floor to great depths where they are heated, releasing carbon dioxide gas that finds its way back into the atmosphere through volcanic releases[13]. Carbon dioxide and water are greenhouse gases that absorb much of the infrared radiation released from the surface of the Earth. Therefore as the amount of water and carbon dioxide in the atmosphere declined, the Earth's surface cooled to more moderate temperatures.

Taking a Big Leap

The length of a day has been increasing ever since the Earth was formed because of frictional forces associated with ocean tides. The length of the year hardly increases at all, however, because there are no significant frictional forces impeding the Earth as it revolves around the sun. Because the days were shorter in duration but the length of the year was about the same, there were more days in the distant past! About four billion years ago, each day was only five hours long. Four hundred million ago, each year contained 400 days that were almost 22 hours long. Today we enjoy 365 24-hour days each year, and a bonus day on leap years. This slowing rate of rotation probably yielded calmer winds that were less capable of kicking up little water droplets from the ocean surface that supply clouds with moisture.

Singin' the Blues

Day Two has passed and there is still no need for antagonism between science and the Bible. The Bible may actually provide a quick glimpse at changes in the atmosphere that are consistent with an era roughly 3.8 billion years ago, when Earth was probably covered with an ocean, a clear atmosphere and clouds.

The stage was set for another transformation of biblical proportions.

References
1. J. William Schopf; "When Did Life Begin?" in Life's Origin—The Beginnings of Biological Evolution, edited by J. William Schopf, University of California Press, Berkeley, California, 2002, 175
2. Jon Erickson; Plate Tectonics—Unraveling the Mysteries of the Earth, Revised Edition 2001, Checkmark Books, New York, 183
3. J. William Schopf; "When Did Life Begin?" in Life's Origin—The Beginnings of Biological Evolution, edited by J. William Schopf, University of California Press, Berkeley, California, 2002, 175
4. Michael Zeilik; Astronomy—The Evolving Universe, Ninth Edition, Cambridge University Press, Cambridge, UK, 2002, 162
5. Peter D. Ward, Donald Brownlee, Rare Earth—Why Complex Life Is Uncommon in the Universe, Copernicus, Springer-Verlag New York, Inc., New York, NY, 2000, 157-189
6. Michael Zeilik; Astronomy—The Evolving Universe, Ninth Edition, Cambridge University Press, Cambridge, UK, 2002, 161-163
7. Mark A. Garlick; The Story of the Solar System, Cambridge University Press, New York, 2002, 70
8. Michael Zeilik, Astronomy—The Evolving Universe, Ninth Edition, Cambridge University Press, Cambridge, UK, 2002, 153
9. Robert H. Dott, Jr., Roger Batten; Evolution of the Earth, Fourth Edition, 1981, McGrawHill Book Company, New York, 186
10. Jon Erickson; Plate Tectonics—Unraveling the Mysteries of the Earth, Revised Edition 2001, Checkmark Books, New York, 184
11. Peter D. Ward, Donald Brownlee; Rare Earth—Why Complex Life Is Uncommon in the Universe, Copernicus, Springer-Verlag New York, Inc., New York, NY, 2000, 201-20212.
12. Jon Erickson; Plate Tectonics—Unraveling the Mysteries of the Earth, Revised Edition 2001, Checkmark Books, New York, 190-193
13. Peter D. Ward, Donald Brownlee; Rare Earth—Why Complex Life Is Uncommon in the Universe, Copernicus, Springer-Verlag New York, Inc., New York, NY, 2000, 208-212

Chapter 9. Day Three: Land Ho!

Genesis 1:9-10 And God said, "Let the water under the sky be gathered to one place, and let dry ground appear." And it was so. God called the dry ground "land", and the gathered waters he called "seas". And God saw that it was good.

Land appeared out of the ocean.

The Genesis Observer had been sailing the ocean that covered a substantial portion of the surface of the young Earth. On the third day of creation, ground rose out of the waters! The Genesis Observer had dry land to explore. An immense ocean preceding the appearance of land is also implied in the 24th and 104th Psalms. *Psalm 24:1-2 The earth is the Lord's, and everything in it, the world, and all who live in it; for he founded it upon the seas and established it upon the waters. Psalm 104:5-9 He set the earth on its foundations; it can never be moved. You covered it with the deep as with a garment; the waters stood above the mountains. But at your rebuke the waters fled, at the sound of your thunder they took to flight; they flowed over the mountains, they went down into the valleys, to the place you assigned for them. You set a boundary they cannot cross; never again will they cover the earth.*

What can science tell us of the origin of land?

Crack Me Up

Roughly four billion years ago, the continents began to form[1,2]. Although a thin crust encapsulated the entire Earth, most of it lay beneath the ocean floor. At this time the surface of Earth was probably covered with a single body of water peppered with volcanic islands[3-5] and the extent of the continental crust was only about 10% of its present size[6]. The crust, a mosaic of large, interlocking segments referred to as plates, became thicker and attained enough stability for continents to emerge. Roughly 3.8 billion years ago relatively little permanent growth in the continents had yet occurred[7], but stable portions of continents then formed as the planet continued to cool during the next three hundred million years. Some portions of the continental crust formed during this period have persisted until today[8].

Several forces contributed to the building of continents. The planet's initial crust was primarily composed of basalt; a dark, dense volcanic rock[9]. Portions of the basalt were apparently melted by geologic forces and meteoric impacts. Upon cooling and solidification, the basalt completed its transformation into granite. Granite is less dense than basalt, providing the buoyancy that lifted the granite above the underlying basalt. Granite is also thicker than an equivalent mass of basalt spread out over the same area; therefore the granite was able to lift the level of the continents above sea level[10].

The slow, persistent movements of the segments of Earth's crust could have also contributed to continent building. These tectonic plates and the continents they support move due to the slow-motion circulation of soft rock in the mantle. This flow exerts tremendous forces on the crust that are capable of moving entire continents laterally. For example, North America and Europe are moving apart from one another at a measly rate of an inch or so per year, a speed slightly greater than that attained by an 11-year old child who has been asked to take out the trash. Plates can also slide against one another in opposite directions along faults. They can get stuck for a while but when they finally have a chance to suddenly slip, an earthquake results. Although these plates have moved about at incredibly slow speeds, they have done so for even more incredibly long periods of time. Their movements have formed mountains, dug ocean trenches, and built land masses. Clear evidence of this type of tectonic activity dates back 3.6 billion years, and there is compelling evidence of a 500 million year growth spurt of continent formation that began three billion years ago that produced nearly three quarters of today's continental landmass[11]. Plate tectonics have also induced global rearrangements of the continents[12]. Scientists have been able to reconstruct the movement of ancient continents by using fossils, the dating of rocks, the shapes of continents, mineral deposits, evidence of erosion by glaciers, and rocks containing iron-rich crystals that were oriented toward the magnetic pole when they formed. Although it is difficult to trace the movements of the continents billions of years ago, it appears that about 700 million years ago there was a single continent, Rodinia, which subsequently broke into several continents that meandered about before rejoining into a supercontinent called Pangea. About 300 million years ago Pangea broke into several continents, which have drifted to their current locations. Ron Redfern's beautifully illustrated book chronicles the movements of these land masses during the last 700 million years[13]. Plate tectonics still fuel the engines of geologic change today.

Smooth Landing

Continents began to form on a watery Earth about four billion years ago as the crust became cooler, thicker, and more stable. One and a half billion years later, a sizable portion of the permanent continental crust had been established. Not only did plate tectonics form the land, but it also made our planet a hospitable environment for life[14].

There is no need to fret over the Bible's simple observation that land emerged from beneath the surface of the waters. That appears to be what actually happened.

References
1. Jon Erickson; Plate Tectonics—Unraveling the Mysteries of the Earth, Revised Edition 2001, Checkmark Books, New York, 27, 28
2. Robert H. Dott, Jr., Roger Batten, Evolution of the Earth, Fourth Edition, 1981, McGrawHill Book Company, New York, 113
3. Jon Erickson; Plate Tectonics—Unraveling the Mysteries of the Earth, Revised Edition 2001, Checkmark Books, New York, 27, 181-190
4. Peter Andrews, John Barber, Michael Benton, Marianne Collins, Christine Janis, Ely Kish, Akio Morishima, J. John Sepkoski, Jr., Christopher Stringer, Jean-Paul Tibbles; The Book of Life—An Illustrated History of the Evolution of Life on Earth, general editor Stephen Jay Gould, W.W. Norton and Co., New York, NY, 2001, 38
5. Peter D. Ward, Donald Brownlee; Rare Earth—Why Complex Life Is Uncommon in the Universe, Copernicus, Springer-Verlag New York, Inc., New York, NY, 2000, 201-202
6. Jon Erickson; Plate Tectonics—Unraveling the Mysteries of the Earth, Revised Edition 2001, Checkmark Books, New York, 27
7. Jon Erickson; Plate Tectonics—Unraveling the Mysteries of the Earth, Revised Edition 2001, Checkmark Books, New York, 28
8. Robert H. Dott, Jr., Roger Batten; Evolution of the Earth, Fourth Edition, 1981, McGrawHill Book Company, New York, 186
9. Jon Erickson; Plate Tectonics—Unraveling the Mysteries of the Earth, Revised Edition 2001, Checkmark Books, New York, 28
10. Robert H. Dott, Jr., Roger Batten; Evolution of the Earth, Fourth Edition, 1981, McGrawHill Book Company, New York, 132
11. Jon Erickson; Plate Tectonics—Unraveling the Mysteries of the Earth, Revised Edition 2001, Checkmark Books, New York, 29-31
12. Jon Erickson; Plate Tectonics—Unraveling the Mysteries of the Earth, Revised Edition 2001, Checkmark Books, New York, 1-26
13. Ron Redfern, Origins: The Evolution of Continents, Oceans and Life, University of Oklahoma Press, 2001, 52-261
14. Peter D. Ward, Donald Brownlee; Rare Earth—Why Complex Life Is Uncommon in the Universe, Copernicus, Springer-Verlag New York, Inc., New York, NY, 2000, 191-220

Chapter 10. Day Three: Green Peace

Genesis 1:11-13 Then God said, "Let the land produce vegetation: seed-bearing plants and trees on the land that bear fruit with seed in it, according to their various kinds." And it was so. The land produced vegetation: plants bearing seed according to their kinds and trees bearing fruit with seed in it according to their kinds. And God saw that it was good. And there was evening, and there was morning—the third day.

The land that arose out of the waters became fertile ground for plants and trees.

The Genesis Observer jumped out of his boat and began walking on the rich soil that supported a wide array of plants and trees. These verses have also been fertile ground for contention. There are three very divisive issues tucked away in this little passage; the process by which plant life appeared, the observation that seeds grow into the type of tree or plant that they came from, and the timing of the appearance of seed-bearing plants and trees relative to other forms of life.

Fresh Produce

There is no doubt about the identity of the Creator of Life, *"Then*

God said...", but there is nothing but doubt concerning how He created it. The description of the how plant life was formed simply indicates that *"The land produced vegetation:...".* This vague statement seems to allow for a natural method of the vegetation being produced, rather than restricting the creation of plants and trees to instantaneous miracles or supernaturally directed processes.

A Kind Word

The terse statement describing the reproduction of life, *"according to their kinds"* has become an anti-evolutionist motto. If this phrase was a little bit shorter, you would probably see it plastered on creationist bumper stickers. "Kind" is commonly associated with "species" by creationists, which seems to be a logical viewpoint in the context of reproduction. After all, apple trees beget apple trees of the same species. Therefore creationists consider microevolution, or small changes within a species caused by evolution, to be biblically permissible. (This grand theological concession has undoubtedly been influenced by the fact that microevolution has been observed and measured in the lab and in the wild!) But did macroevolution, evolution leading to the transformation of one species into another, occur? Nearly every red-blooded creationist would say "No!" because Genesis indicates that life can only produce life after its kind, which amounts to a scriptural prohibition of macroevolution.

Is this the only way that these verses can be interpreted? What lesson was God teaching through this observation that anyone, even ancient Hebrews, could understand? A fundamental attribute of life is clearly stated; plants give rise to plants after their kind. Everyone agrees that apple seeds produce apple trees, even the most heinous evolutionists! But is this biblical insight meant to establish the bounds of life's diversification over millions or billions of years? Maybe not. The history of modern man is a fleeting moment in geologic time. Genesis One may simply be providing a quick summary of the reproductive process that anyone, including the Genesis Observer, could appreciate. There is no reason, other than desiring to combat the evils of evolution, to insist that these verses were meant to define the extent of biological changes that could occur over hundreds of thousands, millions, or billions of years.

Out of Order

Although the beginning of life may have been hinted at in the second verse of Genesis One when the Spirit of God was hovering over the waters, the first explicit description of life in Genesis is associated with plants and trees found on the land. Therefore Young Earth Creationists have no choice but to believe that apple trees and orange trees were pioneer life forms. Skeptical scientists also favor this creationist viewpoint because it is so demonstrably wrong. Life, both the tiny microscopic forms and the larger, complex visible forms, was established surfside long before the plants and trees described on Day Three[1]. Consider the organisms that inhabited Earth during the three and a half billion years following life's origin roughly four billion years ago.

Precambrian Period, 4,000,000,000 to 600,000,000 years ago

The fossil and chemical record of old rocks is irrefutable concerning the earliest residents; single-celled bacteria without nuclei were the first known forms of life. Isotopic evidence of life dates back nearly four billion years. Bacteria fossils appear in rocks formed during the Precambrian period at least three and a half billion years ago. About two billion years later a small but incredibly significant change occurred; bacteria with nuclei appeared when the successful merger of two or more kinds of bacteria cells occurred[2]. During the latter part of this period, anaerobic bacteria, photosynthetic bacteria, and green algae had appeared[3].

Vendian Period, 600,000,000 to 540,000,000 years ago

Multi-cellular life inhabited the oceans, with the most notable example being Edicaran fauna[4]. Although named after the Edicara Hills of Australia where they were first discovered, similar fossils have been found in several continents[5]. A notable increase in the number of species occurred during this period[6], a trend that would become even more pronounced during the subsequent Cambrian Period.

Cambrian Period, 540,000,000 to 500,000,000 Years Ago

A proliferation of larger ocean-dwelling life forms occurred during the Cambrian Period[7-9]. After more than three billion years of boring microscopic bacteria, algae, and multicellular life, the oceans gave rise to a multitude of large, complex species. The Cambrian Period has been referred to as the period of visible life because a hypothetical observer (a secular version of our Genesis Observer) would have been able to see many of these large complex organisms, such as shellfish, sponges, brachiopods and coral. Although the majority of organisms detected in Cambrian fossils, such as trilobites, became extinct, some have persisted to modern times.

The fossil record is clear; microscopic life was flourishing in waters billions of years before the seed-bearing plants and fruit trees were thriving on land. Larger, visible forms of ocean life (that are correlated with Day Five) appeared several hundred million years before the plants and trees attributed to Day Three[10]. There is absolutely no doubt that fruit trees were not the first forms of life on Earth.

Is the Bible wrong, or do creationists read too much into Genesis One? You guessed it—creationists read too much into Genesis One. The Genesis Observer consigned the appearance of the land and the vegetation it would eventually support to the same day of creation. *Yes*, there was a huge time gap between the appearance of continents and the appearance of trees. *Yes*, life in the ocean preceded life on the land. *Yes*, fruit-bearing trees were not the first forms of life on the planet. Could it be, however, that Genesis presents the order of visible life out of sequence because the six days of creation are arranged within a *literary framework* rather than a chronological timeline? Although the overall sequence of events in Genesis One appears to be reasonable at first glance, starting with a lifeless Earth and ending with the creation of man, the chronological sequence of specific events during the creation week defers to the poetic framework of the six days. As it turns out, land and plants were consigned to Day Three.

Problem	Preparation	Population
Genesis 1:2	Days 1–3	Days 4–6
Darkness	1a creation of light (day)	4a creation of sun
	1b separation from darkness (night)	4b creation of moon, stars

Watery abyss	2a creation of firmament	5a creation of birds
	2b separation of waters above from waters below	5b creation of fish
Formless Earth	**3a separation of earth from sea**	6a creation of land animals
	3b creation of vegetation	6b creation of humans
"without *form* and *void*"	Formlessness is formed	Void is filled

If you are still reluctant to let the Bible "off the hook" for presenting the sequence of life out of order, then you may think that this mix-up proves that the Bible is not divinely inspired. If so, let me ask you two questions. Answer them honestly. Here's the first.

What did you do last year? Take a minute and consider how you would reply.

Now think about your answer. Did you delete boring activities? Did you conveniently forget embarrassing episodes? Did you overlook mundane details? Did you conceal illegal activities? Did you hide your darkest secret—an addiction to SpongeBob Squarepants reruns? You probably thought of your activities in an order that reflected their importance, although you may have also listed some or most of them according to their sequence. Should your reply be considered a legend, myth or fairy tale if you only spoke of only some of your accomplishments and did not present them in a precise chronological order? Of course not! Why then should believers obsess over the precise sequence of events within Genesis One, giving others the impression that if they are out of order then the Bible is not the Word of God?

Here is my second question. Remember to tell the truth.

What is the last exciting science book that you read?

Admit it; many technical books can be boring if you are not a geek. You're probably struggling to stay awake while reading this book, which is why I made the text so short and the appendices so long! If you wanted to relate a grand achievement to the general public, would your first instinct be to convey it in a manner that only a highly technical audience would appreciate? I don't think so. Why, then, do creationists insist that Genesis is an account designed to appease the technical curiosity of twenty first century scientists? I think that God placed observations of an evolving Earth in a six-day poetic framework to make it a better read.

Maybe He thought that the poetic principle of six days of work followed by a day of rest was more important principle for us to understand than knowing when trilobites first appeared.

Give It Up

For the peaceful co-existence between science and the Bible to continue, you need to stop pretending that the order of creation events in Genesis is chronological; it isn't! The scriptures yielded to literary elegance rather than sequential precision.

You will also have to acknowledge that the Bible never says that plant life instantaneously appeared. The Bible does say that the land produced life, however, leaving the door open for some slow, natural mechanism.

Finally, you will also have to admit that the observation of life begetting life "according to its kind" may have been intended to reflect what is obviously true on a time-scale that is commensurate with a man's lifespan, or the duration of modern civilization. "According to its kind" need not correspond to a biblical restriction on the limits of genetic diversity over unimaginably long periods of time.

References
1. Peter Andrews, John Barber, Michael Benton, Marianne Collins, Christine Janis, Ely Kish, Akio Morishima, J. John Sepkoski, Jr., Christopher Stringer, Jean-Paul Tibbles; The Book of Life—An Illustrated History of the Evolution of Life on Earth, general editor Stephen Jay Gould, W.W. Norton and Co., New York, NY,2001,36-63, J. John Sepkowski, Jr., Ch. 1, "Foundations—Life in the Oceans"
2. Niles Eldredge; The Triumph of Evolution and the Failure of Creationism; Henry Holt and Company; 2000; New York, NY; 39-41
3. Kenneth Miller; Finding Darwin's God—A Scientist's Search for Common Ground Between God and Evolution; 1999, Cliff Street Books, Harper Collins; New York, NY, 38,39
4. Kenneth Miller; Finding Darwin's God—A Scientist's Search for Common Ground Between God and Evolution; 1999, Cliff Street Books, Harper Collins; New York, NY, 38,39
5. Niles Eldredge; The Triumph of Evolution and the Failure of Creationism; Henry Holt and Company; 2000; New York, NY; 42-47
6. Peter Andrews, John Barber, Michael Benton, Marianne Collins, Christine Janis, Ely Kish, Akio Morishima, J. John Sepkoski, Jr., Christopher Stringer, Jean-Paul Tibbles; The Book of Life—An Illustrated History of the Evolution of Life on Earth, general editor Stephen Jay Gould, W.W. Norton and Co., New York, NY,2001,51-52
7. Niles Eldredge; The Triumph of Evolution and the Failure of Creationism; Henry Holt and Company; 2000; New York, NY; 42-47
8. Peter Andrews, John Barber, Michael Benton, Marianne Collins, Christine Janis, Ely Kish, Akio Morishima, J. John Sepkoski, Jr., Christopher Stringer, Jean-Paul Tibbles; The Book of Life—An Illustrated History of the Evolution of Life on Earth, general editor Stephen Jay Gould, W.W. Norton and Co., New York, NY,2001,51-57]
9. Kenneth Miller; Finding Darwin's God—A Scientist's Search for Common Ground Between God and Evolution; 1999, Cliff Street Books, Harper Collins; New York, NY, 38,39
10. Kenneth Miller; Finding Darwin's God—A Scientist's Search for Common Ground Between God and Evolution; 1999, Cliff Street Books, Harper Collins; New York, NY, 38,39

Chapter 11. Day Four: First Star I See Tonight

Genesis 1:14-19 And God said, "Let there be lights in the expanse of the sky to separate the day from the night, and let them serve as signs to mark seasons and days and years, and let them be lights in the expanse of the sky to give light on the earth." And it was so. God made two great lights— the greater light to govern the day and the lesser light to govern the night. He also made the stars. God set them in the expanse of the sky to give light on the earth, to govern the day and the night, and to separate light from darkness. And God saw that it was good. And there was evening, and there was morning—the fourth day.

Who Turned On the Lights

The sun, moon and stars became visible from Earth's surface.

The Genesis Observer was only able to distinguish light and darkness on Day One as the thick clouds cover began to dissipate. On Day Four, the cloud cover had cleared enough to provide an unimpeded view of celestial objects. The sun was the first great light that ruled the day; the moon was the second great light, illuminating the night. Together, the sun, moon and stars governed day and night and marked the seasons. Although this order of events of Days One and Four appears to be sequential, this sequence of observations is probably influenced primarily by the literary framework of Genesis One. The following table correlates the problem of Earth's primordial darkness being solved by the preparation of light on Day One that was to emanate from the population of celestial objects created on Day Four.

Problem	Preparation	Population
Genesis 1:2	Days 1-3	Days 4-6
Darkness	**1a creation of light (day)**	**4a creation of sun**
	1b separation from darkness (night)	**4b creation of moon, stars**
Watery abyss	2a creation of firmament	5a creation of birds
	2b separation of waters above from waters below	5b creation of fish
Formless Earth	3a separation of earth from sea	6a creation of land animals
	3b creation of vegetation	6b creation of humans
"without *form* and *void*"	Formlessness is formed	Void is filled

Still not convinced that a literary framework, rather than historical chronology, influenced the order of events described in the creation week? Consider this. The sun, moon, and stars were in place *billions* of years before plants and trees took root. Even the dense cloud cover that initially blocked the sun from view had dissipated several *billion* years before land plants and fruit trees showed up[1]. Therefore the events of Day Four, whether they correspond to the actual origination of the sun, moon and stars or the time when they would have been visible from Earth's surface, preceded those of Day Three.

What can science tell us about the appearance of the celestial lights in the heavens?

Obscure Information

About 4.6 billion years ago, the hot, molten Earth's first atmosphere was so light that it was lost to outer space. The sun, moon and stars would have been visible from the infant Earth, but the planet was inhospitable for life. The planet then out-gassed enough steam and carbon dioxide to engulf the entire surface of Earth in a thick blanket of clouds. As the Earth cooled enough for water vapor to condense, oceans formed, the cloud cover thinned, and sunlight was able to reach the surface of the Earth. These conditions correlate with the Earth's condition roughly four billion years ago as life was set to appear in the oceans. Although day and night were discernible, the bright celestial objects were probably hidden from view by overcast skies. As the atmosphere continued to clear, the sun, moon and stars became visible.

Lighten Up

How could light have appeared on Day One, even though the sources of light—sun, moon and stars—were not made until Day Four? Perhaps the Genesis Observer was describing things as He saw them from Earth's surface. Roughly four billion years ago the dense cloud cover enabled light to make it through, but celestial objects were not in plain view. This constituted the day One observation. The sun, moon and stars became visible as the atmosphere continued to clear, and this observation was assigned to Day Four. It is more probable, though, that the order of these events was selected to fit the six-day literary framework rather than a chronological timeline. In either case, Day Four should present no problem for Bible believers.

References
1. Peter Andrews, John Barber, Michael Benton, Marianne Collins, Christine Janis, Ely Kish, Akio Morishima, J. John Sepkoski, Jr., Christopher Stringer, Jean-Paul Tibbles; The Book of Life—An Illustrated History of the Evolution of Life on Earth, general editor Stephen Jay Gould, W.W. Norton and Co., New York, NY,2001, Michael Benton, Life and Time, 30–31

Chapter 12. Day Five: Joining the Teem

Genesis 1:20-23 And God said, "Let the water teem with living creatures, and let birds fly above the earth across the expanse of the sky." So God created the great creatures of the sea and every living and moving thing with which the water teems, according to their kinds, and every winged bird according to its kind. And God saw that it was good. God blessed them and said, "Be fruitful and increase in number and fill the water in the seas, and let the birds increase on the earth." And there was evening, and there was morning—the fifth day.

Sea World

The creatures in the oceans, rivers, lakes and seas caught the attention of our Genesis Observer. Although microscopic life previously evaded his attention, these animals were easily seen with the naked eye. There is no doubt that God made life in the sea; but once again there is no comment on how He did it. Like the plant life described on Day Three, these verses state that the sea life would reproduce with gusto, yielding life according to its kind. There is no mention of the specific type of creatures in the water, so it is questionable as to whether this verse correlates to the initial surge of life in the waters a half billion years ago. Perhaps these creatures were the contemporary animals that the author of Genesis was familiar with. In either case, it clearly acknowledges that God is the Creator of all life that fills the oceans, seas, lakes and rivers.

The Birds

The mysterious creation of birds is also attributed to Day Five. Like the animals in the ocean, the birds were to reproduce; yielding offspring that looked just like Mom and Dad.

Out of Order, Again!

The fossil evidence indicates that animals in the oceans preceded land animals, which preceded the appearance of birds. Why, then, would the life in the waters and the sky be lumped together? Once again, the literary framework of the creation week provides the most convincing and consistent explanation. Day Five of the creation week corresponds to Day Two in the simple pattern that correlates the Population with the Preparation required to address the Problem found in Genesis 1:2.

Problem	Preparation	Population
Genesis 1:2	Days 1–3	Days 4–6
Darkness	1a creation of light (day)	4a creation of sun
	1b separation from darkness (night)	4b creation of moon, stars
Watery abyss	2a creation of firmament	5a creation of birds
	2b separation of waters above from waters below	5b creation of fish
Formless Earth	3a separation of earth from sea	6a creation of land animals
	3b creation of vegetation	6b creation of humans
"without *form* and *void*"	Formlessness is formed	Void is filled

What else can science tell us about the appearance of large animals in the waters and the birds in the air?

Underwater Explosion

Cambrian Period, 540,000,000 to 500,000,000 Years Ago

After three billion years of mundane microscopic organisms ruling the planet, an outburst of life occurred that is usually referred to as the Cambrian Explosion. The relationship between the life that debuted during the Cambrian period and contemporary life is startling. Living organisms are classified into three domains, Archea (the extremophiles), Bacteria, and Eucara[1]. The Eucara domain houses the kingdoms of the plants, animals, fungi, and protists. Each of these kingdoms are further refined into smaller groups referred to a phyla or division, which in turn is broken down into class, order, family, genus and species. Amazingly, the lineage of nearly all modern phyla, or body architectures, can be traced back to the Cambrian Explosion. Consider humans. Although none of our species existed 500 million years ago, our chordate phylum did. Chordates have a rod-like support structure composed of cartilage at some time during their life that runs parallel to the main cable of the nervous system. The chordate's digestive system starts with the mouth at the front of the body and ends with the anus at the back end. Further, the left side of a chordate is quite similar to the right side.

Why did the chordates, and all of the other phyla, suddenly appear in the fossil record without warning? Just how quickly did they appear? Why did the emergence of these body types happen just over half a billion years ago?

It's a Miracle!

Intelligent Design advocates *love* the Cambrian Explosion because they believe it confirms the instantaneous, miraculous appearance of animals in the waters. The Cambrian Explosion of life has even been touted as a direct repudiation of evolution because there was no gradual transition from small, simple organisms to large complicated organisms[2,3]. Although Intelligent Design creationists acknowledge that Earth is ancient, they typically say that the process of evolution cannot account for the rapid appearance of such a large number of diverse, complex species[4-6]. Other creationists don't go quite so far, and only point out that the Cambrian Explosion is more of an enigma than evidence for evolution[7].

Could the creationists be right? Was God so bored with billions of years of bacteria that He zapped complex, large, visible life into existence? Maybe there are no intermediate fossils between the Precambrian and Cambrian Periods because there were no transitional life forms between the Precambrian and Cambrian Periods! Maybe the Cambrian Explosion proves that evolution is false.

Unsolved Mystery

Maybe not. The Cambrian Explosion of life has also captured the attention of scientists. Why didn't Earth remain the abode of single-celled bacteria for all time? Was the Cambrian Explosion an inevitable event, or was it a freak accident? It may be one of the most baffling parts of the history of life on Earth, but it is hardly so mysterious that it is demands the resignation of scientific examination in favor of a faith-based solution[8,9]. The Cambrian Explosion was a brief event in the history of Earth, but it was not irregular, instantaneous, or 24 hours in duration[10]. It took at least 10 million years for the fauna of the early Cambrian Period, such as the trilobites, to become established[11]. The increase in the number of orders of life that appeared during a 60 million year-wide period of time associated with the Vendian Period and the Cambrian Period shows a geometric rise in the number of orders of life, not an instantaneous burst of diversity[12,13].

But why did it happen, and why did it happen when it happened? This type of increase in the number of species may be associated with the ability of animals of increased size and mobility to exploit oceans of easily accessible and digestible resources[14]. The fossil record repeatedly demonstrates that the consequences of life entering an uninhabited environment include a rapid rise in population and species. Such bursts of evolution have occurred numerous times in the history of life on Earth when there has been an "empty environment, untapped resources, and easy access to potential benefits."[15]

The establishment of the basic architectures of life during the Cambrian Explosion is a bit more difficult to understand[16]. For example, three hundred million years after the Cambrian Explosion a great extinction occurred that left behind a few thousand surviving species. Although an explosion in the population of living organisms and number of species ensued, not a single new phylum appeared! Why is it that the 30 or so basic body designs of life, such as sponges, jellyfish, annelids, mollusks, arthropods and chordates, originated only during the Cambrian Explosion? Why did large, complex life emerge at this time? Perhaps the preponderance of phyla during the Cambrian Explosion was related to differences in the way genetic commands are processed. For example, in contemporary life forms, DNA controls the rate and order in which proteins and other organic molecules are made. Cells within the organism transmit instructions in a cascading network in which a gene can activate or stop the work of other genes, which in turn can activate or stop the work of others genes. A genetic mutation in such a chain of command may not have fatal consequences because the correct genetic information can be transmitted correctly through one of the alternate pathways. These fail-safe systems may not have been present in organisms that lived during the Cambrian Explosion, however. Genetic errors may have been acted on directly; leading in most cases to an animal not suited for survival, but in some cases an animal with new traits that provided an advantage over its peers. These unchecked genetic experiments could have yielded the dramatic and numerous changes in morphology during the Cambrian Explosion.

Are these explanations peppered with good old-fashioned guesses? You bet! Could they end up being refined, corrected or replaced with better ideas? Certainly; especially as more fossils are found and more is learned about the mechanisms that developed and propagated genetic information. But there is not a conspiracy of silence concerning the inability of science to provide indisputable answers to these questions associated with the Cambrian Explosion. Scientists plainly state that they are still searching for answers[17,18]. I'm willing to give them another few centuries to sort it out, especially because the Bible is silent on the precise mechanisms by which life in the waters originated, flourished or diversified.

The Birds

Let's return to the history of life on this planet as reported by the

Genesis Observer. On Day Five, the skies were filled with birds. Therefore our feathered friends were sighted before the land animals that will appear on Day Six. The fossil record reveals, however, that animal life was thriving on the land long before birds ever showed up!

Ordovician Period, 500,000,000 to 430,000,000 Years Ago

Jawless fish appeared, along with coelenterates (animals having saclike bodies with only one opening and tentacles), arthropods (insects, crustaceans, arachnids, and myriapods, that are characterized by a tough, protective exoskeleton and a segmented body with pairs of jointed appendages) and cephalopods (critters like the octopus, squid, cuttlefish, or nautilus, having a large head, large eyes, tentacles, and often an ink sac used for protection or defense). Corals and seaweed were thriving in the oceans, while primitive plants began to take root on land.

Silurian Period, 430,000,000 to 400,000,000 Years Ago

Fishes with jaws appeared in the waters, and coral reefs were thriving. Insects, centipedes and millipedes were creeping around. Plants with water-conducting tissues populated the land.

Devonian Period, 400,000,000 to 350,000,000 Years Ago, The Age of Fishes

Fishes flourished in the waters, and land plants were doing so well that they formed forests. Amphibians and tetrapods appeared. Sharks and bony fish began to emerge.

Carboniferous Period, 350,000,000 to 280,000,000 Years Ago

Amphibians were commonplace during this period, as were plants such as horsetails and ferns. Insects began to fly and reptiles began to crawl. Large swamps developed that would subsequently be crushed and baked into coal. Plants with exposed seeds, like conifers, also debuted.

Permian Period, 280,000,000 to 225,000,000 Years Ago, The Age of Amphibians

Amphibians and reptiles ruled the day. Gymnosperms, plants with exposed seeds, dominated the plant life. Phytoplankton and plants oxygenated the air to a level comparable to that found in today's atmosphere. At the end of this period, the most massive extinction of life during the Earth's history occurred. Trilobites, 50% of all animal families, 95% of marine species, and many trees became extinct.

Triassic Period, 225,000,000 to 180,000,000 Years Ago, The Age of Reptiles

Frogs, dinosaurs, flies and mammals make their debut. A wide range of reptiles appeared. Ferns, cycads and ginkophytes were the dominant plants. Ammonites, cephalopods characterized by their multi-chambered shells, were present. A minor extinction of about one third of the animal families occurred during this period, giving room for dinosaurs to take charge. The earliest mammals appeared.

Jurassic Period, 180,000,000 to 135,000,000 Years Ago, The Age of Reptiles

Dinosaurs gained dominance as the first birds appear. The first flowering plants also appeared.

Cretaceous Period, 135,000,000 to 63,000,000 Years Ago, The Age of Reptiles

Dinosaurs dominated early in this period. The feathered dinosaurs, crocodilians, butterflies, ants and bees appeared. Birds continued to fill the heavens, and flowering plants made their debut. Another mass extinction, usually attributed to an asteroid impact, put an end to the dinosaurs and half of the marine invertebrate species.

Bird Droppings

The fossil record is unequivocal; birds of Day Five did not exist before land animals of Day Six. Neither did the birds of Day Five appear at the same time as sea animals of Day Five. If one holds to a literal interpretation of Genesis One, it appears that God can't simply get things straight. The literary framework yet again provides the solution. The creation of the sky on Day Two is correlated with the birds in the sky on Day Five; it's as simple as that.

Problem	Preparation	Population
Genesis 1:2	Days 1–3	Days 4–6
Darkness	1a creation of light (day)	4a creation of sun
	1b separation from darkness (night)	4b creation of moon, stars
Watery abyss	**2a creation of firmament**	**5a creation of birds**
	2b separation of waters above from waters below	5b creation of fish
Formless Earth	3a separation of earth from sea	6a creation of land animals
	3b creation of vegetation	6b creation of humans
"without *form* and *void*"	Formlessness is formed	Void is filled

Five Down, One to Go

What is required to maintain our reconciliation of science and biblical faith? You must again be willing to accept that the biblical order of events during the creation week is constrained primarily by poetry rather than chronology. You may also want to distance yourself from those who associate the Cambrian Explosion with an instantaneous, inexplicable, supernatural burst of sea life; it's the same strategy that has made the church look silly throughout its history as it deduced science from scripture. It simply isn't wise to putty God into the gaps of modern science.

Five days down, one to go. Day Six is the most contentious day of the creation week, however, because land mammals appeared. You are one of them!

References
1. Peter D. Ward, Donald Brownlee; Rare Earth—Why Complex Life Is Uncommon in the Universe, Copernicus, Springer-Verlag New York, Inc., New York, NY, 2000, 6-7
2. N. Eldredge; The Triumph of Evolution and the Failure of Creationism; Henry Holt and Company; 2000; New York, NY; 42-46
3. Robert T. Pennock, Tower of Babel—The Evidence Against the New Creationism, MIT Press, Massachusetts Institute of Technology, 2000,154,160,163,228
4. Michael J. Behe; Darwin's Black Box—The Biochemical Challenge to Evolution; Touchstone, New York, NY, 1996, 27-28
5. Ross, H.; The Genesis Question—Scientific Advances and the Accuracy of Genesis; Navpress 1998, Colorado Springs, CO; pg. 150
6. Mere Creation—Science, Faith & Intelligent Design, edited by William A. Dembski, InterVarsity Press, Downers Grove, IL, 1998, 23,158-159,443
7. G.L. Schroeder; The Science of God; Simon and Schuster; New York, NY; 1997; 41-71, 29-33
8. Niles Eldredge; The Triumph of Evolution and the Failure of Creationism; Henry Holt and Company; 2000; New York, NY; 42-46
9. Robert T. Pennock, Tower of Babel—The Evidence Against the New Creationism, MIT Press, Massachusetts Institute of Technology, 2000,154,160,163,228
10. Peter Andrews, John Barber, Michael Benton, Marianne Collins, Christine Janis, Ely Kish, Akio Morishima, J. John Sepkoski, Jr., Christopher Stringer, Jean-Paul Tibbles; The Book of Life—An Illustrated History of the Evolution of Life on Earth, general editor Stephen Jay Gould, W.W. Norton and Co., New York, NY,2001, J. John Sepkowski, Jr., Foundations—Life in the Oceans, 52
11. Niles Eldredge; The Triumph of Evolution and the Failure of Creationism; Henry Holt and Company; 2000; New York, NY,44-45
12. Peter Andrews, John Barber, Michael Benton, Marianne Collins, Christine Janis, Ely Kish, Akio Morishima, J. John Sepkoski, Jr., Christopher Stringer, Jean-Paul Tibbles; The Book of Life—An Illustrated History of the Evolution of Life on Earth, general editor Stephen Jay Gould, W.W. Norton and Co., New York, NY,2001, J. John Sepkowski, Jr., Foundations—Life in the Oceans, 52
13. Niles Eldredge; The Triumph of Evolution and the Failure of Creationism; Henry Holt and Company; 2000; New York, NY, 44
14. Peter Andrews, John Barber, Michael Benton, Marianne Collins, Christine Janis, Ely Kish, Akio Morishima, J. John Sepkoski, Jr., Christopher Stringer, Jean-Paul Tibbles, The Book of Life—An Illustrated History of the Evolution of Life on Earth, general editor Stephen Jay Gould, W.W. Norton and Co., New York, NY,2001,36-63, J. John Sepkowski. Jr., Ch. 1, "Foundations—Life in the Oceans"
15. Peter Andrews, John Barber, Michael Benton, Marianne Collins, Christine Janis, Ely Kish, Akio Morishima, J. John Sepkoski, Jr., Christopher Stringer, Jean-Paul Tibbles; The Book of Life—An Illustrated History of the Evolution of Life on Earth, general editor Stephen Jay Gould, W.W. Norton and Co., New York, NY,2001, 56, J. John Sepkowski, Jr., Ch. 1, "Foundations—Life in the Oceans"
16. Peter Andrews, John Barber, Michael Benton, Marianne Collins, Christine Janis, Ely Kish, Akio Morishima, J. John Sepkoski, Jr., Christopher Stringer, Jean-Paul Tibbles; The Book of Life—An Illustrated History of the Evolution of Life on Earth, general editor Stephen Jay Gould, W.W. Norton and Co., New York, NY, 2001,57, J. John Sepkowski, Jr., Ch. 1, "Foundations—Life in the Oceans"
17. Peter Andrews, John Barber, Michael Benton, Marianne Collins, Christine Janis, Ely Kish, Akio Morishima, J. John Sepkoski, Jr., Christopher Stringer, Jean-Paul Tibbles; The Book of Life—An Illustrated History of the Evolution of Life on Earth, general editor Stephen Jay Gould, W.W. Norton and Co., New York, NY,2001, 58, J. John Sepkowski, Jr., Ch. 1, "Foundations—Life in the Oceans"
18. Peter D. Ward, Donald Brownlee; Rare Earth—Why Complex Life Is Uncommon in the Universe, Copernicus, Springer-Verlag New York, Inc., New York, NY, 2000, 125-156

Chapter 13. Day Six: Animal House

Genesis 1:24, 25 And God said, "Let the land produce living creatures according to their kinds: livestock, creatures that move along the ground, and wild animals, each according to its kind." And it was so. God made the wild animals according to their kinds, the livestock according to their kinds, and all the creatures that move along the ground according to their kinds. And God saw that it was good.

Ground Beef

On Day Six the Genesis Observer reports on the creation of land-bound animals. The three groupings include livestock (such as cattle, oxen, goats, and sheep), creatures moving along the ground (probably creepy crawly reptiles, rodents and bugs), and wild animals (lions and tigers and bears, oh my!). Dinosaurs are not described because the writers of the Flintstones were wrong! Humans and dinosaurs did not coexist. "Biblical" and "scientific" claims of Young Earth Creationists to the contrary are entertaining but false[1].

The process of creating these animals is, as always, obscure. The Word of God declares that, *"God made the wild animals...livestock...and all the creatures...",* yet the Word of God states that God's will was to, *"Let the land produce living creatures…"*. So which is it? Did God create the animals, or did the land produce them? Perhaps both! Perhaps God, in His role as Creator, decided to establish a planet that could bring forth life on its own. These verses, along with the earlier, similar passage concerning the creation of vegetation, imply that God was not in danger of losing His job if He used a slow, natural, impersonal, unguided, ruthless mechanism to accomplish His goals.

The timing of the appearance of the land mammals is on the last day of creation. If you constrain these animals to be mammals, then one may consider this as a confirmation of the relatively recent appearance of these animals in the fossil record. But if you throw insects, amphibians and reptiles into the mix, then God has things out of order—again—because insects, amphibians and reptiles of Day Six showed up before the birds of Day Five. Once again it appears that the literary framework provides the simplest and best explanation. The land animals of Day Six correlate with the appearance of land and vegetation on Day Three.

Problem	Preparation	Population
Genesis 1:2	Days 1–3	Days 4–6
Darkness	1a creation of light (day)	4a creation of sun
	1b separation from darkness (night)	4b creation of moon, stars
Watery abyss	2a creation of firmament	5a creation of birds
	2b separation of waters above from waters below	5b creation of fish
Formless Earth	3a separation of earth from sea	6a creation of land animals
	3b creation of vegetation	6b creation of humans
"without *form* and *void*"	Formlessness is formed	Void is filled

What does the fossil record tell us about the appearance of land animals?

Many Mingling Mammals

Although the livestock are certainly mammals, some insects,

amphibians and reptiles may be eligible for the "wild animals" and "creatures that move along the ground" categories. When did they show up? Insects started crawling around about 400,000,000 years ago, followed by the amphibians and reptiles. The large mammals began taking center stage after the dinosaurs bit the dust.

Tertiary Period, 63,000,000 to 1,500,000 Years Ago, The Age of Mammals

The great extinction event that did in the dinosaurs provided a stage for mammals with an opportunity to diversify and multiply. During this period, large mammals, primitive primates, rodents, whales, pigs, rhinos, horses, dogs, bears, monkeys and apes appeared. At the end of the Tertiary Period, the upright animals referred to as *Australopithecus* made their debut; hairy hominids that bore an uncanny resemblance to that person in the mirror.

What is required to continue our reconciliation of science and the Bible? One may have to concede that natural processes may have been responsible for the appearance of animals that live on the land. Insects and reptiles may be among the creepy land animals of Day Six, but these appeared before the birds of Day Five! This is yet another confirmation that the days of Genesis fit a literary pattern that correlates the land-dwelling animals of Day Six with the appearance on land on Day Three. As we continue to the end of Day Six, we approach a species that is quite unique in God's eyes: humans. We're next!

References
1. [Appendix M]

Chapter 14. Day Six: Man According to the Bible

Genesis 1:26-31 Then God said, "Let us make man in our image, in our likeness, and let them rule over the fish of the sea and the birds of the air, over the livestock, over all the earth, and over all the creatures that move along the ground." So God created man in his own image, in the image of God he created him; male and female he created them. God blessed them and said to them, "Be fruitful and increase in number; fill the earth and subdue it. Rule over the fish of the sea and the birds of the air and over every living creature that moves on the ground." Then God said, "I give you every seed-bearing plant on the face of the whole earth and every tree that has fruit with seed in it. They will be yours for food. And to all the beasts of the earth and all the birds of the air and all the creatures that move on the ground— everything that has the breath of life in it—I give every green plant for food." And it was so. God saw all that he had made, and it was very good. And there was evening, and there was morning—the sixth day.

Who 'Da Man?

The making of man is presented as the climatic event of the creation week. These verses reveal what makes us "man" in God's eyes, and this perspective is quite different than what makes us "human" in the eyes of science. Overlooking this subtle distinction has caused most of the tension between scientists and believers concerning human evolution. Let's clarify matters by looking at the *biblical qualities of man* in this chapter, and the *scientific characteristics of humans* in the next chapter.

Man Could be Men!

There is no reason that these verses in Genesis One must be rendered as God creating only a couple of folks. These verses refer to man, or "adam", as "them" several times. *Gen 1:26-31 Then God said, "Let us make man in our image, in our likeness, and let them rule over the fish of the sea and the birds of the air, over the livestock, over all the earth, and over all the creatures that move along the ground." God blessed them and said to them,...* The term "man" can be considered as mankind rather than two people. Genesis One does not constrain the creation of any animal in the seas, sky or land to a single pair—it is perfectly reasonable to assume that in some unspecified manner, God created a population of humans.

The Population of Man was Small

The initial population of spiritual men and women must have been relatively small because they were commanded to multiply and fill the Earth. *"Be fruitful and increase in number; fill the earth."* A small population of mankind was instructed to crank out the kids, explore the Earth, and wisely manage the planet's bounty.

Man Could be Women!

Sounds like a tabloid headline, doesn't it? Another indication that "man" refers to mankind is the explicit declaration that "man" can be male or female! In Genesis One the term "adam" refers to both males and females made in God's image. *So God created man in his own image, in the image of God he created him; male and female he created them.*

Man Could be Manager

Man was given dominion over this planet, especially the wildlife, and the responsibility to rule over it wisely. *"Be fruitful and increase in number; fill the earth and subdue it. Rule over the fish of the sea and the birds of the air and over every living creature that moves on the ground."* This is not, as liberal theologians and scientists love to imply, a verse conveniently slipped into the text by ancient Republican scribes that would one day allow greedy Americans to pollute, plunder, pillage, strip mine, deforest, and eradicate all species—including Democrats—who stand in their way. Yes, life on Earth did just fine for three and a half billions years without our management, but like it or not, God recognized the capabilities of our species and made mankind accountable for the responsible stewardship of life on Earth.

Man Would Eat Fruit and Vegetables

God advised man to have a diet rich in fiber—yuk! *Then God said, "I give you every seed-bearing plant on the face of the whole earth and every tree that has fruit with seed in it. They will be yours for food…"* Creationists typically insist that this passage clearly indicates that early mankind and his animal neighbors were vegetarian and remained so until God gave the green light to Noah to start barbequing after the flood. *Genesis 9:3-4 Everything that lives and moves will be food for you. Just as I gave you the green plants, I now give you everything. But you must not eat meat that has its lifeblood still in it.* The fossil record—as best exemplified by fossilized vomit, stomach contents and dung—clearly demonstrates that beasts of old were not vegetarian. The archeological evidence for carnivorous humans is also compelling; after all it is doubtful that those ancient spears and arrows were fashioned for hunting wheat! Skeptics seize upon these scriptures as evidence of the Bible's fallibility. Some believers, however, tend to view these instructions less literally. Some think that these dietary guidelines simply serve as a reminder that man and the animal kingdom were ultimately dependent upon the plant kingdom. Others think that early man was commanded by God to be vegetarian, but was more than happy to ignore the Almighty and devour a couple of pounds of red juicy meat anyway! Take Abel. He raised flocks and sacrificed animals to the Lord and would have been a serious candidate for a carnivorous appetite. Some consider God's vegetarian instructions and prophetic Old Testament passages describing vegetarian predators in the kingdom of the

Messiah as symbols of peace in the presence of the Lord, lending credence to those who believe Genesis One is indeed completely mythical. e.g. *Isaiah 11:6 The wolf will live with the lamb, the leopard will lie down with the goat, the calf and the lion and the yearling together, and a little child will lead them*

Man Was Very Good

God was delighted with all that He had made during the Day Six, including man. *God saw all that he had made, and it was very good. And there was evening, and there was morning—the sixth day.*

Man Was Made in God's Image

The most astounding trait of man is that we alone were made in God's image. This is the big ticket item that distinguishes us from all other forms of life. What is God's image, though? Man's appearance certainly does not resemble God's. Despite the countless paintings that depict Him as an agile 86 year old Caucasian with lightning emanating from His fingertips and tornadoes funneling out of His nostrils, God is not the Galactic Grey-Haired Geriatric Geezer. What else about man is in the image of God? Intelligence? Language? Creativity? Morality? The desire to build relationships? Conscience? Consciousness? Self awareness? Perception of our place in nature? Participation in our own destiny? Perhaps. But God is not flesh and blood, and any attribute founded in our physiology is unlikely to be the distinguishing characteristic that makes us so exceptional in His eyes.

Let's consider God during the creation events. As God pondered the creation of man, He said *Genesis 1:26 "Let us make man in our image, in our likeness,…"*. If there is only one God, then who is "us"? Probably the three men I admire most, the Father, Son and Holy Ghost. All three persons of the Godhead are credited with creation. God the Father is obviously the Creator, *Genesis 1:1 In the beginning God created the heavens and the earth.* God the Holy Spirit was also joining in the action, *Genesis 1:2 Now the earth was formless and empty, darkness was over the surface of the deep, and the Spirit of God was hovering over the waters.* The pre-incarnate Son of God was also referred to as the Creator. *John 1:1-4 In the beginning was the*

Word, and the Word was with God, and the Word was God. He was with God in the beginning. Through him all things were made; without him nothing was made that has been made. In him was life, and that life was the light of men.

What is a common characteristic of God the Father, God the Son and God the Holy Spirit? What about Spirit? Jesus spoke of His Father, saying, *John 4:24 God is spirit, and his worshipers must worship in spirit and in truth.* The Holy Spirit is spirit—that's a no-brainer. During creation, the Son of God only had a spiritual nature; He did not become human in form until He was born. Although Jesus, the eternal Son of God, was made in human likeness to accomplish our salvation two thousand years ago, He did not have a human form during the creation events billions of years ago. Jesus exchanged His glory for human likeness, even the likeness of sinful man, when He came to Earth to die for our sins. *Philippians 2:4-8 Each of you should look not only to your own interests, but also to the interests of others. Your attitude should be the same as that of Christ Jesus: Who, being in very nature God, did not consider equality with God something to be grasped, but made himself nothing, taking the very nature of a servant, being made in human likeness. And being found in appearance as a man, he humbled himself and became obedient to death—even death on a cross! Romans 8:3 For what the law was powerless to do in that it was weakened by the sinful nature, God did by sending his own Son in the likeness of sinful man to be a sin offering. And so he condemned sin in sinful man. John 1:14 The Word became flesh and made his dwelling among us.*

A common denominator of the Holy Trinity, the creative union of Father, Son and Holy Spirit, is Spirit. Maybe the unique feature that sets us apart from all other life and enables us to be classified as made in the image of God is our spirit. Man alone has a spirit; a supernatural, eternal, real spirit. When plants and animals die, their future is fertilizer. When you die, the fate of your sad sack of flesh is no better, as God explained to Adam, *Genesis 3:19 By the sweat of your brow you will eat your food until you return to the ground, since from it you were taken; for dust you are and to dust you will return."* But the part of you that is made in God's image has a different destiny, *Hebrews 9:27 Just as man is destined to die once, and after that to face judgment.* You will face judgment after you die; your dog won't (although my chair-eating dog deserves it). Your spirit will persist after your death, even as your flesh and bones are getting recycled.

Man is More than Human

Many of the seemingly irreconcilable differences between the scientific and biblical perspectives of man's origins stem from word games played with the term "spirit". Christians understand the term "spiritual" as a description of our intangible, miraculous constitution that can commune with God and will answer to God—for better or for worse—after our death. Some scientists may pay lip service to our "spiritual" nature, but they are usually patronizing the dimwitted religious crowd that isn't smart enough to know that their "spirit" is no more than purely natural brain activity—or lack thereof. For these skeptical scientists, our spirit evolved along with our brain because our spirit is a part of our brain. For them, the spirit is simply hope, pep, wishful thinking, creativity, compassion, problem-solving skills, befuddlement, a way of coping with death, a vain desire for life after death, a wish to get rich, a way to deal with grief, a relief for guilt, an anesthetic for loneliness, or a way to scare the hell out of people while you exploit them.

Let's try to keep things straight in the rest of this book by using the term "religious" when referring to any *natural* capacity to engage in activities that one may associate with a higher power, while reserving the term "spiritual" for descriptions of our eternal, *supernatural* nature that can know the Creator or reject Him wholeheartedly. Of course, this is nothing but a silly shell game for those who do not believe in God or an eternal spirit within humans, so they can interchange the two terms with a clear conscience.

Likewise, the words "human" and "man" can cause some confusion. We can clear the air if we use the word "human" to speak only of our species' *natural* attributes, including our bodies and minds. I'm even willing to throw in some religious tendencies that humans may have developed naturally. The term "man", however, will be reserved for references to humans who possess a supernatural, spiritual nature.

Therefore, the equation for the making of man is simple;
man = human + spirit!

Jesus' Science Class

Breaking man down into two parts, one natural and one supernatural, certainly is not a new idea. Jesus spoke of the dual nature of man when discussing being born again. He drew a clear distinction between our natural, physical, human nature and our supernatural, intangible, spiritual nature.

John 3:1-8 Now there was a man of the Pharisees named Nicodemus, a member of the Jewish ruling council. He came to Jesus at night and said, "Rabbi, we know you are a teacher who has come from God. For no one could perform the miraculous signs you are doing if God were not with him." In reply Jesus declared, "I tell you the truth, no one can see the kingdom of God unless he is born again." "How can a man be born when he is old?" Nicodemus asked. "Surely he cannot enter a second time into his mother's womb to be born!" Jesus answered, "I tell you the truth, no one can enter the kingdom of God unless he is born of water and the Spirit. Flesh gives birth to flesh, but the Spirit gives birth to spirit. You should not be surprised at my saying, 'You must be born again.' The wind blows wherever it pleases. You hear its sound, but you cannot tell where it comes from or where it is going. So it is with everyone born of the Spirit."

Jesus made it clear; flesh gives birth to flesh, but the Spirit gives birth to spirit. The spiritual nature of man is miraculous and supernatural, while the physical nature of man is composed of flesh and blood. Nicodemus thought this "born again" thing was a bit strange and let Jesus know that he was not willing to visit the nearest AAA office to get a Trip-Tik for another voyage through his mother's birth canal. But Jesus only reiterated his message. He explained that the Spirit of God—like the wind—could not be directly observed, yet remained undeniably influential in everyday life. Spiritual renewal has transformed the hearts and minds of men and women for thousands of years—restoring lives, marriages, families and nations. Yet the Spirit of God remains beyond the reach of direct observation, just as Jesus said.

Standard Spiritual Equipment

Our spiritual nature, housed in a human body, fashions us in the image of God. The New Testament also provides clear attributes of man's spiritual capabilities and responsibilities, especially in the first chapter of Paul's letter to the church in Rome. In this text, Paul described the spiritual state of every spiritual man or woman that has ever lived, even if they have never heard of the scriptures or the gospel.

Romans 1:20-25 For since the creation of the world God's invisible qualities—his eternal power and divine nature—have been clearly seen, being understood from what has been made, so that men are without excuse. For although they knew God, they neither glorified him as God nor gave thanks to him, but their thinking became futile and their foolish hearts were darkened. Although they claimed to be wise, they became fools and exchanged the glory of the immortal God for images made to look like mortal man and birds and animals and reptiles. Therefore God gave them over in the sinful desires of their hearts to sexual impurity for the degrading of their bodies with one another. They exchanged the truth of God for a lie, and worshiped and served created things rather than the Creator— who is forever praised. Amen.

Man knows there is a powerful, divine God; it's spiritual instinct. God's power and divinity are clearly evidenced by *what* has been made, not *how or when* we think it was made. Man is held accountable to thank, glorify and worship the Creator. Why? It's not that a glance at God's creation moves our hearts to think that the world was created only six thousand years ago, or that a second look may persuade us that it was intelligently designed billions of years ago. In some mysterious manner, our spirit senses God when we look upon the glories of the heavens and Earth—*just because they are there.* Whether we are fully aware of its functions or completely baffled by its behavior, our spirit can perceive the Hand of the Almighty in His creation. Although we cannot fathom the ways of the universe, we can remain convinced of God's presence and our own eternal nature. *Ecclesiastes 3:11 He has made everything beautiful in its time. He has also set eternity in the hearts of men; yet they cannot fathom what God has done from beginning to end.* That's right— one can be a mature spiritual Christian while remaining absolutely clueless, indifferent, or incorrect about how God's creation originated or functions!

Of course, man has always been free to reject the knowledge of God. In Paul's day, many exchanged the glory of God for the worship of objects, serving their carnal desires with all of their hearts. They pursued their sexual desires without restraint, seeing no wrong in the degradation of their own bodies. Little has changed in two thousand years.

Chapter 15.
Human According to Science

I See Dead People

Scientists are unable to detect the spirit in a living person, let alone a fossil. Although many scientists believe in God, the eternal spirit of man, and the revelation of God through His creation, others are skeptical about this intangible spiritual nature, and some are quite certain that it does not exist. Therefore it should neither surprise nor offend you that scientists who study the origin of man concentrate on the physical trail of hard evidence that our human ancestors have left behind. They discern the appearance and capabilities of the human body in the fossil record. They are dead-people-paparazzi, examining the remains, scrutinizing the dwelling places, sifting through the trash, and categorizing the tools of folks that died long ago. They recover fragments of DNA from frozen folks who died in a cold environment thousands of years ago. They estimate brainpower by studying the size of the skull of early humans because above the human neck, size does matter. They sort through remnants of human activity hidden in caves, graves and garbage dumps that illuminate the social, cultural, artistic, political, hunting, and agricultural activities of early humans. They also have a different perspective on human beliefs, relying on religious artifacts, such as burial items that may have been selected for use in an afterlife, and the human capacity to ponder the mysterious, anticipate mortality, desire social order, and yearn for life after death. With this perspective in mind, the fossil record indicates that human-like animals have been around for a few million years during the Tertiary and Quaternary Periods.

Tertiary Period, 63,000,000 to 1,500,000 Years Ago, The Age of Mammals

Mammals became the prominent animals of the planet. During the latter portion of this period, the first upright, large-brained hominids appeared. The first hominid typically associated with the ancestry of man, *Australopithecus*, made its debut late in this period.

Quaternary Period, 1,500,000 Years Ago to Now, The Age of Humans

Mammoths, mastadons and sloths appeared. Various human species sprouted in Africa, and *Homo sapiens* appeared during the latter part of the Quaternary Period. About ten thousand years ago, a mass extinction of large mammals and birds occurred, usually attributed to the ravages of Ice Ages. The civilization of modern man is usually lumped into the last ten thousand years or so; we are the new kids on the block.

Setting the Record Straight

The fossil record, archeological finds, fragments of DNA in very young fossils, and the genetic characteristics of our closest living relatives in the animal kingdom provide a wealth of information about the origins of humans[1-5]. There is a multiple million-year trail of evidence that reveals human evolution; we did not suddenly appear out of the clear blue sky or in a lush green garden. That is a scientific fact, not a statement of faith. An extensive data base of human fossils[6-8] has been used to construct a family tree with nearly twenty species spanning millions of years[9]. Despite this evidence of multiple human species, it is not an easy task to establish the precise relationship between these species because there was not a linear progression from one to the next to the next to the next.

Rather, these lines of descent form a tree with numerous branches, some of which gave rise to other species while others were halted by extinction. At the end of the day, however, there was, and is, a sole surviving species: *Homo sapiens*. Where did we come from? Our ancestors parted ways with the common ancestor we share with our closest relative, the chimpanzees, roughly five or six million years ago[10, 11]. Appendix N presents details of the extinct human and human-like species that have lived during the past four and a half million years. About four million years ago, one particular genus, *Australopithecus*, appeared and walked on two legs, freeing up its hands for tasks other than movement. About two million years ago, the *Homo* genus of big-brained toolmakers arrived. Roughly 150,000 years ago, *Homo sapiens* appeared in Africa, characterized by their slimmer, more mobile frame. After the demises of *Homo erectus* of Eastern Asia and Australasia some 40,000 years ago, the *Homo neanderthalensis* species of Western Eurasia some 30,000 years ago, and the *Homo floresiensis* species on the island of Flores[12] about 13,000 years ago, *Homo sapiens* emerged as the sole surviving human species.

Are You My Mother?

Human evolution is not only documented in the fossil record, but also within the cells of every living person on Earth, including you! Bryan Sykes, a professor of genetics at the Institute of Molecular Medicine at Oxford University has recently provided a fascinating overview of the genetic clues to our common ancestry hidden within the recesses of our mitochondrial DNA[13] and summaries of these advances also appear in other recent books on human evolution[14,15] and DNA[16]. This research began to captivate the public in 1987 when Allan Wilson, an evolutionary biochemist, and two of his students, Rebecca Cann and Mark Stoneking, published a paper that demonstrated the usefulness of the mitochondrial DNA of living individuals to determine both the time and location of our common ancestors[17]. Cann and Wilson recently summarized the current understanding of the genetic studies of mitochondrial DNA that confirm the African origins of our species[18].

Mitochondria are small structures in a cell that power the cell's operation that reside in the cytoplasm (the portion of each cell that is inside of the cell membrane but outside of the DNA-rich nucleus). The DNA within the mitochondria has several attributes that make it uniquely suited for genetic studies of ancestry. Mitochondrial DNA is a short code of genetic information that contains only about sixteen thousand bases, a small number compared to the three billion bases in the human genome within the cell's nucleus. More importantly, mitochondrial DNA is derived solely from the mother, while both Mom and Dad both contribute to the nuclear DNA. Without Dad getting everything all mixed up, as dads have a tendency of doing, Mom can efficiently transmit her mitochondrial DNA code to the kids. For instance, if you go back five generations, as many as thirty two great-great-great-grandparents contributed to your nuclear DNA, but only one, your great-great-great-grandma, contributed to your mitochondrial DNA. This results in an uncluttered genetic trail of maternal ancestry. The reproduction of mitochondrial DNA from generation to generation may not be perfect, however. Mutations can occur during the generation of the mitochondrial DNA, and the rate at which such mutations occur can be combined with measurements of the number of mutations to trace maternal ancestries back over the past several hundred thousand years.

The revelations extracted from this analysis of mitochondrial DNA are stunning. For example, the mitochondrial DNA of Neanderthals is so different from ours that there was not enough time for it to have mutated into contemporary *Homo sapien* DNA. Therefore we can say with assurance that we did not descend directly from this extinct species or from an interbreeding of the *Homo sapien* and *Homo neanderthalensis* species[19].

Who, then, were our mitochondrial ancestors? 95% of today's European population can trace their ancestry to one of seven clan mothers who lived between 10,000 and 45,000 years ago—dubbed the Seven Daughters of Eve[20]. It is possible to trace the roots of these seven clans, and the maternal ancestors of twenty six other clans from around the world, back even further to find the most recent common mitochondrial ancestor of all humans. The earliest female root of the today's mitochondrial DNA, nicknamed Mitochondrial Eve, lived about 150,000 years ago. It is even possible to determine where she lived, based on the diversity of contemporary mitochondrial DNA as a function of location. The place where humans have lived the longest is where the mitochondrial DNA would have had the greatest opportunity to mutate, leaving behind the richest diversity of mito-chondrial DNA. 40% of human clans are found in Africa, therefore Mitochondrial Eve lived in Africa[21] and she is therefore also known as African Eve.

Why Adam?

A similar technique can be used to trace our paternal ancestors if the Y-chromosome is used. These little chunks of our genetic code remain oblivious to the influence of Mom's DNA and exist only to make men. The Y-chromosome carries the SRY gene, which prevents all embryos from developing into females (perhaps the clearest evidence of Intelligent Design yet) by turning on genes on other chromosomes that produce male piping. There are two types of mutations that can be used to fingerprint the Y-chromosome. The first is a change in the expected base, which is tedious to eval-uate because it happens sporadically along the entire length of the Y-chromosome. The second type is the generation of multiple reproductions of a sequence of bases in the DNA, which can be readily counted.

Scientists used DNA from men living in Europe and the Middle East to assess their paternal ancestry[22]. Their study found ten groups of characteristic DNA that pointed to ten lineages of male ancestors. When did they live? During the same period of time as the Seven Daughters of Eve![23] European citizens can trace about 20% of their ancestry to the Neolithic (New Stone Age) farmers and 80% from Paleolithic (Old Stone Age) hunters fol-lowing either the maternal or paternal genetic clues present in human mitochondria. Such studies of the Y-chromosome point to a more ancient male common ancestor who lived in Africa, otherwise known as "African Adam"[24], who may have lived about 60,000 years ago[25].

African Adam and African Eve Are Not from Eden

It is at this point that some creationists come along like academic ambulance chasers and claim that African Adam and African Eve are actually the Adam and Eve of the Bible. Some would even suggest that Noah and Eve would be their more accurate identities because Noah and his sons were the only men on Earth when they disembarked, while their wives had a mixed ancestry that led to Eve as their most recent common ancestor. This explains why African Adam lived at a much more recent time that African Eve.

Forget about it!

Mitochondrial Eve (African Eve) was not the sole woman on Earth. She was the only woman of a small population whose mitochondrial DNA was successfully transmitted to all of us living today. Neither was Mitochondrial Eve created instantly! She also had a mother, a grandmother, a great-grandmother, a great-great-grandmother, and...well...you get the idea. Neither was Y-chromosome Adam (African Adam) the first man, an instantly created man, a parentless man, or the only man on Earth.

Further, both Mitochondrial Eve and African Adam were absolutely clueless about their title because it could only be awarded in retrospect; there was no way that anyone living back then could have known whose descendents would be surviving well into the future.

Don't get ideas about a thing going on between these two African ancestors. African Adam and African Eve didn't know one another and weren't even alive at the same time[26], with African Eve clocking in at 140,000 years ago and African Adam at 60,000 years ago.

It must also be kept in mind that relatively small segments of DNA, the mitochondria and the Y-chromosome, are being considered in these studies. In essence, we have descended into our ancestry from mother-to-mother-to-mother-to-mother to find Mitochondrial Eve, while searching from father-to-father-to-father-to-father to find Y-chromosome Adam. But casting aside our concerns over an easily traceable gene, what's to stop us from going from finding our most recent common ancestor searching in a repeating pattern of [mother to father], or [mother to mother to father to father]? Had we followed such a strategy, we would have arrived at two completely different most recent common ancestors[27].

Things get even trickier when you consider when "today" is when you say "all people alive today". Depending on what year you select for "today", the identities of those deemed Mitochondrial Eve and Y-Chromosome Adam change![28] Let's say that Agnes Chad was the name of the most recent mitochondrial ancestor of all people living in 2005, and let's imagine that Agnes was born 142,324 years ago. Agnes was "our" Miss Mitochondrial Eve for 2005! What if we had selected all humans alive 20,000 years ago as the group in search of "their" most recent mitochondrial mother? Many women who were living 20,000 years may not have had Agnes Chad in their maternal ancestry and may not have given rise to an unbroken chain of female descendants that would extend to the year 2005. Therefore their search for their most recent common maternal ancestor would lead back into history further than our search. "Our" Mitochondrial Eve for 2005 A.D.—Agnes Chad —could not be "their" Mitochondrial Eve for 18,000 B.C. "Their" most recent maternal ancestor, Miss Mitochondrial Eve for 18,000 B.C., would have been one of Agnes' ancestors! Rather than 20,000 years ago, let's consider Agnes' birthday 142,324 years ago as the point in time when humans would look back in time for the most recent common maternal ancestor. The newborn and still slimy Agnes certainly could not have been the most recent common ancestor of the mitochondrial DNA of all women alive when she was born! Her generation would have had their own Mitochondrial Eve who lived long before Agnes was a twinkle in her parents' eyes.

Rather than focusing on the ancestry of a small portion of our DNA, let's set our sights on the most recent common ancestor of everyone alive today. This search would be like an old-fashioned effort to document a family tree. If everyone alive today was able to trace down their genealogy, would the most recent name appearing in everyone's family tree be a resident of the Garden of Eden? No. Why? Although the calculations are not precise, it can be said with certainty that this ancestor lived "some tens of thousands of years ago, conceivably somewhere in the low hundreds of thousands, no more"[29]. This most recent common ancestor, who may have lived outside of Africa, was in the company of others, some of whom would have been an ancestor of at least some people alive today

What if we are determined to find the single common ancestor of *every human that has ever lived?* Only 40,000 years ago four distinct human species, *Homo sapien, Homo neanderthalensis, Homo erectus,* and *Homo floresiensis,* were alive, a sure sign that finding our most recent common ancestor will reach into the distant past. How far back in time would we have to travel, from ancestor to ancestor to ancestor, until all humans ended up at the same doorstep, looking for the Mother of All Mothers? The human genome found within the cell nucleus is derived from thousands of African Eve's contemporaries and their ancestors[30], and a recent study based on a study of several hundred markers in the portions of our DNA that do not encode genetic information indicates that we have descended from a *population* of only several thousand humans that lived in northern Africa as long as 140,000 years ago[31]. Therefore we must go back even further. If we traverse roughly six million years, or about 250,000 generations[32, 33], we would meet an archancestress[34] who would have had a child from whom all of our ancient human-like and human ancestors descended[35]. Don't even think about equating this female with the biblical Eve; this archancestress was not even a *Homo sapien* and her other child would have been the ancestor of our cousins, the bonobo and common chimpanzee[36, 37]! We would not be at the Tree of Life in Eden, but rather at a branch point in the evolutionary tree of life where humans diverged from the chimps in Africa. Even that breakup could have been messy! A recent analysis of human and chimp DNA indicates that the two lineages may have parted ways, then interbred for a while before permanently separating into two distinct species again about 6.3 million years ago[38].

There is no way, absolutely no way at all, to follow the paths leading to our most recent common ancestors of our DNA or portions of our DNA and find a couple abiding at the Garden of Eden. It is impossible. Attempts to correlate the results[39] with Adam and Eve or Noah and Eve are either naïve, erroneous, or deliberate attempts to mislead other creationists. There is no escaping the fact that the trail of archaeological, fossil and genetic evidence of human origins goes to a time, a continent, a population and a species far removed from any of the creationist versions of Adam and Eve.

Man, This is Hard to Believe

There is a rich fossil history of human species and their predecessors. There is a remarkable amount of genetic evidence within our cells that also points back to our ancestors. Both of these trails lead to

Homo sapiens who were running around about 160,000 years ago that would, after a trip to the barber and the mall, blend right in with today's crowd. Their predecessors date back roughly six million years, to the time when humans branched from the lineage that would give rise to the chimps.

And that's only a part of a much longer story, as eloquently told by Richard Dawkins[40]. We could travel back further and further in time, discovering that we share most recent common ancestors with gorillas seven million years ago, orangutans 14 million years ago, gibbons 18 million years ago, Old World monkeys 25 million years ago, New World monkeys 40 million years ago, tarsiers 58 million years ago, lemurs 63 million years ago, colugos and tree shrews 70 million years ago, rodents and rabbits 75 million years ago...all the way back to the most recent common ancestor of all life on Earth, which had an ancestry of its own that led back to the mysterious origin of life.

How does this affect our belief in the special standing of man in God's eyes? Scientists have shown us that the *body* of *humans* emerged via a *natural* process. Genesis and Jesus have told us that the *spirit* of *man* originated with a *supernatural* act of God. We must accept that God let life evolve for billions of years until an animal arose that He deemed worthy of receiving an eternal spirit.

References
1. Ian Tattersall; Becoming Human—Evolution and Human Uniqueness; Harcourt Brace, Orlando Florida, 1999
2. Robert Boyd, Joan B. Silk; How Humans Evolved, 2nd Edition, W.W. Norton & Company, New York, 2000
3. Peter Andrews, John Barber, Michael Benton, Marianne Collins, Christine Janis, Ely Kish, Akio Morishima, J. John
   Sepkoski, Jr., Christopher Stringer, Jean-Paul Tibbles; The Book of Life—An Illustrated History of the Evolution of
   Life on Earth, general editor Stephen Jay Gould, W.W. Norton and Co., New York, NY,2001,218-251
4. Jared Diamond; The Third Chimpanzee—The Evolution and Future of the Human Animal, HarperPerennial, 1993, New
   York, NY,11-58
5. Appendix N
6. Jeffrey H. Schwartz, Ian Tattersall; The Human Fossil Record, Volume 1, Terminology and Craniodental Morphology
   of Genus Homo (Europe), Wiley-Liss, New York, NY, 2002
7. Jeffrey H. Schwartz, Ian Tatterasall; The Human Fossil Record, Volume 2, Craniodental Morphology of Genus Homo
   (Africa and Asia), Wiley-Liss, New York, NY, 2003
8. Ralph L. Holloway, Douglas C. Broadfield, Michael S. Yuan, Jeffrey H. Schwartz; The Human Fossil Record, Volume
   3, Brain Endocasts -The Paleoneurological Evidence, Wiley-Liss, New York, NY, 2004
9. I. Tattersall, J. Schwartz; Extinct Humans; Westview Press; Boulder Colorado; 2001
10. Carl Zimmer, Evolution—The Triumph of an Idea, HarperCollins Publishers, 2001, 260
11. Steve Olsen; Mapping Human History—Genes, Race and Our Common Origin, A Mariner Book, Houghton
    Miller, Boston, MA, 2002, 18-19
12. Appendix N
13. B. Sykes; The Seven Daughters of Eve—The Science That Reveals Our Genetic History; Norton 2002; New York, NY
14. I. Tattersall, J. Schwartz; Extinct Humans; Westview Press; Boulder Colorado; 2001, 228-231
15. Robert Boyd, Joan B. Silk; How Humans Evolved, 2nd Edition, W.W. Norton & Company, New York, 2000, 478-480
    James D. Watson with 16. Andrew Berry; DNA—The Secret of Life, Alfred A. Knopf, New York, 2003, 228-260
17. R.L.Cann, M. Stoneking, A.C. Wilson; Science (1987) Mitochondrial DNA and Human Evolution, Nature 325 (1987),
    31-36
18. R.L. Cann, Allan C. Wilson; The Recent African Genesis of Humans—Genetic Studies Reveal thatan African Woman
    from less than 200,000 Years Ago Was Our Common Ancestor, Scientific American, 13(2),2003, Special Edition, New
    Look at Human Evolution, 54-61
19. James D. Watson with Andrew Berry, DNA—The Secret of Life, Alfred A. Knopf, New York, 2003, 229-233
20. B. Sykes; The Seven Daughters of Eve—The Science That Reveals Our Genetic History; Norton 2002; New York, NY
21. B. Sykes; The Seven Daughters of Eve—The Science That Reveals Our Genetic History; Norton 2002; New York,
    NY, 271-286
22. O. Semino, G. Passarino, P. Oefner, A. Lin, S. Arbuzova, L. Beckman, G. De Benedictus, P. Francalacci, A. Kouvatsi,
    S. Limborska, M. Marcikiae, A. Mika, B. Mika, D. Primorac, A. Santachiara-Benerecetti, L. Cavalli-Sforza, P.
    Underhill, The Genetic Legacy of Paleolithic Homo sapiens sapiens in Extant Europeans: a Y Chromosome
    Perspective, Science 290, Nov. 10, 2000, 1155-1159
23. B. Sykes; The Seven Daughters of Eve—The Science That Reveals Our Genetic History; Norton 2002; New York,
    NY, 185-194
24. I. Tattersall, J. Schwartz; Extinct Humans; Westview Press; Boulder Colorado; 2001, 230
25. Richard Dawkins; The Ancestor's Tale—A Pilgrimage to the Dawn of Evolution, Houghton Mifflin Company, Boston,
    MA, 2004, 54
26. Steve Olsen; Mapping Human History—Genes, Race and Our Common Origin, A Mariner Book, Houghton Miller,
    Boston, MA, 2002, 26
27. Richard Dawkins; The Ancestor's Tale—A Pilgrimage to the Dawn of Evolution, Houghton Mifflin Company, Boston,
    MA, 2004, 100-105
28. Richard Dawkins, The Ancestor's Tale—A Pilgrimage to the Dawn of Evolution, Houghton Mifflin Company, Boston,
    MA, 2004, 54
29. Richard Dawkins with Yan Wong, The Ancestor's Tale—A Pilgrimage to the Dawn of Evolution, Houghton Mifflin
    Company, Boston, MA, 2004, 44
30. Steve Olsen; Mapping Human History—Genes, Race and Our Common Origin, A Mariner Book, Houghton Miller,
    Boston, MA, 2002, 47-48
31. Discover, The Year in Science, 100 Top Science Stories of 2003, No. 7. Our Genes Prove It, We Are Family, January
    2004, 56
32. Richard Dawkins, A Devil's Chaplain—Reflections on Hope, Lies, Science and Love, Houghton Mifflin, 2003, 20-26
33. Richard Dawkins, The Ancestor's Tale—A Pilgrimage to the Dawn of Evolution, Houghton Mifflin Company, Boston,
    MA, 2004, 100
34. Richard Dawkins, A Devil's Chaplain—Reflections on Hope, Lies, Science and Love, Houghton Mifflin, 2003, 24
35. Richard Dawkins, A Devil's Chaplain—Reflections on Hope, Lies, Science and Love, Houghton Mifflin, 2003, 24
36. Richard Dawkins, A Devil's Chaplain—Reflections on Hope, Lies, Science and Love, Houghton Mifflin, 2003, 24-25
37. Richard Dawkins, The Ancestor's Tale—A Pilgrimage to the Dawn of Evolution, Houghton Mifflin Company, Boston,
    MA, 2004, 100-105

38. Nick Patterson, Daniel J. Richter, Sante Gnerre, Eric S. Lander, David Reich, Genetic evidence for complex speciation of humans and chimpanzees, Nature, May 17, 2006, doi:10.1038/nature04789

39. Hugh Ross, A Matter of Days—Resolving a Creation Controversy, NavPress, Colorado Springs, CO, 2004, 221–226

40. Richard Dawkins, The Ancestor's Tale—A Pilgrimage to the Dawn of Evolution, Houghton Mifflin Company, Boston, MA, 2004, 26–581

Chapter 16. Rest Stop

Stop and Rest

Genesis 2:1-3 Thus the heavens and the earth were completed in all their vast array. By the seventh day God had finished the work he had been doing; so on the seventh day he rested from all his work. And God blessed the seventh day and made it holy, because on it he rested from all the work of creating that he had done.

We have completed our review of God's work during the creation week. The perspective of the Genesis Observer is no longer needed because man is now on the scene. This pattern of work and rest would set a precedent for man summarized in the fourth commandment. *Exodus 20:8-11 "Remember the Sabbath day by keeping it holy. Six days you shall labor and do all your work, but the seventh day is a Sabbath to the LORD your God. On it you shall not do any work, neither you, nor your son or daughter, nor your manservant or maidservant, nor your animals, nor the alien within your gates. For in six days the LORD made the heavens and the earth, the sea, and all that is in them, but he rested on the seventh day. Therefore the LORD blessed the Sabbath day and made it holy."*

Our overview of the creation week has shown that the Bible and science provide distinct, complementary perspectives on our origins. The Bible clearly declares *Who* is Lord over creation, *why*

He made it, a few brief observations about *what* was made, and an unequivocal declaration of man's unique *spiritual* status. The scriptures leave us clueless about *how* and *when* anything was made, however, including the human body and our mysterious brain. Science provides buckets of data concerning *what* is in the universe on our Earth, *when* creation unfolded, *how* the universe, the solar system, Earth, life, and humans have changed and are changing, and *where* we have been during our wanderings on this planet. Although science has unveiled clues concerning early religious customs and imaginations of our human ancestors, the eternal, spiritual, supernatural nature of man that is so well characterized in the Bible leaves no fossil behind. The riches of our spirit can only be explored by faith in the revealed Word of God, while the bounty of the universe is best understood through the eyes of science.

The reconciliation of science and the scriptures found in Genesis One is a relatively easy task because that text does not identify individuals nor does it constrain the initial population of humanity to two solitary people. Resolving the issues in Genesis Two and Three is much more contentious though. It's also much more entertaining and interesting because it gets personal. Genesis Two and Three introduce us to Adam and Eve in the Garden of Eden. Are they the first Mr. and Mrs., or are they just a myth-ter and myth-ess? We have already seen that they could not have been the biological ancestors of all humans. Does that mean they were not real people? Liberal theologians, including liberal SCUMBAGs, would certainly discount the existence of this pair. As a proud conservative SCUMBAG, I am convinced that they were real folks! I think there is a strong biblical case for believing that this couple actually lived. What may surprise you, though, is that a belief in Adam and Eve does *not* require the denial of human evolution.

Chapter 17.
Garden Variety Humans

The next two chapters of Genesis bring us to a new venue, the Garden of Eden. Opinions of the Garden of Eden typically divide believers with a sincere respect for the Word of God into three groups; those who believe that the Garden of Eden yields exquisite details of how God supernaturally manufactured the first man and woman, those who consider the Garden to be a mythical land inhabited by two mythical people who demonstrate the relationships between mankind and God, and those who feel no burning compulsion to decide one way or the other despite being badgered by members of the first two groups. Read it yourself and see what you think.

Genesis 2:4-25 This is the account of the heavens and the earth when they were created. When the LORD God made the earth and the heavens- and no shrub of the field had yet appeared on the earth and no plant of the field had yet sprung up, for the LORD God had not sent rain on the earth and there was no man to work the ground, but streams came up from the earth and watered the whole surface of the ground— the LORD God formed the man from the dust of the ground and breathed into his nostrils the breath of life, and the man became a living being. Now the LORD God had planted a garden in the east, in Eden; and there he put the man he had formed. And the LORD God made all kinds of trees grow out of the ground—trees that were pleasing to the eye and good for food. In the middle of the garden were the tree of life and the tree of the knowledge of good and evil. A river watering the garden flowed from Eden; from there it was separated into four headwaters. The name of the first is the Pishon; it winds through the entire land of Havilah, where there is gold. (The gold of that land is good; aromatic resin and onyx are also there.) The name of the second river is the Gihon; it winds through the entire land of Cush. The name of the third river is the Tigris; it runs along the east side of Asshur. And the fourth river is the Euphrates. The LORD God took the man and put him in the Garden of Eden to work it and take care of it. And the LORD God commanded the man, "You are free to eat from any tree in the garden; but you must not eat from the tree of the knowledge of good and evil, for when you eat of it you will surely die." The LORD God said, "It is not good for the man to be alone. I will make a helper suitable for him." Now the LORD God had formed out of the ground all the beasts of the field and all the birds of the air. He brought them to the man to see what he would name them; and whatever the man called each living creature, that was its name. So the man gave names to all the livestock, the birds of the air and all the beasts of the field. But for Adam no suitable helper was found. So the LORD God caused the man to fall into a deep sleep; and while he was sleeping, he took one of the man's ribs and closed up the place with flesh. Then the LORD God made a woman from the rib he had taken out of the man, and he brought her to the man. The man said, "This is now bone of my bones and flesh of my flesh; she shall be called 'woman,' for she was taken out of man." For this reason a man will leave his father and mother and be united to his wife, and they will become one flesh. The man and his wife were both naked, and they felt no shame.

Genesis 3:1-24 Now the serpent was more crafty than any of the wild animals the LORD God had made. He said to the woman, "Did God really say, 'You must not eat from any tree in the garden'?" The woman said to the serpent, "We may eat fruit from the trees in the garden, but God did say, 'You must not eat fruit from the tree that is in the middle of the garden, and you must not touch it, or you will die.'" "You will not surely die," the serpent said to the woman. "For God knows that when you eat of it your eyes will be opened, and you will be like God, knowing good and evil." When the woman saw that the fruit of the tree was good for food and pleasing to the eye, and also desirable for gaining wisdom, she took some and ate it. She also gave some to her husband, who was with her, and he ate it. Then the eyes of both of them were opened, and they realized they were naked; so they sewed fig leaves together and made coverings for themselves. Then the man and his wife heard the sound of the LORD God as he was walking in the garden in the cool of the day, and they hid from the LORD God among the trees of the garden. But the LORD God called to the man, "Where are you?" He answered, "I heard you in the garden, and I was afraid because I was naked; so I hid." And he said, "Who told you that you were naked? Have you eaten from the tree that I commanded you not to eat from?" The man said, "The woman you put here with me—she gave me some fruit from the tree, and I ate it." Then the LORD God said to the woman, "What is this you have done?" The woman said, "The serpent deceived me, and I ate." So the LORD God said to the serpent, "Because you have done this, "Cursed are you above all the livestock and all the wild animals! You will crawl on your belly and you will eat dust all the days of your life. And I will put enmity between you and the woman, and between your offspring and hers; he will crush your head, and you will strike his heel." To the woman he said, "I will greatly increase your pains in childbearing; with pain you will give birth to children. Your desire will be for your husband, and he will rule over you." To Adam he said, "Because you listened to your wife and ate from the tree about which I commanded you, 'You must not eat of it' "Cursed is the ground because of you; through painful toil you will eat of it all the days of your life. It will produce thorns and thistles for you, and you will eat the plants of the field. By the sweat of your brow you will eat your food until you return to the ground, since from it you were taken; for dust you are and to dust you will return." Adam named his wife Eve, because she would become the mother of all the living. The LORD God made garments of skin for Adam and his wife and clothed them. And the LORD God said, "The man has now become like one of us, knowing good and evil. He must not be allowed to reach out his hand and take also from the tree of life and eat, and live forever." So the LORD God banished him from the Garden of Eden to work the ground from which he had been taken. After he drove the man out, he placed on the east side of the Garden of Eden cherubim and a flaming sword flashing back and forth to guard the way to the tree of life.

Historical Attributes

So what is it, history or allegory? Few believers are willing to admit with their mouths what they know in their hearts; it's hard to tell! The Garden of Eden narrative has attributes of biblical history and biblical symbolism. Historical aspects include a specific geographic location, an inventory of nearby natural resources, and the identification of characters by name; details not found in other biblical texts that are universally accepted as allegorical. Further, the history of Adam and Eve extends beyond the Garden of Eden into Genesis Four and Five, which document Adam's marriage, children, neighbors, family feuds and death. There are also numerous references to Adam in the Bible that seemingly present Adam as a historical person; an incredibly important one at that. The Apostle Paul, in his letter to the Romans, wrote extensively about the chilling effect of Adam's disobedience. In the following text, the first "one man" refers to Adam, the second "one man" is Jesus.

Romans 5:12-19 Therefore, just as sin entered the world through one man, and death through sin, and in this way death came to all men, because all sinned—for before the law was given, sin was in the world. But sin is not taken into account when there is no law. Nevertheless, death reigned from the time of Adam to the time of Moses, even over those who did not sin by breaking a command, as did Adam, who was a pattern of the one to come. But the gift is not like the trespass. For if the many died by the trespass of the one man, how much more did God's grace and the gift that came by the grace of the one man, Jesus Christ, overflow to the many! Again, the gift of God is not like the result of the one man's sin: The judgment followed one sin and brought condemnation, but the gift followed many trespasses and brought justification. For if, by the trespass of the one man, death reigned through that one man, how much more will those who receive God's abundant provision of grace and of the gift of righteousness reign in life through the one man, Jesus Christ. Consequently, just as the result of one trespass was condemnation for all men, so also the result of one act of righteousness was justification that brings life for all men. For just as through the disobedience of the one man the many were made sinners, so also through the obedience of the one man the many will be made righteous.

A similar message was delivered to the church at Corinth.

1 Corinthians 15:12-22 But if it is preached that Christ has been raised from the dead, how can some of you say that there is no resurrection of the dead? If there is no resurrection of the dead, then not even Christ has been raised. And if Christ has not been raised, our preaching is useless and so is your faith. More than that, we are then found to be false witnesses about God, for we have testified about God that he raised Christ from the dead. But he did not raise him if in fact the dead are not raised. For if the dead are not raised, then Christ has not been raised either. And if Christ has not been raised, your faith is futile; you are still in your sins. Then those also who have fallen asleep in Christ are lost. If only for this life we have hope in Christ, we are to be pitied more than all men. But Christ has indeed been raised from the dead, the firstfruits of those who have fallen asleep. For since death came through a man, the resurrection of the dead comes also through a man. For as in Adam all die, so in Christ all will be made alive.

Through Adam's disobedience, we have sin, condemnation, spiritual death, judgment, and the need of a Savior. These highlight some of the core truths of Christianity; man is inherently sinful and in need of a Savior. Therefore many Christians, especially creationists, would argue that if Adam is just an allegorical figure, then there is no single act of disobedience in the Garden of Eden. Without that act, there is no consequential judgment and condemnation by God. Without this condemnation, there is no sinful nature. Without a sinful nature, there is no spiritual death. Without spiritual death, there is no need for spiritual regeneration and no need for salvation. What, then, was accomplished by the single act of Christ's death on the cross? A short walk down this path illustrates why many consider it as a slippery slope that leads to liberal theologies promoting Jesus as an ancient Mister Rogers—a real nice guy but hardly deity. This conclusion is so repulsive to many Christians that they insist on a purely literal rendering of the Garden of Eden, regardless of any scientific evidence supporting human evolution.

Historical Problems

There are some biblical problems associated with treating the Garden of Eden and its inhabitants as pure history, though. The most obvious dilemma is that the Garden must be reconciled with the creation story in Genesis One. This would imply that the vague creation of man on Day Six of the creation week was vividly detailed in the Garden of Eden. But a different order of events seems to emerge in these versions of the creation story. In Genesis

One, mankind, both male and female, was created during Day Six after all of the plants, trees and animals were created. In Genesis Two and Three, however, man was made and then the Garden was planted and then the animals and then Eve. This does not seem to faze most creationists because they note that this may have been a description of creation events only in the locality of the Garden of Eden and that the text simply says the animals Adam named "had been made", not that they "were then made".

But what of the activities that filled Day Six? If Adam and Eve were made on the sixth day of creation, then all of the events between Adam's origination and God's instructions to the first couple must have happened within 24 hours. Let's see, that's the creation of Adam from the ground, the impartation of life in his body, Adam receiving horticultural instructions, the creation of birds and beasts from the dirt of the ground, an animal parade, the naming of the beasts, a reflective moment when Adam realized that having sex with a baboon was not very appealing, application of divine anesthesia, a biopsy, the creation of Eve using a portion of Adam's tissue and other unspecified raw materials, their first date, and instructions from God on running the planet. Try scheduling that on your calendar for next Friday!

What of that passage containing the famous "get your own place" advice that is still repeated in wedding ceremonies, much to the delight of exhausted parents? *Genesis 2:3-5 The man said, "This is now bone of my bones and flesh of my flesh; she shall be called 'woman,' for she was taken out of man." For this reason a man will leave his father and mother and be united to his wife, and they will become one flesh. The man and his wife were both naked, and they felt no shame.* Why is there advice for a husband to move out from Mom and Dad's place when he gets married if Adam and Eve were manufactured as parentless, fully functioning adults? I know, I know, marriage in general requires that newlyweds not live with their parents, so this was advice for their descendents. It still strikes me as odd that that the only people who never had parents were the ones admonished to move away from them.

What happened to the Garden of Eden, anyway? If you believe the Garden of Eden and the Tree of Life were actually located on Earth, where did they go? There is not a shred of biblical evidence that the Garden of Eden was relocated, demolished or flooded. In fact, the opposite impression is given. When last spotted by the evicted first family, the Garden of Eden stood firm with cherubim and a flaming sword barring access to the Tree of Life. But the Garden of Eden is never seen again after Adam and Eve are evicted. The Tree of Life does not appear again until the last book of the Bible, the Revelation of Jesus Christ written by the Apostle John, who conveyed this message from Christ to the church, *Revelation 2:7 He who has an ear, let him hear what the Spirit says to the churches. To him who overcomes, I will give the right to eat from the tree of life, which is in the paradise of God. According to a John's angelic tour guide, Jesus was right! Revelation 22:1-2 Then the angel showed me the river of the water of life, as clear as crystal, flowing from the throne of God and of the Lamb down the middle of the great street of the city. On each side of the river stood the tree of life, bearing twelve crops of fruit, yielding its fruit every month. And the leaves of the tree are for the healing of the nations.* The Tree of Life is in heaven, not Iraq. Perhaps the simple message of the Tree of Life in the Garden of Eden was that eternal life is found only in the presence of God.

Speaking of the possibilities of symbolism in the Garden of Eden, let's see if that is a reasonable position to hold.

Symbolic Attributes

You do not have to be a theologian to sense symbolism in scriptures. The creation of Adam and Eve symbolized God's authority as Creator of mankind. The life that was breathed into Adam was spiritual and/or physical. The Tree of Life and the Tree of Knowledge of Good and Evil symbolized, you guessed it, life and the knowledge of good and evil. Man and woman were made for one another. Man was given dominion over Earth and was expected to be a faithful steward. There is a strong temptation to question God and His Word, especially when the opportunity to acquire power seems to present itself. All men and women are inherently sinful and in need of a Savior. The lowly spiritual status of Satan relative to God was symbolized by the lowly stature of the serpent. The fruit-chomping represents sinful disobedience. When a man gets in trouble, his first instinct is to blame his wife. Eviction from the Garden of Eden represented the loss of intimate communion with God. The animals that were sacrificed to make skins that covered Adam's and Eve's nakedness foreshadowed the need for a perfect sacrifice to cover our sin. The prophetic promise of One who would crush Satan pointed to the Savior. Adam's name meant man and sounded like the Hebrew word for ground (adamah), hinting that God made man from inanimate material. The death penalty imposed by God was spiritual desolation, although some consider the ancient explanation for physical death to be associated with this judgment. Man was expected to work diligently to satisfy his needs. Planting a garden? Expect weeds! Childbirth was to be a real pain. Marriage was established as heterosexual and monogamous. The sexual relationship between husband and wife was to bind the pair together physically, emotionally and spiritually until death. The barred access to the Tree of Life indicated that sinful man could not approach God on his own merits. Finally, the chances of a successful marriage were bolstered by not living with your in-laws.

Symbolic Problems

But if the Garden of Eden is completely symbolic, what is the point of including all of those little historic, geographic, and geologic details? Why is the story of Adam and Eve continued in two additional chapters that contain mundane and embarrassing details of their family life? If Adam was not a real person, why was his story so highly touted in the New Testament? Are the early portions of Genesis, up to and including Chapter 11[1] merely a collection of myths, or do they contain elements of history?

The Odd Couple

Is the Garden of Eden historical or allegorical? I think it may be both. Perhaps the Garden of Eden is a spiritual setting with a cast of historical characters. Genesis Two and Three is overwhelmingly symbolic, but perhaps it contains a small bit of history in that Adam and Eve were real people. They miraculously received a spiritual nature, they were our spiritual representatives before God, and they were the first known ancestors of Abraham. Genesis does *not* demand, however, that Adam and Eve were the only humans, the first and only humans, the sole humans granted a spiritual nature, or the only genetic ancestors of all mankind.

This interpretation really isn't a new idea. There are many other people who have previously concluded that Adam may have been a natural human into whom God breathed a supernatural spirit. I have been around creationists long enough to know what goes through their mind when they hear such comments about Adam and Eve. "What an obvious attempt to twist the scriptures in order to appease evolutionists!" The best way to refute this charge is to demonstrate that considering Adam to be a human whose body of natural origin was supernaturally imbued with an eternal spirit was first proposed *centuries before Darwin was born*. What's more surprising is that this viewpoint, which is detailed in ancient Hebrew commentaries, was based solely on the book of Genesis.

How in the world did they come up with that idea? Let's find out.

References
1. Hugh Brody. The Other Side of Eden—Hunters, Farmers, and the Shaping of the World. North Point Press, A Division of Farrar, Straus, and Giroux. New York, NY, 2000, 63–97

Chapter 18.
The Adam's Family

I Was Raised by Animals

One can make the biblical case that Adam existed and had a unique role in the history of man's spirituality *without requiring that he was the first and only human.* What if the "breath of life" that entered Adam was solely in reference to the spiritual nature that God miraculously gave him as an adult? What if becoming "man" is something more than gaining a human physiology or high-powered brain? What if being made in God's image requires the acquisition of an eternal spirit—not just a religious curiosity? Could it be that the Garden of Eden doesn't concern our biology at all? Perhaps Adam was not the original *Homo sapien*, but rather a spiritual pioneer in the Middle East and mankind's spiritual representative before God. Could it be that there was a recent and sudden appearance of a spiritual man emerging from a population of non-spiritual humans with identical physiology? Gerald Schroeder, a physicist and biblical scholar who pondered how the text of Genesis and the findings of science correlated, has offered one of the most interesting and compelling presentations of this viewpoint. Schroeder himself reasoned that non-spiritual humans with bodies indistinguishable from ours but lacking a spiritual nature may have preceded Adam[1], but he was a bit wary to share such a provocative notion with others. He finally summoned the courage to ask a prominent rabbi if the Garden of Eden could be an account of Adam miraculously receiving his supernatural spirit from God as a young man, perhaps 20 years after being born of human parents. Much to Schroeder's surprise and relief, the rabbi informed him that Hebrew scholars had suggested such an interpretation roughly a thousand years ago based solely on the wording of Genesis. Ancient commentaries, including the Talmud (ca. 500 A.D.), Rashi (ca. 1050 A.D.), Maimonides (ca. 1190 A.D.) and Nahmanides (ca. 1260 A.D.) postulated that generations of spiritless, human-like animals preceded Adam. They thought that it was reasonable to conclude that Adam was born the old-fashioned way, but was unique in that he was chosen by God to suddenly receive a spiritual nature as a young adult.

How did ancient Hebrew scholars extract images of non-spiritual, human-like animals from Genesis, as opposed to the sudden creation of humans? *How did they look into the Garden of Eden and see a natural process for the origin of the human body followed by the recent impartation of a spiritual nature, while today's creationists see nothing but mud pies turning into man?* Schroeder lays out the clues that emerge from a careful reading of Genesis. After all, why can't a careful and thorough examination of Genesis by Hebrew scholars be of more merit than the simplistic, literal rendering so highly touted by creationists? Let's take at look at Schroeder's summary of why these ancient scholars believed that Adam may have abruptly received a spirit while retaining a long human ancestry[2]. Although Schroeder has made some notable blunders in his scientific explanations of various phenomena[3], his summary of these Hebrew commentaries provides an interesting perspective for distinguishing between our supernatural spirit and human physiology.

Man was Made Before He was Created

Creation usually implies the making of something from nothing. For example, the heavens and the Earth were first created out of nothing. *Genesis 1:1 In the beginning God created the heavens and the earth.* Then the common features of Earth and the life it supports were made from this substance into the forms we recognize today. *Exodus 31:16-17 The Israelites are to observe the Sabbath, celebrating it for the generations to come as a lasting covenant. It will be a sign between me and the Israelites forever, for in six days the LORD made the heavens and the earth, and on the seventh day he abstained from work and rested.* When it came to man, however, God apparently got it backwards. First man was made, and then he was created! *Genesis 1:26-27 Then God said, "Let us make man in our image, in our likeness, and let them rule over the fish of the sea and the birds of the air, over the livestock, over all the earth, and over all the creatures that move along the ground." So God created man in his own image, in the image of God he created him; male and female he created them.* Perhaps this is a hint that man's body was made, and then his spirit was created! The human body could have been formed from the inanimate materials that God created and then elevated to the status of man via the introduction of the intangible human spirit. No hint is given on how much time elapsed between the two events, however. Maybe a second or a minute. Perhaps five or six million years.

Man was Made and Made Again

There is a spelling difference of a word translated as "formed" that implies a difference in the makeup of animals and man. Animals were "formed" from the adamah, the Hebrew word for the dust of the ground, *Genesis 2:19 Now the LORD God had formed out of the ground all the beasts of the field and all the birds of the air. He brought them to the man to see what he would name them; and whatever the man called each living creature, that was its name.* Man was also formed from the adamah, *Genesis 2:7 the LORD God formed the man from the dust of the ground and breathed into his nostrils the breath of life, and the man became a living being.* Although both man and animal were made from adamah, the Hebrew word translated as "formed" is different for animals than it is for man. When applied to animals, the word translated as "formed" is "ya-tsar", and this "ya-tsar" has a single letter "yud". When applied to man, however, "ya-tsar" has a double "yud". The letter "yud" is also the abbreviation of God's name that is most closely translated as "eternal." The ancient scholars considered the "double yud" as an indicator of man's dual nature; a temporal physical body and an eternal spirit. Until both parts of the formation were complete, humans were only animals. After the inclusion of the eternal spirit, the human being became a spiritual man.

Two-for-One

God made the animals with a "nefesh", the Hebrew term for a soul. For example, animals are referred to as living "creature", or living "nefesh". *Genesis 1:20-21 And God said, "Let the water teem with living creatures, and let birds fly above the earth across the expanse of the sky." So God created the great creatures of the sea and every living and moving thing with which the water teems, according to their kinds, and every winged bird according to its kind. And God saw that it was good. Genesis 1:24 And God said, "Let the land produce living creatures according to their kinds: livestock, creatures that move along the ground, and wild animals, each according to its kind." And it was so.* Man was different. *Genesis 1:26-27 Then God said, "Let us make man in our image, in our likeness, and let them rule over the fish of the sea and the birds of the air, over the livestock, over all the earth, and over all the creatures that move along the ground." So God created man in his own image, in the image of God he created him; male and female he created them.* These verses indicate that man received a "nefesh" just like the animals, but the following passage shows that he subsequently received a "neshama", the "breath" of life. *Genesis 2:7 the LORD God formed the man from the dust of the ground and breathed into his nostrils the breath of life, and the man became a living being.* First man received a "nefesh", but then man received the "neshama". Animals and humans can share some of the "nefesh" experiences, such as happiness, excitement, fear and boredom, but only man can commune with God. Only man can experience spiritual renewal. Only man can live eternally. The supernatural "neshama" is a unique attribute of mankind that points to our spirituality.

Getting an Upgrade

One Hebrew word is typically omitted from the translation of the following verse because most translators considered it to be inconsequential. *Genesis 2:7 the LORD God formed the man from the dust of the ground and breathed into his nostrils the breath of life, and the man became a living being.* The Hebrew actually reads that Adam "became *to* a living being." Nahmanides noted that the word "to", denoted by the letter "lamud", indicated a change in form. He actually surmised that our origins may have begun as a mineral and our development then passed to plant to fish to animal and finally to man upon receipt of a "neshama". (This progression from inanimate material to animate substance and on through lower life forms before becoming man is strikingly similar to the process of you-know-what!) Alternately, Nahmanides proposed that when the scriptures declare that Adam "became to a living being", it may have indicated that non-spiritual humans with identical physical characteristics preceded spiritual man. They were human, but not quite man because they lacked a spiritual nature.

Getting It Together

The dual nature of man—soul and spirit—may be implied by the use of the word "us" in the following passage, *Genesis 1:26 Then God said, "Let us make man in our image, in our likeness, and let them rule over the fish of the sea and the birds of the air, over the livestock, over all the earth, and over all the creatures that move along the ground."* Could this verse be God personifying the spiritual and material dimensions of man? Perhaps the "us" is the union of animal nature and the spiritual nature that is unique to man. (As we noted previously, most Christians would take issue with this interpretation because they ascribe the usage of "us" to the three persons of the Holy Trinity.)

Please Won't You Be My Neighbor

Still not convinced? For those of you who are certain that the Bible unequivocally teaches that Adam and Eve were miraculously created as the *first* and *only* man and woman on the face of the Earth, how do you explain their neighbors?

Genesis 4:1-17 Adam lay with his wife Eve, and she became pregnant and gave birth to Cain. She said, "With the help of the LORD I have brought forth a man." Later she gave birth to his brother Abel. Now Abel kept flocks, and Cain worked the soil. In the course of time Cain brought some of the fruits of the soil as an offering to the LORD. But Abel brought fat portions from some of the firstborn of his flock. The LORD looked with favor on Abel and his offering, but on Cain and his offering he did not look with favor. So Cain was very angry, and his face was downcast. Then the LORD said to Cain, "Why are you angry? Why is your face downcast? If you do what is right, will you not be accepted? But if you do not do what is right, sin is crouching at your door; it desires to have you, but you must master it." Now Cain said to his brother Abel, "Let's go out to the field." And while they were in the field, Cain attacked his brother Abel and killed him. Then the LORD said to Cain, "Where is your brother Abel?" "I don't know," he replied. "Am I my brother's keeper?" The LORD said, "What have you done? Listen! Your brother's blood cries out to me from the ground. Now you are under a curse and driven from the ground, which opened its mouth to receive your brother's blood from your hand. When you work the ground, it will no longer yield its crops for you. You will be a restless wanderer on the earth." Cain said to the LORD, "My punishment is more than I can bear. Today you are driving me from the land, and I will be hidden from your presence; I will be a restless wanderer on the earth, and whoever finds me will kill me." But the LORD said to him, "Not so; if anyone kills Cain, he will suffer vengeance seven times over." Then the LORD put a mark on Cain so that no one who found him would kill him. So Cain went out from the Lord's presence and lived in the land of Nod, east of Eden. Cain lay with his wife, and she became pregnant and gave birth to Enoch. Cain was then building a city, and he named it after his son Enoch.

Sadly, the first child of the first couple ended up murdering his brother Abel, leaving Adam, Eve and Cain as the surviving family members. Why, then, was Cain so worried about confronting vengeful people wherever he wandered in that region? Where did Cain's wife come from? Who inhabited the city that Cain was building? Creationists point to the following verses for their answer. *Genesis 3:20 Adam named his wife Eve, because she would become the mother of all the living. Genesis 5:1-4 This is the written account of Adam's line. When God created man, he made him in the likeness of God. He created them male and female and blessed them. And when they were created, he called them "man." When Adam had lived 130 years, he had a son in his own likeness, in his own image; and he named him Seth. After Seth was born, Adam lived 800 years and had other sons and daughters.* According to creationists, Adam and Eve were cranking out the kids left and right. Cain's wife, Abel's avengers, and Cain's city

dwellers were therefore the children, grandchildren and great grandchildren of Adam and Eve. Creationists correctly point out that
there was no restriction against marrying relatives at this point, so
inbreeding was perfectly acceptable.

I would suggest an alternate view that is a bit more reasonable
than assuming that everyone waiting in line for one of Eve's babies
to grow up to keep them company. Genesis Four makes no apol-
ogy for Adam and Eve having human contemporaries, so why
should we? The Bible plainly presents the events of Adam, Eve and
Cain in the context of a community of other people. Maybe these
neighbors did not have a spiritual nature, but perhaps they did. In
either case, Adam and Eve were just two of many people living at
that time; they were not the only people on Earth.

Adam's Other Women

Did Adam make it with other ladies? Let's take a look.

*Genesis 4:25,26, 5:1-3 Adam lay with his wife again, and she gave birth
to a son and named him Seth, saying, "God has granted me another child
in place of Abel, since Cain killed him." Seth also had a son, and he
named him Enosh. At that time men began to call on the name of the
LORD. This is the written account of Adam's line. When God created
man, he made him in the likeness of God. He created them male and
female and blessed them. And when they were created, he called them
"man." When Adam had lived 130 years, he had a son in his own likeness, in his own image; and he named him Seth.*

After the family tragedy involving their boys, Adam had sexual relations with his wife Eve. Again. Schroeder points out that the
Talmud questions the point of adding the word "again" to this sentence. If Eve was Adam's only woman, who else could Adam have
been having sexual relations with[4]? Would any man you know
refuse to have sex for 130 years because he was annoyed with his
wife? We can't even abstain for 130 hours without going crazy! The
Talmud postulates that during his years of separation from Eve,
Adam was busy having an extended mid-life crisis, mating with
non-spiritual beings and producing human children without a
spiritual nature.

We Are Not Alone

There is a case to be made for a biblical interpretation of Genesis that allows for Adam's natural physical origin and supernatural spiritual origin, and such a case was made long before Darwin showed up. It certainly is not the only conclusion that one can arrive at based on the scriptures, and it definitely was not the most popular viewpoint of Christians. It was, however, a well established interpretation of ancient Hebrew scholars. Further, it complements the scientific evidence of humanity's ancient lineage much better than any creationist interpretation of the Garden of Eden. But if humans ascended to man upon the receiving an eternal spirit, when did it happen? When did our species rise to immortality? Our bodies were millions of years in the making since we diverged from the ancestor we share with the chimpanzees. When did our spirit show up? Of course no one knows for sure because a date is not provided in the Bible, but there are some interesting clues.

References
1. G.L. Schroeder; The Science of God; Broadway Books, 1998; 125-145
2. G.L. Schroeder; The Science of God; Broadway Books, 1998; 125-145
3. Mark Perakh; Unintelligent Design, Prometheus Books, Amherst New York, 2004, 173-191
4. G.L. Schroeder; The Science of God; Broadway Books, 1998; 141

Chapter 19.
Adam's First Date

Stupid Human Tricks

Genesis provides some clues as to the timing of man's spiritual ascent. The skills of Adam and his immediate descendants provide compelling indications concerning when he lived because scientists have uncovered evidence as to when these human capabilities emerged.

Genesis Two and Three have already shown us that early spiritual men and women talked with one another, spoke with God, called each other by name, tended gardens, pulled weeds, herded livestock, aspired to monogamous marriages, sewed clothes, and blamed their spouse when things went wrong. If one adheres to the King James Version rendering of Genesis 3:19, Adam was even starting fires, making ovens, and baking bread! *Genesis 3:19 KJV In the sweat of thy face shalt thou eat bread.* Genesis Four begins with two fundamental tasks associated with early spiritual man, raising livestock and farming, although there is no biblical indication that these skills were necessarily invented at this time. *Genesis 4:2 Abel kept flocks, and Cain worked the soil.* Later in Genesis 4, we find a host of job descriptions and skills associated with the early descendants of Adam. *Genesis 4:17-26 Cain lay with his wife, and she became pregnant and gave birth to Enoch. Cain was then building a city, and he named it after his son Enoch. To Enoch was born Irad, and Irad was the father of Mehujael, and Mehujael was the father of Methushael, and Methushael was the father of Lamech. Lamech married two women, one named Adah and the other Zillah. Adah gave birth to Jabal; he was the father of those who live in tents and raise livestock. His brother's name was Jubal; he was the father of all who play the harp and flute. Zillah also had a son, Tubal-Cain, who forged all kinds of tools out of bronze and iron. Tubal-Cain's sister was Naamah. Lamech said to his wives, "Adah and Zillah, listen to me; wives of Lamech, hear my words. I have killed a man for wounding me, a young man for injuring me. If Cain is avenged seven times, then Lamech seventy-seven times." Adam lay with his wife again, and she gave birth to a son and named him Seth, saying, "God has granted me another child in place of Abel, since Cain killed him." Seth also had a son, and he named him Enosh. At that time men began to call on the name of the LORD.*

The morality of early spiritual man degenerated quickly into murder, polygamy, and atheism, but their skills and career paths were blossoming. Adam and Eve and their early descendents were an upright-walking, language-talking, garment-weaving, animal-hunting, crop-planting, weed–pulling, fire-starting, bread-baking, beast-herding, city-building, tent-making, harp-playing, flute-toot-ing, bronze-molding, iron-working, tool-toting, soul-saving lot. Let's see if the dates that some of these *Homo sapien* skills first appeared, according to scientists, can give us a clue about when Adam lived. We'll assume that Homo sapiens originated 150,000 years ago, so that will be the upper limit of this table even though earlier human species may have had the attribute. I've listed the names of the people in the correct genealogical order, from the most ancient to the most recent.

Attribute or Skill	Bible Character that Exhibited this Attribute or Skill	Number of Years Ago that Homo sapiens First Exhibited the Attribute or Skill
Upright posture	Adam	>>150,000
Language	Adam	150,000—40,000
Gardening/Agriculture	Adam, Cain	10,000—9,000
Clothing	Adam	23,000
Needles for sewing	Adam	30,000—18,000
Bread	Adam	10,000
Shepherding	Abel	10,000—9,000
Cities	Cain	9,000
Tents	Jabal	>>150,000
Raising livestock	Jabal	10,000—9,000
Harp	Jubal	6,000—5,000
Flute	Jubal	40,000—35,000
Bronze tools	Tubal-Cain	5,500—4,000
Iron tools	Tubal-Cain	5,000—4,000

Please don't read too much into these passages. For example, I don't think that when Genesis says *Zillah also had a son, Tubal-Cain, who forged all kinds of tools out of bronze and iron,* that it literally means "Zillah also had a son, Tubal-Cain, who was the first human being on the planet's surface who ever forged an object out of either bronze or iron and he alone passed this trade secret on to others and then founded Iraqi Ironworkers Local 001." This verse may simply mean that Tubal-Cain was the first known descendent of Adam that demonstrated significant metal-working skills in the Middle East. Further, there is not universal agreement on the precise dates when these attributes originated. With this more relaxed perspective in mind, the information in this table provides a ballpark idea of when Adam and his immediate descendants, Cain and Abel, showed up. I would not be the first to place the Adam within the Neolithic Revolution—the transition from the Old Stone Age to the New Stone Age—in the ancient Near East about 8000 to 7500 B.C. *Therefore, if Adam existed, he probably lived about 9,500 to 10,000 years ago*[1]. There's no way that he lived more than 20,000 years ago. The bread baking, city making, livestock raising, cattle grazing, seed sowing, crop growing skills that his family exhibited simply weren't developed at that time.

The Sum of All Years

Genealogies can also be used to determine the year in which spiritual life was breathed into Adam. One starts by summing the ages of paternity in the chain of succession between Adam, the first spiritual man in the lineage of the Jews, and Terah, Abraham's (Abram's) father[2]. The result, 1946 years, is the duration of the interval between Adam and Abraham. Abraham was probably born sometime between 1900 BC and 2200 BC, therefore one can quickly determine that Adam was made in the image of God about 4000 BC, or 6000 years ago. A comparison of genealogies within the Bible indicates that it is not uncommon to skip over generations now and then. Therefore the 6000 year estimate is a lower limit. If the genealogies were missing half of the links in the chain of ancestry, then Adam would have lived about 12,000 years ago. It seems reasonable (at least to me) to assert that spiritual man first appeared roughly 6,000—12,000 years ago. This result is in rough agreement with the dating of Adam and Eve's family based on their demonstrated skills and attributes.

Not So Fast...

Science can neither confirm not deny the existence of God or a spirit because it is supernatural. Nonetheless, the suggestion that there was a sudden impartation of spirituality into humans about 6,000 years ago does not sit well with some investigators. Why? If the Spirit of God is as influential as the Bible purports, then tangible and notable changes in the course of human history would have probably occurred at a point in time when God gave humans a spiritual nature. Mark Perakh[3] is one of many who argue that the notion of spiritual humans being preceded by spiritless human-like animals about 6,000 years ago is sheer nonsense. Perakh claims that Schroeder associates the impartation of the spirit 6000 years ago with the advent of the attributes that distinguish us from our pre-Adamic ancestors. Perakh then correctly points out that an impressive increase in the capabilities in humans occurred during the last 40,000 years[4], and all of the achievements commonly associated with humans, such as language, art, city building, and agriculture, were exhibited much earlier than 6,000 years ago. Perakh's criticism of Schroeder is a bit unfair, though. Schroeder does *not* claim that humans instantly gained the ability to speak, make stone tools, or create art 6,000 years ago. He plainly acknowledges that humans made pottery and were engaged in agriculture before 4,000 B.C.[5]. Neither does Schroeder contend that humans gained their ability to speak or draw when the spirit was received. Schroeder simply maintains that about 6,000 years ago God added supernatural spirituality to the laundry list of other human attributes that already differentiated people from animals. I agree with Schroeder's idea in general, but not with his timeline in particular. Based on Adam's skills and the propensity for biblical genealogies to skip over generations, I think that Adam lived about 10,000 years ago rather than 6,000 years ago.

Many archeologists would claim that there is persuasive hard evidence for dating the religious origins of humans, and that this body of evidence points to an era long before 8,000 B.C. Burial sites, graves containing food and supplies, figurines, drawings of creatures with human heads and animal bodies, shrines housing slabs that are reminiscent of altars, and monuments may provide a better gauge for dating the origin of religious belief than man's ability to speak or farm. How old are these ancient indicators of possible religiosity? Forty thousand year old graves contain enough articles to make archeologists wonder if the grieving survivors were providing the dearly departed with tools and treats for their journey. Dickson's fascinating account of the Upper Paleolithic Period, between 35,000—10,000 years ago, in southwestern Europe outlines the possible origin of religious beliefs as reflected in burial practices and art[6]. One of the oldest known structures that was almost certainly built for religious purposes is about 27,000 years old. The shrine, located in Spain, is so big that it certainly required a cooperative effort to complete. It housed objects not needed for run-of-the-mill Stone Age existence, and contained a heavy limestone slab and an unusual stone sculpture of a half human-half beast head[7]. The evidence of religious activity becomes more prevalent and obvious when sites less than 10,000 years old are examined.

In light of this evidence, it is no surprise that some modern creationists, most notably Hugh Ross, are eager to stretch back Adam's out-of-thin-air appearance to 40,000 BC or so. In this way, all of these ancient shades of religious activity can be considered post-Adamic expressions of true spirituality and the acceptance or rejection of God by men and women made in the image of God. All of the remarkable changes that occurred in human history at this time (e.g. advanced stone tools; complex artifacts made of shaped bone, antler, and ivory; beads and pendants; remarkably sophisticated and beautiful art; systematic hunting; and sites containing hearths, pits, huts, and tents) could also be attributed to the supernatural touch of God upon humanity. There are some huge problems with plunging Adam 40,000 years into the past, however. For example, the genealogies on Genesis would have to skip a whopping six out of seven generations to push Adam's birthday from 6000 years ago to 40,000 years ago! There are examples of generation-skipping in Bible genealogies, but jumping over six out of seven ancestors? I don't think so. It's also obvious that Adam and Eve and their sons Cain and Abel knew how to plant gardens, raise crops and herd animals. Although there was indeed a revolution in the skills of humans 40,000 years ago, farming and shepherding would not be practiced for another 30,000 years. Finally, there simply is no evidence whatsoever for the notion that humans became extinct 40,001 years ago, forcing God to replace them with a solitary couple in the Garden of Eden the following year.

Catch 22

There's no way that Adam lived 40,000 years ago. 40,000 years ago most of the skills attributed to Adam were not developed. If Adam lived 10,000 years ago, though, then he would have been familiar with clothing, language, shepherding, bread, and crops. The genealogies would have only been missing about half of the names in the family tree; still a high fraction but a reasonable value. Adam would have not been the sole person on Earth, either; he would have been in the good company of many other men and women. *But how could the non-spiritual humans that preceded Adam have made the statues, shrines, artwork, and burial items that seem to convey religious belief?* Let's take a look at the prehistoric religious artifacts dating back to the Old Stone Age and explore what impact that it has on the proposed 10,000 year old advent of man's spirituality.

Gimme That Old Time Religion

What are we to make of those religious artifacts dating back 20,000, 30,000 or 40,000 years? If the spirit was first breathed into mankind only about 10,000 years ago, what compelled humans to seemingly express religious thoughts tens of thousands of years earlier? What is it that drove humans to carve small statues and draw images that strongly suggest a belief in gods or an afterlife? I think the scientists may be right—again—when they attribute these finds to the evolution of the human brain working in conjunction with a set of skilled hands. Perhaps our earliest religious aspirations were indeed bundled in genes such as those involved in the brains' manufacture of monoamines that regulate mood and motor control, as suggested by Dean Hamer[8]. (Hamer acknowledges that his findings that trace religious hunger to our evolving DNA neither prove nor disprove the existence of God. "If there's a God, there's a God. Just knowing what brain chemicals are involved in acknowledging that is not going to change the fact."[9]) Perhaps puzzled Paleolithic parents eventually formed some shades of religion when they pondered the wonders of creation, considered the finality of death, feared the elements against which they struggled, revered the beasts that they preyed upon, sought refuge from the daily struggles of survival, or marveled at the mystery of childbirth. Perhaps the gods of the Old Stone Age motivated our ancestors to shun destructive behavior and restrain their murderous acts. Early religion may have been birthed by a purely natural process—the evolution of the human brain—in mere mortals who did not have a shred of a supernatural spirit in their being. Religion in its most primitive form could have simply been a mutation that benefited groups of humans by providing them an evolutionary advantage; a sense of optimism[10].

But did these ancient humans possess a spirit, or were they mere mortals that possessed religious thought? Did they possess an eternal spiritual nature given to them by God, or was their soul no more than an overactive imagination? As religious concepts began to take root in humans tens of thousands of years ago, were fanciful gods evolving in their heads or was God revealing Himself to them? Were the statuettes and cave drawings mere creativity, or a sign that humans were beginning to express a belief in God or to reject His revelation? There is no scientific way to verify or falsify a supernatural soul in our human ancestors, so let's take a look at a few of the ideas that have been promoted by skeptics and saints concerning the relationship between these ancient religious activities and the eternal spirit of man.

Perhaps the human compulsion for religion developed as our brains evolved without the help of God—because there never was a God in the first place. For those of you who don't believe anything unless you can prove it, this is right up your alley! You can simply dismiss all expressions of religion and spirituality associated with humans as mere brain chemistry. Not surprisingly, this leaves science alone as the final arbiter of truth, much to the delight of skeptical, agnostic, and atheistic scientists. These fine investigators may respect religion or degrade it, but in either case it becomes apparent that religion and spirituality are classified as purely natural phenomena. Not just the primitive religion of the Old Stone Age, mind you. The entirety of Christianity is considered as a remarkably sophisticated myth that evolved from its polytheistic ancestors. There is no real hope of salvation or eternal life; such doctrines merely reflect our species' collective panic at the thought of our inescapable date with death.

What if there is a God after all? Maybe He let human religious tendencies evolve until we developed an understanding that He exists. The breath of God received by Adam may be symbolic of the birth of the human conscience within our species[11]. We alone received the liberty of choice, and Adam's fall was the myth that illuminated our tendency to make wrong choices. Despite our yearnings for eternal life, we remained mere mortals whose hope for an afterlife was vanquished by death. Our disengaged God may be eternal, but we certainly are not.

Now my favorite! Could it be that God let our species' religious tendencies evolve to a point where they were ready for an upgrade? Did God eventually decide to breathe an eternal spirit into mortal human beings? Did He select us for the marvelous privilege of enjoying His fellowship and receiving His revelation?

I think that God waited until *Homo sapiens* were ready to receive a spirit, and then He gave it to us. How? I don't know. Where? Not sure. How many people received a spirit? No idea! When? Probably 10,000 years ago, but I can't be certain. Why not earlier? I can only guess. Perhaps God took a look at our species 50,000 years ago and declared, in the words of Jack Nicholson's character Colonel Jessup in *A Few Good Men*, "You can't handle the truth!" Perhaps 10,000 years ago God decided that our species had progressed far enough to be promoted from mortal humans with religious tendencies to humans blessed with an intangible, everlasting spiritual nature. Death would still return the body to the ground, but the spirit would return to God. Although it certainly cannot be proven, perhaps our species newborn spirituality contributed in part to the remarkable advances in human civilization at the dawn of the New Stone Age[12].

Get It Together

Let's put it all together while casting creationist and atheistic objections[13] aside. If Adam was indeed real, he would have lived roughly 10,000 years ago. He had a long and rich heritage of human forefathers who apparently exhibited some primitive religious beliefs that were natural in origin. Adam and Eve *were not* the first humans, they *were not* the only humans, they *were not* the common biological ancestors of all humans, and they *were not* the only humans that God elevated to "man" via the miraculous impartation of a spiritual nature. Adam was a spiritual pioneer, however, in the sense that he received a supernatural, eternal spirit directly from his Creator. He possessed an immortal soul that returned to God upon his death. Adam was unique in that he was selected as man's representative before the Almighty; when Adam fell, we all fell. Adam lived in the company of many other people at the beginning of the New Stone Age, and his descendents spread throughout the Middle East. Abraham, Isaac, Jacob, Ishmael, Jesus, the Arabs and the Jews trace their roots to Adam and Eve, but the structure of this family tree is a matter of faith, not science. (Due to intermarriage with other Middle Eastern peoples it is not possible to correlate the genetic heritage of modern Jews to Jacob, let alone Isaac, Abraham, Noah, or Adam[14,15].) This is the way—the one and only way—that one can believe in Adam and Eve as a historical couple while acknowledging the indisputable scientific findings concerning human origins.

References
1. Davis A. Young; The Antiquity and the Unity of the Human Race Revisited, Christian Scholar's Review XXIV:4, 380–396, May, 1995
2. Appendix O
3. Mark Perakh; Unintelligent Design, Prometheus Books, Amherst New York, 2004, 173–191
4. Appendix N
5. G.L. Schroeder; The Science of God; Simon and Schuster; New York, NY, 1997; 135–145
6. D. Bruce Dickson; The Dawn of Belief—Religion in the Upper Paleolithic of Southwestern Europe, University of Arizona Press, January 1994, 93–158
7. C. Simon, Stone-age Sanctuary, Oldest Known Shrine, Discovered in Spain, Science News, Dec. 5, 1981, 357
8. Dean Hamer, The God Gene—How Faith is Hardwired into Our Genes, Doubleday, New York, NY, 2004, 56–78
9. Quote of Dean Hamer found in: Jeffrey Kluger, Is God in Our Genes? A Provocative Study Asks Whether Religion is a Product of Evolution, Inside a Quest for the Roots of Faith,Time, October 25, 2004, 62–68
10. Dean Hamer; The God Gene—How Faith is Hardwired into Our Genes, Doubleday, New York, NY, 2004, 12–13
11. Lecomte du Nouy; Human Destiny, Longman's, Green and Company, New York, NY, 1947, 103–119
12. Appendix N
13. Appendix P
14. Steve Olsen; Mapping Human History—Genes, Race and Our Common Origin, A Mariner Book, Houghton Miller, Boston, MA, 2002, 106–119
15. Jonathan Marks; What It Means to be 98% Chimpanzee—Apes, People and Their Genes, University of California Press, Berkeley, CA, 2002, 245–249

Chapter 20.
Am I Wrong?

I believe that the origin of the spirit of man is divine. Would I invoke the supernatural for the origin of anything else? Perhaps the answer to just one question; why is there anything, rather than nothing at all? Maybe God asked the same question, and then set the stage for creation to appear in the way that only science can reveal.

Could I be wrong? I believe the arguments made in this book are correct, but then again, I make mistakes every day. I routinely strand my kids at their school's sporting events and spend 18% of each day searching for my car keys! Could this book be an aggregate of my bigger blunders? Am I wrong about the first verse of the Bible corresponding to the Big Bang? Am I merely exhibiting 20-20 hindsight by associating the dark, wet, lifeless condition of our planet four billion years ago with the Genesis 1:2? Is my imagination running wild when I suggest that when God was hovering over the waters of the Earth, life's first forms were brewing? Does the Bible's first mention of light really correspond to the initial penetration of sunlight through the Earth's early cloud cover? Could I be completely off-base by correlating the Bible's description of land emerging from beneath the waters with continent-building tectonic activity? Am I nutty to assert that when

God commanded the land to bring forth life, it corresponded to a completely natural process? Are ancient Hebrew commentaries that promote Adam as a spiritual pioneer with a long human ancestry a classic case of a blind squirrel finding an acorn rather than a great biblical insight?

If I were a red-blooded creationist, I would answer with a hearty "No, I certainly could not be wrong!" In fact, I would warn you that if you disagreed with me, you would be responsible for the fall of Western civilization, the breakup of the institution of marriage, the disintegration of Christianity, tax audits and salmonella. But I'm not positive that I am absolutely correct.

Of course I could be wrong!

If I am wrong, however, it is a result of mistaking poetic descriptions of nature for inspired observations of an evolving planet. If I am in error, it's because I have strained the scriptures in an attempt to defend the authenticity of Adam and Eve; taking two mythical people that represented mankind in God's eyes and transforming them into historical figures. If I am off base, it's because I have made comparisons between scriptures and ancient events that should never have been matched up in the first place. Perhaps my exercise in correlating Genesis with science is indeed peppered with "mental acrobatics". But if conservative SCUMBAGs like me are wrong, then who is right? The Intelligent Design crowd? The atheists?

Was Darwin Wrong?

Darwin was wrong about a lot of things[1]. He was wrong about the source of variations in a species. He was wrong about the mechanism of inheritance of traits. He was wrong about the origin of a Scottish geologic feature known as the Parallel Roads of Glen Roy. But Darwin was not wrong about his central thesis; life—including human life—evolved on Earth via natural selection. When it comes to evolution, Darwin was right.

Likewise, no reasonable, objective person can seriously deny the scientific evidence supporting the antiquity of the expanding universe, the formation of the solar system over four billion years ago, the growth and meandering movements of the continents, and the beginnings of life nearly four billion years ago. These are scientific facts, laws, or theories. They are time-tested, thoroughly substantiated, well documented, peer-reviewed, myth-breaking, soul-shaking testaments of truth. When it comes to science, the scientists are generally right.

Is the Bible Wrong?

The Bible promotes several non-negotiable truths; God is the Creator, He did very well when He slapped this universe into existence, creation declares His glory, and we bear His image. Jesus taught that flesh is born of flesh—a natural process—while the Spirit gives birth to spirit—a supernatural event. When it comes to spiritual truth, the Bible is right.

Are the Creationists Right?

If I'm off base, then are the creationists right? No! Their "science" would still be as wrong as ever, regardless of the purity of their faith and the honorable intentions of their hearts. Even Intelligent Design would remain a compilation of beliefs rather than a scientific theory[2]. Perhaps it is time for the hard core Protestant creationists to take a page from the current Catholic playbook[3] by believing in the miraculous impartation of our spirit, acknowledging the lack of theological consensus among those interpreting Genesis One, and accepting the history and process of evolution as sound science.

Are the Atheistic Scientists Right?

What about those brilliant atheistic scientists who have gained fame and honor, yet deny the existence of a holy and loving God? They may be right about their science, but they're also knee-deep in spiritual error. *Mark 8:36 What good is it for a man to gain the whole world, yet forfeit his soul?*

What About Those Liberal SCUMBAGs?

The acceptance of sound science, the belief in these core values of God's role in creation, and the acknowledgement that the early chapters of Genesis may be rich in divinely inspired spiritual truth but devoid of actual history are the hallmarks of the liberal SCUMBAGs. If I'm wrong, odds are that these folks are right.

References
1. David Quammen, Was Darwin Wrong? No., National Geographic, Nov. 2004, 20
2. Appendix D
3. Michael Ruse; The Evolution-Creation Struggle, Harvard University Press, Cambridge, MA, 2005, 145

Chapter 21.
Teach Your Children Well

If you are a believer and a parent, I hope that you have the courage to instruct your children about their origins because they will be exposed to the creation vs. evolution turmoil whether you like it or not. There are plenty of creationist books and websites that can keep a parent comfortably insulated from the body of scientific literature that explores our origins. You can surround yourself with this blanket of security for the rest of your natural life, but your kids are likely to be a bit more inquisitive than you and even more likely to outlive you. They love to explore and inevitably find things that you tried so hard to hide from them, like your cash, lingerie, car keys and birth control devices. Like it or not, your children are going to find out about evolution. They are likely to hear radically opposed viewpoints of their origins at their school and their house of worship, and I would suggest that parents brush aside the extremists on both sides of this issue and encourage their children to foster their intellect and faith. You can comfortably acknowledge and accommodate the persuasive historical and mechanistic aspects of evolution[1] within a conservative biblical perspective while rejecting or refuting the offensive philosophical and religious opinions of atheistic scientists[2].

Let your children know that there is a loving Creator; He owns
a universe filled with natural wonders and magnificent processes
that they can and should explore. Tell them that the universe
emerged from a Big Bang 13.7 billion years ago and our planet
formed 4.6 billion years ago. Let them know that microscopic life
emerged on Earth about four billion years ago and evolved thereafter. Slightly more than a half billion years ago, the Cambrian
Explosion of life yielded a magnificent diversity of large and complex life forms that shaped the architecture of all subsequent life on
Earth. There is no reason to hide the fact that a number of human-
like and human species evolved during the past few million years,
or that *Homo sapiens* originated in Africa roughly 150,000 years
ago. Tell them that not long thereafter God interrupted human history, as He has a habit of doing in recent times, and supernaturally
sparked our spiritual origins. Let them know that He breathed an
intangible, eternal, spiritual nature into our species, thereby
upgrading us to man—made in His image.

Your kids will inevitably be confronted with the notion that
God could not use the process of evolution to form life in general and man in particular. After all, what kind of a God would let
His work be fashioned by random mutations, unexpected environmental changes, and catastrophic events? Your children may wonder what God's role was in creation if life blossomed naturally,
without supernatural guidance or direction, perhaps within a megaverse of opportunities. Tell them that the existence of the universe
and the evolution of life was His idea in the first place! It's His universe; He owns it, He is aware of every particle in it, and He played
by His own set of rules when He established it. No one, regardless
of their religious background, has the right to declare that God
couldn't have used an all-natural playbook in making everything.
The universe is an expression of His creative will. He is ingenious—far more intelligent than you or I or creationists or skeptics
can ever imagine, and He has every right to make stuff in the way
that He did.

You and your kids are invariably going to contemplate the reconciliation of our immortal spiritual nature with the evolution of
mortal humans. Although Darwin typically associated the origin of
God with the ascent of human imagination and wonder rather
than the actual existence of a Supreme Being, he had some sound

spiritual advice on occasion. In one case, he compared the mystery of when an individual became immortal with the equally mysterious ascent of our species to immortality, saying "He who believes in the advancement of man from some low organized form, will naturally ask how does this bear on the belief in the immortality of the soul...Few people feel any anxiety from the impossibility of determining at what precise period in the development of the individual, from the first trace of a minute germinal vesicle, man becomes an immortal being; and there is no greater cause for anxiety because the period cannot possibly be determined in the gradually ascending organic scale."[3] Darwin was right. Lighten up! No one worries that our children do not have immortal souls because we do not know the exact moment when they receive a spirit from God. (Please, no letters from those of you who do know the precise nano-second when God gives the forming child a spirit.) Likewise, our inability to nail down the timing of our species' initial spirituality does not mean that we don't have a spiritual nature.

The Bible and science are both right about the making of man. We can benefit from spiritual and scientific instruction[4,5]. The evolutionary tree of life relates humans to all organisms that have ever inhabited this planet, while Eden's Tree of Life illuminates man's eternal spiritual nature. Our advent required the evolution of our body and the divine gift of our spirit. Flesh gave birth to flesh, and Spirit gave birth to spirit.

References
1. Appendix Q
2. Appendix R
3. Charles Darwin, The Descent of Man, Great Minds Series, Prometheus Books, Amherst, NY, 1998, 636
4. Appendix S
5. Appendix T

Appendix A. Basic Bible Teachings on Creation

Here are some important biblical themes concerning creation. I think that most Christians who believe in the divine inspiration of the Bible would agree with all of these points.

God is the Creator.

Recognition that God made everything is a standard spiritual feature for men and women. *Romans 1:20 For since the creation of the world God's invisible qualities—his eternal power and divine nature—have been clearly seen, being understood from what has been made, so that men are without excuse.* A glance at God's creation tells our spirit that there is a Creator, and that He has a divine nature and eternal power. The Bible is also quite clear that each person of the Godhead was in on the act. God the Father made all things, *Genesis 1:1 In the beginning God created the heavens and the earth.* The Gospel of John, speaking of Jesus, states with equal clarity that the "Word" (Jesus) created all things, *John 1:1-3 In the beginning was the Word, and the Word was with God, and the Word was God. He was with God in the beginning. Through him all things were made; without him nothing was made that has been made.* The Holy Spirit was also creating, *Genesis 1:2 Now the earth was formless and*

171

empty, darkness was over the surface of the deep, and the Spirit of God was hovering over the waters.

God decided to establish the universe.

God didn't get up from a nap to find a universe growing under His couch. He decided to have the universe emerge, or established the conditions needed for our universe to emerge, or did something else that ultimately led to the universe unfolding before Him. *Psalm 33:6 By the word of the LORD were the heavens made, their starry host by the breath of his mouth. Revelation 4:11 "You are worthy, our Lord and God, to receive glory and honor and power, for you created all things, and by your will they were created and have their being."* In some unspecified, mysterious, untestable, unverifiable manner, the universe resulted from a spiritual decision made by the Creator. The precise linkage between God's creative will and nature's origins and workings will never be understood.

God created the universe for His pleasure.

God created the universe for His own good pleasure. *Revelation 4:11 "Thou art worthy, O Lord, to receive glory and honour and power: for thou hast created all things, and for thy pleasure they are and were created." KJV* Creation was His idea. He made it happen. He owns it. He rules over it. It gives Him great pleasure. We should give Him his due honor and praise for a job well done without regard for how or when He made it!

Creation reveals God's existence and character to all people.

God did such a good job making everything that His existence is obvious. Even a casual glance of the night sky tells us that there is a powerful and glorious God. *Psalm 19:1 The heavens declare the glory of God; the skies proclaim the work of his hands.* Our spirits can sense His eternal nature in the quiet splendor of a night sky. And no one gets off the hook; the recognition that there is a powerful and divine Creator is a standard feature of all mankind. *Romans 1:18-20 The wrath of God is being revealed from heaven against all the godlessness and wickedness of men who suppress the truth by their wickedness, since what may be known about God is plain to them, because God has made it plain to them. For since the creation of the world God's invisible qualities—his eternal power and divine nature—have been clearly seen, being understood from what has been made, so that men are without excuse.*

Those were the easy ones. I think the following themes are a bit more contentious.

The Bible does not contain detailed scientific information.

God's Word contains history, poetry, prophecy, prayers, laws, commandments, parables, instructions, encouragements, observations, personal letters, warnings, visions and spiritual truths. No one would doubt that. I also believe that the early chapters of Genesis contain a few fragmentary, divinely inspired glimpses of creation events. Even if I am right, scientific principles cannot be extracted from these scriptures; the information simply isn't there. The Bible never commands us to deduce the physics, geology or biology of creation events, though. The wonders of creation speak to our spirits that God is the creator, and the Holy Spirit doesn't need pseudo-scientific nonsense to persuade folks that He is real. In the following rebuke of Job, God openly mocks those who claim to have spiritual insight into how He created Earth! *Job 38:1-7 Then the LORD answered Job out of the storm. He said: "Who is this that darkens my counsel with words without knowledge? Brace yourself like a man; I will question you, and you shall answer me. Where were you when I laid the earth's foundation? Tell me, if you understand. Who marked off its dimensions? Surely you know! Who stretched a measuring line across it? On what were its footings set, or who laid its cornerstone-while the morning stars sang together and all the angels shouted for joy?* God's complete lesson on this point consumes Job 38 and 39, and both chapters are presented in their entirety in Appendix F.

The Bible contains divinely inspired allegories, symbols, metaphors and parables that teach valuable spiritual lessons, including truths concerning creation.

Many passages are plainly presented as allegorical, such as the parables of Christ, while other portions of scripture burst with symbolism, such as the Book of Revelation. Some of the events described in the early chapters of Genesis can be perplexing because they seem to contain historical and symbolic details, such as the Garden of Eden story. Nonetheless, the use of symbolism to explain truth does not mean that the Bible is a pack of lies. This has been a common accusation against Christianity for thousands of years, and even Peter addressed those who taught that Christ's life, death, resurrection and return were a collection of myths, *II Peter 1:16 We did not follow cleverly invented stories when we told you about the power and coming of our Lord Jesus Christ, but we were eyewitnesses of his majesty.*

Holy Spirit-filled Christians, not scientists, are commissioned by Christ Himself to persuade unbelievers that God exists.

Many Christians whine about scientists and school teachers refusing to help the church persuade folks that God exists. Get over it. It is the responsibility of the Holy Spirit and the church, not bewildered biologists and biology teachers, to convince us of God's presence. Immediately before ascending into heaven, the risen Christ said, *Acts 1:8 But you will receive power when the Holy Spirit comes on you; and you will be my witnesses in Jerusalem, and in all Judea and Samaria, and to the ends of the earth.* He spoke those words to his disciples, not the American Association for the Advancement of Science. Frankly, scientists are the last people I want convincing my kids that God exists! Their god would be a calculator-toting, pocket-protected, galactic geek made in their own image that could care less about the pathetic lives of humans!

Appendix B. How Many Hours are in a Day?

Yes, a "day" usually refers to a spin of the globe in the Bible. I find no fault with those who, using the scriptures alone, conclude that the days of creation were simply that; days! Some may hold that they are literal days that marked the actual passage of time required for God to make stuff, while others (including myself) think that days were a poetic device used to frame the creation story. But there are some interesting reasons for believing that a day in the Bible may refer to a much longer period of time[13]. Let's take a look at them.

Jesus violated the 24-hours-per-day rule! *Luke 13:31-33 At that time some Pharisees came to Jesus and said to him, "Leave this place and go somewhere else. Herod wants to kill you." He replied, "Go tell that fox, 'I will drive out demons and heal people today and tomorrow, and on the third day I will reach my goal.' In any case, I must keep going today and tomorrow and the next day—for surely no prophet can die outside Jerusalem!* Jesus intended to preach to the lost, heal the sick and exorcise the demon-possessed before dying on the cross for our sins. But this conversation with the Pharisees took place many months before His death. Jesus was using "today", "tomorrow" and "the next day" to speak of the time when He was speaking, the following months, and His crucifixion, respectively.

Decades after His resurrection, Jesus did it again in His message to a first-century church. *Revelation 2:8-11 "To the angel of the church in Smyrna write: These are the words of him who is the First and the Last, who died and came to life again. I know your afflictions and your poverty—yet you are rich! I know the slander of those who say they are Jews and are not, but are a synagogue of Satan. Do not be afraid of what you are about to suffer. I tell you, the devil will put some of you in prison to test you, and you will suffer persecution for ten days. Be faithful, even to the point of death, and I will give you the crown of life. He who has an ear, let him hear what the Spirit says to the churches. He who overcomes will not be hurt at all by the second death.* Nobody that I know insists that these ten days constituted a 240-hour period. Many believe that they symbolize a longer period of time and may have been a reference to the ten Roman emperors that persecuted the early church. These ten days could have lasted many decades.

Moses had something to say about the length of a day. *Psalm 90:4 For a thousand years in your sight are like a day that has just gone by, or like a watch in the night.*

David also had trouble limiting a day to 24 hours. *Psalm 86:6 Hear my prayer, O LORD; listen to my cry for mercy. In the day of my trouble I will call to you, for you will answer me.* Do you really think that David was in trouble for only 24 hours? My own teenagers get into trouble for no less than 72 hours per incident!

Solomon's forty-year reign was also described as a day. *II Chronicles 9:20 All King Solomon's goblets were gold, and all the household articles in the Palace of the Forest of Lebanon were pure gold. Nothing was made of silver, because silver was considered of little value in Solomon's day.*

Further, the duration of the seventh day of the creation week is unlike the first six. *Genesis 2:2-3 By the seventh day God had finished the work he had been doing; so on the seventh day he rested from all his work. And God blessed the seventh day and made it holy, because on it he rested from all the work of creating that he had done.* Unlike the first six days, the seventh was not marked by morning and evening. In fact, there is no mention of when or if the seventh day ended. It may be continuing, even until today, in clear violation of the 24-hour-per-day rule!

Even the aggregate of the six days appears to be called a day. In the second chapter of Genesis, we find *Genesis 2:4 This is the history of the heavens and the earth when they were created, in the day that the Lord God created the earth and the heavens. (New King James Version)*

These examples do not sway those who believe the first six days of Genesis One were good old-fashioned days. Why? The Hebrew word used for day, *yom*, typically denotes just that, a day! Each day of the creation week was also marked by morning and evening; it is really hard to distinguish months, years, eras, and epochs by morning and evening! And despite arguments to the contrary offered up by old-Earth Intelligent Design creationists like Hugh Ross[4], there were indeed Hebrew words for long periods of time available to the author of Genesis. Mark Perakh, a brilliant physicist who is fluent in Hebrew and several other languages, points out that there were other words available to the author of Genesis to describe long periods of time[5]. The most common Hebrew word for "epoch" is *tkufa*, but the words *sfira* and *idan* (of Aramaic origin but also used in biblical Hebrew) were also available[6].

It seems to be likely that in Genesis One, a day is simply a day. I think that the day is a literary tool, however, rather than a literal 24-hour time period associated with creation events.

References
1. Hugh Ross; The Fingerprint of God; 1989; Whitaker House; New Kensington, PA; 145–155
2. Hugh Ross; A Matter of Days—Resolving a Creation Controversy, NavPress, Colorado Springs, CO, 2004
3. Hugh Ross; Creation and Time—A Biblical and Scientific Perspective on the Creation-Date Controversy; NavPress Publishing Group, Colorado Springs, CO, 1994, 143–147
4. Hugh Ross; The Genesis Question—Scientific Advances and the Accuracy of Genesis; Navpress 1998, Colorado Springs, CO, 65
5. Mark Perakh; Unintelligent Design, Prometheus Books, Amherst New York, 2004, 173–191
6. Mark Perakh; Unintelligent Design, Prometheus Books, Amherst New York, 2004, 183

Appendix C.
Flood Insurance

Noah's Flood

Young Earth Creationists use Noah's Flood to account for mountain ranges, the fossil record, sedimentary rock layers, the Grand Canyon, movement of the continents, a transformation of the Earth's water cycle, and the triumph of the '69 Mets. The most thorough refutations of Flood Geology are actually produced by Old Earth Intelligent Design creationists who know that the fossil record is ancient and are annoyed by the bad press associated with the pseudo-science of Young Earth Flood Geology[1-3]. Let's take a quick look at the story of Noah and just a few of the biblical and scientific problems associated with a recent, worldwide flood.

Genesis 6:1-22 When men began to increase in number on the earth and daughters were born to them, the sons of God saw that the daughters of men were beautiful, and they married any of them they chose. Then the LORD said, "My Spirit will not contend with man forever, for he is mortal; his days will be a hundred and twenty years." The Nephilim were on the earth in those days—and also afterward—when the sons of God went to the daughters of men and had children by them. They were the heroes of old, men of renown. The LORD saw how great man's wickedness on the earth had become, and that every inclination of the thoughts of his heart was only evil all the time. The LORD was grieved that he had made man on the earth, and his heart was filled with pain. So the LORD said, "I will wipe mankind, whom I have created, from the face of the earth—men and animals, and creatures that move along the ground, and birds of the air—for I am grieved that I have made them." But Noah found favor in the eyes of the LORD. This is the account of Noah. Noah was a righteous man, blameless among the people of his time, and he walked with God. Noah had three sons: Shem, Ham and Japheth. Now the earth was corrupt in God's sight and was full of violence. God saw how corrupt the earth had become, for all the people on earth had corrupted their ways. So God said to Noah, "I am going to put an end to all people, for the earth is filled with violence because of them. I am surely going to destroy both them and the earth. So make yourself an ark of cypress wood; make rooms in it and coat it with pitch inside and out. This is how you are to build it: The ark is to be 450 feet long, 75 feet wide and 45 feet high. Make a roof for it and finish the ark to within 18 inches of the top. Put a door in the side of the ark and make lower, middle and upper decks. I am going to bring flood-waters on the earth to destroy all life under the heavens, every creature that has the breath of life in it. Everything on earth will perish. But I will establish my covenant with you, and you will enter the ark—you and your sons and your wife and your sons' wives with you. You are to bring into the ark two of all living creatures, male and female, to keep them alive with you. Two of every kind of bird, of every kind of animal and of every kind of creature that moves along the ground will come to you to be kept alive. You are to take every kind of food that is to be eaten and store it away as food for you and for them." Noah did everything just as God commanded him.

Genesis 7:1-24 The LORD then said to Noah, "Go into the ark, you and your whole family, because I have found you righteous in this generation. Take with you seven of every kind of clean animal, a male and its mate, and two of every kind of unclean animal, a male and its mate, and also seven of every kind of bird, male and female, to keep their various kinds alive throughout the earth. Seven days from now I will send rain on the earth for forty days and forty nights, and I will wipe from the face of the earth every living creature I have made." And Noah did all that the LORD commanded him. Noah was six hundred years old when the flood-waters came on the earth. And Noah and his sons and his wife and his *sons' wives entered the ark to escape the waters of the flood. Pairs of clean and unclean animals, of birds and of all creatures that move along the ground, male and female, came to Noah and entered the ark, as God had commanded Noah. And after the seven days the floodwaters came on the earth. In the six hundredth year of Noah's life, on the seventeenth day of the second month—on that day all the springs of the great deep burst forth, and the floodgates of the heavens were opened. And rain fell on the earth forty days and forty nights. On that very day Noah and his sons, Shem, Ham and Japheth, together with his wife and the wives of his three sons, entered the ark. They had with them every wild animal according to its kind, all livestock according to their kinds, every creature that moves along the ground according to its kind and every bird according to its kind, everything with wings. Pairs of all creatures that have the breath of life in them came to Noah and entered the ark. The animals going in were male and female of every living thing, as God had commanded Noah. Then the LORD shut him in. For forty days the flood kept coming on the earth, and as the waters increased they lifted the ark high above the earth. The waters rose and increased greatly on the earth, and the ark floated on the surface of the water. They rose greatly on the earth, and all the high mountains under the entire heavens were covered. The waters rose and covered the mountains to a depth of more than twenty feet. Every living thing that moved on the earth perished—birds, livestock, wild animals, all the creatures that swarm over the Earth, and all mankind. Everything on dry land that had the breath of life in its nostrils died. Every living thing on the face of the earth was wiped out; men and animals and the creatures that move along the ground and the birds of the air were wiped from the earth. Only Noah was left, and those with him in the ark. The waters flooded the earth for a hundred and fifty days.*

Genesis 8:1-22 But God remembered Noah and all the wild animals and the livestock that were with him in the ark, and he sent a wind over the earth, and the waters receded. Now the springs of the deep and the floodgates of the heavens had been closed, and the rain had stopped falling from the sky. The water receded steadily from the earth. At the end of the hundred and fifty days the water had gone down, and on the seventeenth day of the seventh month the ark came to rest on the mountains of Ararat. The waters continued to recede until the tenth month, and on the first day of the tenth month the tops of the mountains became visible. After forty days Noah opened the window he had made in the ark and sent out a raven, and it kept flying back and forth until the water had dried up from the earth. Then he sent out a dove to see if the water had receded from the surface of the ground. But the dove could find no place to set its feet because there was water over all the surface of the earth; so it returned to Noah in the ark. He reached out his hand and took the dove and brought it back to himself in the ark. He waited seven more days and again sent out the dove from the ark. When the dove returned to him in the evening, there in its beak was a freshly plucked olive leaf! Then Noah knew that the water had receded from the earth. He waited seven more days and sent the dove out again, but this time it did not return to him. By the first day of the first month of Noah's six hundred and first year, the water had dried up from the earth. Noah then removed the covering from the ark and saw that the surface of the ground was dry. By the twenty-seventh day of the second month the earth was completely dry. Then God said to Noah, "Come out of the ark, you and your wife and your sons and their wives. Bring out every kind of living creature that is with you—the birds, the animals, and all the creatures that move along the ground—so they can multiply on the earth and be fruitful and increase in number upon it." So Noah came out, together with his sons and his wife and his sons' wives. All the animals and all the creatures that move along the ground and all the birds—everything that moves on the earth—came out of the ark, one kind after another. Then Noah built an altar to the LORD and, taking some of all the clean animals and clean birds, he sacrificed burnt offerings on it. The LORD smelled the pleasing aroma and said in his heart: "Never again will I curse the ground because of man, even though every inclination of his heart is evil from childhood. And never again will I destroy all living creatures, as I have done. As long as the earth endures, seedtime and harvest, cold and heat, summer and winter, day and night will never cease."

Genesis 9:1-19 Then God blessed Noah and his sons, saying to them, "Be fruitful and increase in number and fill the earth. The fear and dread of you will fall upon all the beasts of the earth and all the birds of the air, upon every creature that moves along the ground, and upon all the fish of the sea; they are given into your hands. Everything that lives and moves will be food for you. Just as I gave you the green plants, I now give you everything. But you must not eat meat that has its lifeblood still in it. And for your lifeblood I will surely demand an accounting. I will demand an accounting from every animal. And from each man, too, I will demand an accounting for the life of his fellow man. Whoever sheds the blood of man, by man shall his blood be shed; for in the image of God has God made man. As for you, be fruitful and increase in number; multiply on the earth and increase upon it." Then God said to Noah and to his sons with him: "I now establish my covenant with you and with your descendants after you and with every living creature that was with you—the birds, the livestock and all the wild animals, all those that came out of the ark with you—every living creature on earth. I establish my covenant with you: Never again will all life be cut off by the waters of a flood; never again will there be a flood to destroy the earth." And God said, "This is the sign of the covenant I am making between me and you and every living creature with you, a covenant for all generations to come: I have set my rainbow in the clouds, and it will be the sign of the covenant between me and the earth. Whenever I bring clouds over the earth and the rainbow appears in the clouds, I will remember my covenant between me and you and all living creatures of every kind. Never again will the waters become a flood to destroy all life. Whenever the rainbow appears in the clouds, I will see it and remember the everlasting covenant between God and all living creatures of every kind on the earth." So God said to Noah, "This is the sign of the covenant I have established between me and all life on the earth." The sons of Noah who came out of the ark were Shem, Ham and Japheth. (Ham was the father of Canaan.) These were the three sons of Noah, and from them came the people who were scattered over the earth.

Yes, the Bible teaches that there was a flood. Yes, one can read these chapters and surmise that the flood may have been global. Yes, that may be a reasonable conclusion based on scriptures alone. But no, is it not the only conclusion that these scriptures can support. There are a few biblical clues that the flood was regional, rather than global, in extent. Keep in mind that Genesis was delivered to a small group of Israelites who were clueless about the size of this planet. Straight from the lips of God comes this question to Job, *Job 38:18 Have you comprehended the vast expanses of the earth? Tell me, if you know all this.* Therefore it is risky business to assume that the words commonly translated as "earth" in the Bible have worldwide implications. Although it may have consumed the complete "world" that the author of Genesis was familiar with, the flood was not necessarily a planet-bathing event. The terms commonly translated as "earth" in the flood account were also used in reference to a region (see the bold words in the following passages).

Consider Cain's reaction to his sentence of exile after God convicted him for the murder of his brother. *Genesis 4:13, 14 Cain said to the LORD, "My punishment is more than I can bear. Today you are driving me from the land, and I will be hidden from your presence; I will be a restless wanderer on the earth, and whoever finds me will kill me."* Had he been driven from the planet, Cain would have been the first astronaut. The story of Joseph and the famine also limits the extent of the "earth", which is termed "country", "world" and "region" in the following text. *Genesis 41:56,57 When the famine had spread over the whole **country**, Joseph opened the storehouses and sold grain to the Egyptians, for the famine was severe throughout Egypt. And all the countries came to Egypt to buy grain from Joseph, because the famine was severe in all the **world**...Genesis 47:11-13 So Joseph settled his father and his brothers in Egypt and gave them property in the best part of the land, the district of Rameses, as Pharaoh directed. Joseph also provided his father and his brothers and all his father's household with food, according to the number of their children. There was no food, however, in the whole **region** because the famine was severe; both Egypt and Canaan wasted away because of the famine.* Do you really think that there is a strong biblical basis for believing that this famine extended to present-day Kansas?

The same principle may apply to the flood account. For example, the depth of the floodwaters does not necessarily signify a global flood. *Genesis 7:18-20 The waters rose and increased greatly on the earth, and the ark floated on the surface of the water. They rose greatly on the earth, and all the high mountains under the entire heavens were covered. The waters rose and covered the mountains to a depth of more than twenty feet.* The popular creationist take on these verses envisions floodwaters rising 20 feet above the highest mountain peak on the planet. But the word translated "mountains" can also be rendered as "hills" or "mounds", and some contend that the depth of the waters may be in reference to twenty feet up the sides of the high mountains relative to their base. Therefore a local flood could have easily satisfied these criteria. The extent of the flooding is also described as the waters receded. *Genesis 8:3-5 The water receded steadily from the earth. At the end of the hundred and fifty days the water had gone down, and on the seventeenth day of the seventh month the ark came to rest on the mountains of Ararat. The waters continued to recede until the tenth month, and on the first day of the tenth month the tops of the mountains became visible.* The ark came to rest on "the mountains of Ararat". There are two mountains in Turkey associated with the mountains of Ararat, and their summits are 5137 meters and 3896 meters above sea level. But the Ararat of today may not correspond exactly to the Ararat of Moses' day. Ararat may have corresponded to a large region that encompassed Armenia, Turkey and Iran. So where was Noah, exactly, at this point in time? What were the elevations of the particular hills or mountains in that specific area? Did the ark come to rest on the peak of the mountain, or just somewhere on or near the mountain? Neither the description of the emerging or receding flood can provide any information concerning the exact extent of the flood or the specific resting place of the ark.

The removal of the floodwaters from the region also provides another clue that the flood was regional rather than global. *Genesis 8:1 But God remembered Noah and all the wild animals and the livestock that were with him in the ark, and he sent a wind over the earth, and the waters receded.* Wind cannot sweep global floodwaters into outer space, but a strong wind can help clear regional floodwaters from a flat region toward an ocean or sea.

What about the survivors who were not on the ark? Even if all of the people in the region died during this catastrophe, there would have been plenty of other survivors in areas of the world far removed from the devastation. There is a good chance that the Bible even names a group of them! *Genesis 6: 4 The Nephilim were on the earth in those days—and also afterward—when the sons of God went to the daughters of men and had children by them. They were the heroes of old, men of renown.* "Those days" means before the flood, and "afterward" means after the flood, and the Nephilim were around before and after the flood. These were big, bad dudes, like Goliath. There are many theological ideas of how they came to be and who their parents were and what their spiritual standing was, which indicates that the Bible simply doesn't give enough information about them to reach any definitive conclusions. But it is a certainty that they lived before the flood and after the flood, and a pair of them did not crawl onto the ark. The simplest explanation is that they survived the flood because they did not live near Noah. Some think that they were not considered "man" because they had not descended from Adam and did not have a spiritual nature.

Others believe that all humans outside of the ark, including the Nephilim, drowned and propose that at least one of Noah's daughters-in-law was the carrier of a gene capable of turning pleasant normal-sized descendants of Noah into large nasty ogres. Still others think that the Nephilim were the biological product of flood-resistant horny demons impregnating women.

There are also several startling inconsistencies concerning the animals that were eradicated by the alleged worldwide flood. Animals that roamed the ground and skies died, but there is no indication in the Bible that animals living in the waters died. Why, then, is the fossil record dominated by plants and animals that lived in the sea?

What of the relationship between the animals on the ark and the animals that are alive today? Creationists insist that the ark passengers were representative of the animals that died in the flood and were buried in the fossil record, but the fossil record is filled almost exclusively with extinct species. Therefore the wildlife exiting the ark would have had the same appearance as these extinct species captured in the fossil record. But the disembarking animals were also the progenitors of the animals living today because God had stopped making new species long before the flood! Hmmm. That means that Noah's animals must have changed in morphology from the appearance of extinct species into contemporary beasts within a few thousand years! Wait a minute; what's that word for the transformation of one species into another species? Evolution! Ironically, Flood Geology requires hyper-accelerated evolution that occurred within a few thousand years, rather than hundreds of millions, to explain why the forms of life found in the fossil record differ from contemporary life!

There are also problems with the deposition of the flood sediments. How could tens of thousands of strata be uniformly deposited by the receding flood in less than a year? The settling particles would have changed in composition every few minutes as the waters receded!

Why are fossils found in these well-defined layers, with the smallest ones at the bottom rather than the large animals that would have drowned and sank like rocks? Young Earth theologians typically suggest that a synchronized drowning performance worthy of a gold medal was responsible for the well-ordered fossil record.

How can coral reefs, which take years to grow on sedimentary rock, be found sandwiched in the middle of sediment layers deposited by the flood in less than a year?

How can large boulders be found above layers of fine-grained sedimentary rock? The large boulders would have settled most quickly ended up at the bottom of the geologic column.

How could fossils of cracked, parched mud be found if the fossils were all deposited in a deluge of water? How could the ripple marks of creeks and rivers be captured in rocks if a single flood rapidly deposited the fossils?

Finally, where's the boat? Most creationists believe that the ark is still in the vicinity of Mt. Ararat because the Bible says that it came to rest "on the mountains of Ararat". Numerous Ararat adventures abound, including "I saw Noah's ark!" or "I was in Noah's ark!" or "Bandits stole my photos of Noah's ark" or "Gramps took me to Noah's ark" or "Good guys led me to Noah's Ark" or "Bad guys chased me from Noah's Ark" or "I lost my photos of Noah's Ark". Why is it that with the advent of cameras, telescopes, spy satellites, global positioning systems, helicopters, airplanes, topographical maps, mountain climbing gear, and long underwear no one can seem to find the remains of the 450-foot long ark? The common excuses are snow, bandits and Turkish bureaucracy. Creationists have an opportunity to conduct an Indiana Jones adventure that would stun the world, silence their critics and validate Flood Geology. Why don't they simply find the boat? I'm not sure, but I have a feeling they never will because Noah's ark came to rest on a hill in the Middle East and quickly became the first self-serve 84 Lumber franchise. It was likely dismembered by Noah's descendants and used to build fires, homes, porches and pool decks.

Evidence of a Regional Flood?

Noah's flood could not have been planetary in extent, but is there even any evidence of a regional flood? A three-meter thick sediment layer that was deposited 5000 years ago in the vicinity of Ur (Abraham's hometown) indicates that this region of Mesopotamia was flooded[4,5]. Another possibility is associated with a recent find of Robert Ballard, who previously located the wreckage of the Titanic. In 1997, Ballard and his colleagues found submerged evidence of an ancient shoreline 500 feet below the surface of the Black Sea and miles offshore from its current coastline. Apparently, this freshwater lake and surrounding area were suddenly deluged by saltwater as the Ice Age ended 7600 years ago when the rising waters of the Mediterranean surged over the Bosporus (now a strait 20 miles long and a half mile wide that joins these two bodies of water). Although some believe that this overflow was very gradual, transpiring over thousands of years, others assert that ten cubic miles of saltwater surged over each day, a rate that is 200 times the rate of the Niagara Falls spillage, for nearly a year. Although Ballard wisely withheld judgment on the theological implications of his find, others quickly associated it with Noah's flood. The timing was right, the mountains of Ararat were nearby, and the combined rainwater and overflow of the Mediterranean may satisfy the biblical description of the event. Although there certainly is no solid geological evidence that this event (or any other) correlates with Noah's flood, a fascinating discussion of the possibility is provided by William Ryan and Walter Pitman[6].

References
1. Hugh Ross; The Genesis Question—Scientific Advances and the Accuracy of Genesis; Navpress 1998, Colorado Springs, CO
2. Alan Hayward; Creation and Evolution; Bethany House Publishers; 1995; 69–81
3. Hugh Ross; A Matter of Days—Resolving a Creation Controversy, NavPress, Colorado Springs, CO, 2004
4. G.L. Schroeder; The Science of God; Simon and Schuster; New York, NY; 1997; 205–206
5. M. Dewsnap; Uncovering the Deluge, Biblical Archeological Review 22(4):56, July/August 1996
6. William Ryan, Walter Pitman; Noah's Flood—The New Scientific Discoveries about the Event that Changed History, A Touchstone Book, Simon & Schuster, First Touchstone Edition, 2000, New York

Appendix D. Why Intelligent Design Sounds Like a Good (But Really is a Bad) Idea

For those of you who feel compelled to build your faith on the transient bewilderment of physicists to solve problems that you can barely pronounce let alone comprehend, Intelligent Design is designed especially for you! It has some mind-boggling examples of apparently divine fine-tuning to build its case upon. Keep in mind that these are not secrets recently uncovered by Intelligent Design advocates; scientists are the ones who identify and quantify these amazing parameters. Here is a *partial* list of what just happens to be right for life to emerge on Earth.

Godly Odds

1. The cosmological constant, an incredibly tiny, positive number that influences the expansion of the universe. (Apparently fine-tuned to a factor of 1 in 10^{120})

2. The force of gravity between electrons and the atomic nucleus is 10^{31} times weaker than the electrical attraction between them.

3. The early rate of expansion of the early universe.

4. The minute initial excess of protons over anti-protons in the young universe.

5. The initial texture of the young universe.

6. Three dimensions of space, rather than two or four or eleven.

7. The ability of stars to form carbon from hydrogen and helium.

8. The ability of neutrinos to push atoms such as carbon out of stars into space during a supernova, where they could later become an ingredient for life on a planet.

9. The existence of the basic building blocks of everything, electrons, quarks, and photons, each having the "just right" properties to build a universe where chemicals could form.

10. The ratio of the electron mass to the proton mass.

11. The magnitudes of strengths of the four basic forces of nature.

12. The neutron-proton mass difference.

13. The size of the moon.

14. The tilt of the Earth.

15. The distance of Earth from our sun.

16. The size of the Earth.

17. The rate of tectonic activity in Earth's crust.

18. The mass of the sun.

19. The type of galaxy in which we reside.

20. Our position in the galaxy.

21. Our position in the solar system with respect to other planets.

22. The metal-rich composition of Earth.

What could be wrong with attributing all of this to God's supernatural intervention and calling it science? Plenty!

Undefined Design

The most obvious problem with Intelligent Design is that it is a very fuzzy concept. What *is* Intelligent Design anyway? I have dozens of books on the topic and I still do not know what the Intelligent Design way of making something is! The mechanism of evolution is easy to identify; mutation, variation, natural selection. The mechanism of washing your hair is obvious; lather, rinse, repeat. But what are the steps of Intelligent Design; Abra, ca, dabra? Creationists never define it because none of them know what it is! For example, how did worms come to be? How long does it take God to make a worm? What end did He start at, or did He begin at the middle and work out? Some Intelligent Design advocates believe that the Garden of Eden is a literal report on the Intelligent Design of humans. If so, how much dirt was needed to form Adam? Did God add water? Did He use topsoil or clay? Did he start at the head and work down? (The answer is "Yes" according to a little evangelism tract that I recently found; it showed Adam during his creation as no more than a head rising out of a pool of liquid neck!) How long did it take the dirt to turn into flesh and blood? Eve's case is just as puzzling. What portion of Adam's side was removed? How long was he unconscious while she was being made? How was Adam's DNA altered to make Eve? How long did Eve's creation take? Intelligent Design advocates have no answers. If they would concede at this point that it was a religious belief, then I would be happy. But can you call this completely undefined mechanism a contribution to science? No way!

Some Intelligent Design advocates are more sophisticated than those who attribute all of life's workings to miracles. Many do not have a problem with evolution in general or even the evolution of man in particular, but contend that many biological processes, such as blood clotting, were intelligently designed. But how did God do this? When did He intervene? How long did it take to happen? Did God tweak an inefficient clotting process, or did He instantly assemble the entire biochemical cycle? Intelligent Design proponents cannot explain, demonstrate or verify a single step of the Intelligent Design process because they themselves have no idea what that process actually is.

Untestable Design

Another reason that Intelligent Design garners so little respect and so much contempt from scientists is that it is not a testable idea. It cannot be confirmed! God simply won't cooperate with requests from skeptics or saints to miraculously create stuff anymore. Science, however, provides a way of understanding life based on hypotheses that can be tested in the lab or in the wild. Evolution is science because it proposes that the flow of life on Earth has been influenced by a never-ending cycle of mutations, variations and natural selection; an idea that has been rigorously tested, scrutinized, refined, and observed in the lab and in the wild. The Big Bang is a sound scientific idea because there is detectable background radiation in the cosmos bearing witness to this ancient event. Intelligent Design offers no alternative mechanism that can be rigorously evaluated or tested, even in part. It relies on the vague supernatural events in the past coupled with a theology that conveniently prohibits miraculous contemporary creative acts in the present. Intelligent Design cannot be independently assessed in the lab or in the wild. It is simply a faith-based assault on the gaps in knowledge of contemporary science.

Unfalsifiable Design

If you propose an explanation for the origin of life or humans or bunnies, there should be a way to prove that your idea is wrong, if it is indeed incorrect. If there is absolutely no hope that such a test could be ever constructed, even in one's imagination, even a thousand years in the future when extraordinarily powerful analytical tools may be available, even if only indirect evidence could be extracted, then it is probably is not a valid scientific hypothesis. The problem with Intelligent Design is that you just cannot, and never will be able to, *scientifically* prove that there is not an elusive Intelligent Designer! After all, what can you ever devise to prove that an invisible, intangible, undetectable, Intelligent Designer who smoothly blends miracles with natural phenomena does not exist, especially when you claim that He retired from the miraculous creation business about 6000 years ago?

Who's-Kidding-Who Design

In an attempt to bolster their scientific credentials, Intelligent Design advocates do not typically attribute the remarkably complex and fine-tuned characteristics of the universe to the God of the Bible. Rather, they defer to an unspecified intelligence. Gimme a break! That's like my kids saying that they aren't sure that Bob Enick is footing their college bills, but they can affirm that an unspecified bald white male will be forking over the cash. Just for fun, though, let's pretend that we agree with the notion that God isn't the Intelligent Designer. Who else could it be? He/she/it would have to be 13.7 billion years old, powerful enough to generate an entire universe, capable of breathing life into inanimate matter, and willing to monitor the activities of every subatomic particle throughout all time. Who is that smart, old and powerful? Hillary Clinton? Garth Brooks? Arnold Schwarzenegger? Christian ID proponents are talking about God, Jesus and the Holy Spirit and everyone knows it. They would actually garner more respect if they just came out and said it. Even the YECs have the guts to plainly say what they believe; the Father, Son and Holy Ghost created everything! If we play along with this charade, however, the ID crowd would have to concede that other folks calling upon a higher intelligence would have an equal claim to being right. This includes ID adherents of the Jewish faith and the Moslem faith, all of whom would insist that Jesus Christ is neither the Son of God nor the Creator. It also gives credence to secular ID proponents who favor the influence of extraterrestrials, black monoliths, and little green goons from the core of the moon.

Unbiblical Design

Why do so many Christians think that Intelligent Design is biblical? Where does the Bible say that God can only make complex stuff via supernatural acts? What is the scriptural reference that defines the level of complexity that requires miraculous intervention? How long do the odds have to be to imply God's miracle-working power was involved...1 in 100? 1 in 34,567?...1 in a million? Where does the Bible declare that natural phenomena are not glorious if they are well understood? Where in the Bible are the laws of nature classified as ungodly? Where is the prohibition on God making a universe filled with random events? There are multitudes of verses in the Bible that declare God's glory in creation and there are scores of miracles in the Bible, but there is not a single scripture that asks believers to associate puzzling parts of a paramecium or a planet with supernatural slight of hand rather than the mysterious yet natural laws of God's universe. There is no biblical command to defend the faith by attempting to disprove scientists. Intelligent Design hardly deserves a place alongside the strong foundations of our faith, including the deity of Christ, the crucifixion, the resurrection, salvation, eternal life, and the Word of God. The Bible does not tell us *how* God created the universe or anything in it. Consider the Psalm's proclamation of God's glory found in the nighttime sky. *Psalm 19:1-6 The heavens declare the glory of God; the skies proclaim the work of his hands. Day after day they pour forth speech; night after night they display knowledge. There is no speech or language where their voice is not heard. Their voice goes out into all the earth, their words to the ends of the world. In the heavens he has pitched a tent for the sun, which is like a bridegroom coming forth from his pavilion, like a champion rejoicing to run his course. It rises at one end of the heavens and makes its circuit to the other; nothing is hidden from its heat.* Listen to what the Lord said to the prophet Isaiah concerning the formation of the human body. *Isaiah 44:24 "This is what the LORD says- your Redeemer, who formed you in the womb: I am the LORD, who has made all things, who alone stretched out the heavens, who spread out the earth by myself,* God confirms that He is the Creator and that His works are glorious, but He makes no mention of the processes occurring within the womb or in the depths of space. Intelligent Design sounds really religious but it has no biblical merit.

Dumb Design

Why do so many Christians think that Intelligent Design enhances God's image? In some respects, Intelligent Design actually makes God look like a stupid designer or a practical joker. If an almighty, all-knowing God supernaturally designed life, why didn't He do a better job with humans? Why would He create eyes with blind spots? Why are there so many chiropractors? Why can't I smell dog poop before I step in it? Why can I wiggle my five fingers individually but my four little toes move in unison? Why does everything look like a fuzzball when I take off my glasses? Why do I crumple in pain when I get hit between the legs with a wiffle ball? If God formed man in His image from a pile of dirt, why did He fashion us to look like balding apes? Why do I have an extra kidney but not an extra heart? What's the point of little toes and the appendix? Why do salamanders grow new limbs when theirs get ripped off, but I don't sprout a new arm if mine gets chopped off? Honestly, is "Intelligent Design" the first concept that comes to mind when you consider PMS, menopause, zits, morning breath, cramps, gas, ear hair, water retention, moles, childbirth, underarm odor, or old age? Can you name a single teenager that you would characterize as Intelligently Designed? And what about all those annoying differences between men and women? (Yes dear, it's the men who are annoying.) Why aren't our bodies better suited for old age, with options such as better bladders and bigger bones[1]? And why is there so much junk in human DNA with no apparent purpose, such as the million copies of a 280 base repeat sequence that constitutes 10% of your DNA[2]? What of those useless human body parts we all have that appear to point back to a beastly ancestry[3,4], such as tailbones, wisdom teeth, a paltry spattering of body hair. What about those weird little features that only a small percentage of modern humans have[5], such as an extra pair of ribs in the lower neck, or that tiny little point of skin on the inner rim of the ear? And what can we say about those parts that a small part of us are missing, such as the wimpy palmaris muscle in our arms and plantaris muscle in our legs that are essentially useless? Goose bumps are useful for animals because they puff up animal fur, enhancing its insulation and making the critter appear more intimidating. Human goose bumps, however, make us look cold and gimpy. If we are so special in our design, then why do human embryos have the same attributes as embryonic fish, including pharyngeal pouches, a tail and six aortic arches? Why would God make human embryos gain, and then shed, a primate-like coat of hair during the first trimester[6]? Why do we have little chunks of RNA dwelling within the nuclei of our cells doing useless tasks?[7]

Animals have their own odd design features that take the wind out of the sails of Intelligent Design. The panda, for example, uses its opposable thumb in conjunction with its other fingers to remove leaves from bamboo shoots before devouring them. Stephen Jay

Gould pointed out the panda's thumb is nothing more than an awkward, oversized wrist bone that enables the bear to efficiently prepare its dinner[8]. But if God designed panda paws from scratch, why didn't He just give them a real thumb? The panda is not unique; every organism has easily identifiable flaws, weaknesses, imperfections, such as the wings of the flightless penguin or the fingernails of the manatee (the sea cow). These odd features are not the hallmarks of Intelligent Design, rather they serve as reminders of each species' remarkable evolutionary past that worked with what it has at its disposal to yield an acceptable improvement rather than exquisite perfection.

Obsolete Design

The Intelligent Designer's incompetence also extends backwards in time because the fossil record is filled with clunkers that could not survive over the long haul. Why did God not just make these plants and animals more resilient in the first place? Why did He have to create so many species and variations within species over millions of years? Did it really take about twenty versions of human-looking animals spread out over millions of years to get the hang of making a *Homo sapien*? "Haphazard Trial-and-Error" would appear to be a better descriptor of His methods than "Intelligent Design". Creationists counter that God had to make new species to account for environmental changes and disasters. But if God is so smart that he supernaturally designed the Earth to be perfectly suited for life, then why didn't He supernaturally prevent those environmental disturbances and associated extinctions from happening in the first place?

WAP, SAP, NAP or SNAP Design

Let's return to the most persuasive Intelligent Design strategy for proving that God exists; a list of the attributes of the universe, solar system, moon, and Earth that make it capable of sustaining intelligent life like us human dudes! Keep in mind that if conditions weren't right for life, then we wouldn't even be here. The real question is whether these conditions were the result of natural phenomena or supernatural intervention. These arguments are known as anthropic principles, and variants include the weak anthropic principle (WAP), the strong anthropic principle (SAP), the natural anthropic principle (NAP) and the supernatural anthropic principle (SNAP). ID fans of course love the SNAP!

The odds against these features just happening to fall into place are so seemingly improbable that God must have supernaturally designed the form of this planet[9-10]. But a rare Earth does not necessarily mean a supernaturally molded Earth; it may simply mean that our planet's hospitality is the exception, rather than the rule, in the cosmos[11]. You should consider the size of the universe before jumping to the conclusion that natural phenomena alone could not have shaped our world. Our galaxy, the Milky Way, contains roughly a hundred billion (10^{11}) stars, and there are a hundred billion other galaxies that we can detect[12]. But that accounts only for the visible or observable universe—the detectable portion of the entire universe. Some conjecture that the entire universe may be infinite in its extent, but it has been suggested by Alan Guth that the entire universe may be "only" 100,000,000,000,000,000,000,000, or 10^{23}, times bigger than the visible universe[13]. Let's do some quick math and get a very rough estimate of the number of stars in a universe that is 10^{23} times bigger than the visible universe. There are about 100 billion (10^{11}) galaxies in the visible universe, each of which contains about 100 billion stars (10^{11}), and the entire universe may be 100 billion trillion (10^{23}) times bigger than the visible universe. That accounts for about 10^{45} stars! But what about the number of planets associated with these stars? Planets outside of our solar system are obviously much harder to detect than stars or galaxies, but during the 1990s scientists started detecting other solar systems by measuring the slight wobbles in nearby stars caused by the gravitational influence of planets and by changes in the intensity of the starlight if the distant planet happened to pass between its sun and Earth during its revolution. (In the near-future, astronomers hope to block out the glare of a star to directly observe the faint glow of the illuminated planet!) Over 130 planets have been detected in these manners in the regions of space relatively close to Earth[14], which lends much credence to the notion that the universe is filled with solar systems[15]. Based on such surveys, it has been estimated that as many as 10% of stars in our galaxy are encircled by at least one planet, although 10% of sun-like stars may be a more realistic estimate. Let's make it 1% of all the stars to keep the math easy. Our own Milky Way may have a billion planets in it. The visible universe may hold a hundred billion billion, or 10^{20}, planets. If there are about 10^{45} stars in a universe that is 10^{23} times bigger than the visible universe, then there may be about 10^{43} planets. That's ten million billion billion billion billion (more commonly called a bazillion) planets. Given this planetary proliferation in our universe, is it really that unlikely to assume that our planet is naturally well suited for life, regardless of how rare its combination of life-giving attributes may be? Perhaps so, you may say, and given the remarkable attributes of the universe required for life to evolve, you would have a point! The laws of the universe are apparently the same throughout, so the remarkable features of our universe are indeed far more impressive than the fortuitous characteristics of our planet. For example, it is truly astounding that the cosmological constant of the universe is precisely fine-tuned to 119 places after the decimal place, as opposed to the easily imagined sheer luck that the Earth's distance from the sun is within a ten million mile wide range of values that would have sustained life in an ocean of liquid water. Our planet might be a lucky one out of 10^{43} candidates, but the unique universe in which it resides must be a supernaturally crafted miraculous one.

But what if our universe is not unique? What if some of the same cosmologists who enlightened us about the wonders of the cosmological constant and string theory are now revealing that our universe may not be alone? Our immense universe may be but one citizen in a "multiverse" populated by an unimaginably large set of diverse universes, each with its own laws of physics. This "multiverse" or "megaverse" is not a dreamland designed to deny God's existence, but rather the outcome of prediction of the latest versions of string theory. Rather than yielding a single solution for a unique universe, string theory is apparently leading to 10^{500} possibilities, each possibly corresponding to a real universe outside of our own. 10^{500} is a big number, a really big number. If the odds of getting the cosmological constant are 1 in 10^{120}, but you get 10^{500} chances to get it right in the megaverse, then arriving at the "right" cosmological constant may be a sure bet. If the string theorists are right, then our cosmological constant may be more sublime than supernatural; more inevitable[16] than incredible; more mundane than marvelous. If these scientists are right about the vast megaverse of possible universes, do you really think God was compelled to supernaturally adjust the cosmological constant to ensure that Earth was hospitable? I don't. If there is a megaverse, then I think He may have just let it emerge and then kept tabs on his project to see where life would appear! I see no reason why a megaverse should be considered an ungodly way to make a universe where life exists, even if it makes it easier for skeptics to claim that it makes a Creator unnecessary.

Appearance-of-Design Design

The honorary father of Intelligent Design, the Rev. William Paley, presented eloquent and impassioned arguments during the early 1800's that the complexity of organisms was the handiwork of God. Paley was convinced that only God could design the eye, just as he knew that only a watchmaker could design a watch. Although this centuries-old analogy is still presented in many churches as proof that evolution is a lie, it is fatally flawed. There is a fundamental difference between a watch and a human; humans have sex and watches don't. Female clocks do not give birth to wristwatchs. Humans are made in the uterus of their mothers, not in a Swiss *Homo sapien* factory. Therefore the attributes of complexity in a living organism must be examined in light of the process of reproduction that brought it into being. Darwin was well aware of Paley's design argument and he addressed it thoroughly in *On the Origin of Species by Means of Natural Selection, or the Preservation of Favoured Races in the Struggle for Life*, explaining that complex organs could have indeed evolved. Human eyes, for example, did not have to suddenly self-assemble because a sequence of useful eyes, increasing in complexity and capability, was available for natural selection to choose from.

Intelligent Design statistics in the realm of microbiology are just as risky. The advent of technologies that has opened the door to the intricate workings of the cell has provided Intelligent Design fans with a host of examples of complicated biological processes. Michael Behe's book, *Darwin's Black Box*[17], presented a series of biochemical challenges to evolution, including the propulsion systems of sperm and bacteria[18], blood clotting[19], the movement of proteins within cells[20], the immune system[21], and the manufacture of nucleotides[22]. Behe explains the complexity of these five examples in detail, but he reminds the reader that numerous other examples abound, including DNA replication, photosynthesis, and electron transport[23]. Intelligent Design proponents such as Behe insist that these complex systems must have been designed by a higher intelligence because only the completely assembled, intricate, fully functional form of the bio-machine is useful. They are therefore "irreducibly complex." Evolution slowly builds bio-machinery piece-by-piece via random genetic mutations followed by natural selection, and if all the pieces were not in place along the way, then there would have been nothing functional for natural selection to choose. Therefore evolution could not have made these machines, leaving Intelligent Design as the sole explanation. Although his arguments are appealing to Christians desperate for something better than Young Earth Creationism, scientists do not flinch at these Intelligent Design arguments. They strongly disagree with the assertion that there could not have been a trail of simpler, yet still useful and functional, precursors for each and every one of Behe's examples. Richard Dawkins' book *The Blind Watchmaker*[24] presented a case for how evolution can indeed yield complexity by following a path of gradually changing, slowly improving, increasingly complex, functional organs. Kenneth Miller provided a courteous yet uncompromising refutation of Behe's version of Intelligent Design at the organ-level and cellular-level in his book *Finding Darwin's God*[25]. In one example, Miller cites the well-documented evolution of the ear as an example of the failure of Intelligent Design[26]. This five-piece machine—the eardrum, three tiny bones, and the oval window—can be considered irreducibly complex because if one part is missing, you're deaf. Unlike organs made of soft tissue, ear bones can fossilize. Miller explains that Arthur Crompton of Harvard has shown how a single-boned working ear changed over millions of years into a three-boned ear. Two bones from the back portion of the reptilian lower jaw diminished in size and migrated back into the ear, reducing the number of bones in the jaw while increasing the number of bones in the ear. Therefore the five-part ear did not need to be carefully designed and assembled; it was a new and improved ear that originated as a simpler functional ear. Miller also addressed the general evolutionary pathways that could have resulted in the irreducibly complex incredible small biomachines[27] cited by Behe. Miller's critique of Intelligent Design is consistent; evolution modified existing functional structures and improved their form and function so efficiently that they seem to have been designed. Of course scientists can never retrace the exact sequence of these steps, and evolutionists must hand-wave about the details as Behe charges. Nonetheless, they have identified the process through which such complexity arose; evolution. It is evolution—not the wave of a master magician's hand—that gives the appearance of design to life.

Overly Complicated Design

Intelligent Design fans love stuff that is hard to figure out. The more confusing it is, the more likely it is that God did it! But what if a design is more complicated than necessary? Is it really a sign of supernatural intelligence to reject simplicity in favor of complexity? Do we really need all of those distant planets in the far reaches of the solar system for life on Earth to thrive? What's the point of all of those stars in all of those galaxies? If we do abide in a megaverse, what's the point of all of those other universes? Why did God use three billion base pairs to encode the DNA of human being while stacking up 670 billion bases pairs for the lowly amoeba[28]? Why is the process for the replication of DNA so convoluted? Does the blood-clotting chemistry of a human really need to contain such a vast array of reactions to stop a cut from bleeding excessively? If God is so smart, why did He select such cumbersome complexity rather than elegant simplicity?

Straw Man Intelligent Design

A great way to make yourself look smart is to argue with the dumbest people you know that hold an opposing view and hope that no one in your audience finds out how stupid your opponents really are. It is for this reason that Jonathan Wells' popular creationist book, *Icons of Evolution, Science or Myth? Why Much of What We Teach About Evolution is Wrong*[29] is so unimpressive. Rather than trying to engage in an intellectual battle with the host of brilliant scientists who could easily refute Wells and effectively make the case for evolution, Wells drudges up the most famous blunders of evolutionists that he can find and leaves the impression that all contemporary evolutionists still accept these mistakes as truth. Wells rehashes offensive philosophies and theologies propagated by some evolutionists, textbook exaggerations, and fraudulent fossil finds. None of this invalidates human evolution, though, any more than the teachings of the Rev. Sun Myung Moon invalidate Christianity. (I find it somewhat ironic that Wells beats up on the unsavory spiritual convictions of some evolutionists while he himself is an ardent follower of the Rev. Moon[30], and Moon considers himself "greater than Jesus himself" and teaches that "The cross is the symbol of the defeat of Christianity."[31]). Wells never mentions that the self-correcting actions of the scientific community, not creationists, recognized and rejected incorrect and falsified data long ago. Wells also cites differences in scientific understanding of the technical details of human evolution and then deceptively leaves the reader with the impression that these befuddled scientists are in such a stupor that they themselves no longer believe in evolution. What is Wells' alternative explanation for the emergence of the human species? Like all other Intelligent Design advocates, he presents none. Although the fallacies of Wells' book were spotted by scientists as soon as the book hit the stands[32], many conservative Christian organizations have promoted its message by encouraging Christians to buy this book.

I-Am-Smarter-Than-All-Scientists Design

Intelligent Design proponents claim to know what level of complexity requires that direct intervention of an Intelligent Designer. For example, several books by William Dembski[33, 34] provide an "explanatory filter" that simplifies the identification of an intelligently designed system. This philosophical filter is—in essence—a miracle detector! Here's how it works. If the system cannot be fully explained by or deduced from a known process or law, and if it is so complex that chance alone could not have produced it, and if it exhibits a pattern that can be associated with a specification of a higher intelligence, then the system must have been intelligently designed. Dembski maintains that living organisms fit all of these criteria; therefore life has been intelligently designed. If you think about it, this is quite a bold claim. William Dembski's convoluted information theory has determined that scientists cannot explain, and never will be able to explain, the complexities of life. If Dembski is right, then life could not have evolved without God's supernatural nudging.

Nonsense! I find it utterly amazing that Intelligent Design advocates, a group that has not discovered anything at all, think that they are smart enough to tell scientists what can and cannot be attributed to natural causes! Evolutionary science has systematically refuted this type of reasoning[35-37]. Further, Dembski doesn't even come close to disproving evolution. He never explains how God allegedly put complex systems together. His explanatory filter is nothing more than an overly complicated argument that is based upon the very assumption that it allegedly proves; natural mechanisms alone cannot yield complex information that characterizes life.

Could God have miraculously intervened in the creation or evolution of the universe during the last 14 billion years? Why not? But is there any theological reason that compelled Him to do so? No! Is there any scientific mystery that compels investigators to immediately and permanently surrender to the supernatural because there is no possible hypothesis that could ever hope to explain the phenomenon? Creationists will tell you "Yes!" because that's the answer that reassures them emotionally, but scientists of all faiths and of no faith will tell you "No!" Should Christians be betting their faith that scientists will never ever figure stuff out, rather than building their faith on the words of Christ? I doubt it.

God-in-the-Gaps Design

Intelligent Design is a sophisticated modern presentation of an old, effective strategy. If brilliant scientists cannot figure out how it happened naturally, then insist that God did it miraculously. That's just silly. How can anyone seriously claim that the unsolved mysteries and intricate complexities of the universe prove that an Intelligent Designer was supernaturally manipulating matter and energy? History has shown that scientists have often determined the natural causes of phenomena previously thought to be "miraculous", even if it takes decades or centuries? In today's environment, when science discovers the natural causes that govern these amazing phenomena, the Intelligent Designer looks more like an Unnecessary

Designer. Even if the natural causes behind some of these phenomena forever remain beyond the realm of scientific resolution, does
that mean that an Intelligent Designer made it happen with a wave
of His hand? Of course not! Maybe we're just not smart enough to
figure it out!

Hypocritical Design

The strategies of Intelligent Design are laced with hypocrisy.
Intelligent Design proponents resurrect obsolete, exaggerated, fraudulent or erroneous claims of evolutionists as evidence of its weak-
ness[38]—as if they had never retreated from preposterous claims made
by members of their own ranks. Intelligent Design proponents criticize the research results of evolutionists as not showing enough evidence of evolution—as if they are not aware that they have made no
contribution whatsoever to the scientific understanding of our origins. Intelligent Design proponents unveil the personal weaknesses,
offensive politics, or liberal social politics of some scientists as symptoms of their untrustworthiness—as if none of their own advocates
hold ideologies that are repulsive to the Christian faith. Intelligent
Design proponents equate the disputes over the technical details of
evolution that ultimately lead toward resolution with confusion and
conspiracy—as if they are not aware of the irreconcilable differences
in their own ranks between those who believe in the divinely assist-
ed evolution of humans over millions of years and those who believe
that humans were instantly created thousands of years ago. Intelligent
Design proponents point to the gaps of knowledge and putty them
over with miracles—as if the church's centuries-old habit of churning out pseudo-science to explain puzzling phenomena never happened. Intelligent Design proponents point out the mysteries of
nature and the unresolved problems of evolution as proof of the
supernatural—as if scientists are not only acutely aware of these mysteries, but are also the ones who pointed them out in the first place
and remain our best hope of resolving them.

Intellectually Bankrupt Design

Richard Dawkins thinks that creationists who label "the amazing"
as "the miraculous" are intellectually "lazy"[39]. He's right. In my

basement I have over 100 books written by creationists and scientists. My Intelligent Design collection can be summarized as "If I can't figure it out, it must be a miracle." My science books can be summarized as "If I can't figure it out, I'll work until I can." There is no scientific merit in boldly declaring one's decision to forego sorting out the mysteries of nature, yet this attitude is the very hallmark of the Intelligent Design movement. Christians would be better off combating the spiritual errors and biases of individual scientists than trying to overturn great scientific theories with religious rhetoric.

Just Don't Do It Design

The Intelligent Design movement paints itself as the victim of prejudice and unwarranted ridicule. They claim to be unfairly denied a fair hearing in the scientific community. That's untrue. For example, Mark Perakh patiently plows through the scientific errors of the heroes of Intelligent Design—Dembski, Behe, Ross, Johnson, and Schroeder[40], providing them with the detailed critique that they have allegedly longed for. Before you pull out your Kleenex for these poor persecuted proponents of ID, you should realize that most of great ideas of science were given cold receptions at some point—but triumphed nonetheless. What did the proponents of some of these grand ideas of science (e.g. relativity, plate tectonics, the Big Bang, inflationary expansion, the origin of the cell nucleus, and yes, even the process of evolution) have going for them that enabled them to win over the droves of doubters and nay-sayers? What did they do that Intelligent Design advocates can't seem to do? They *proved* that their ideas were right! They collected data, not opinions. Their ideas explained the data. Their ideas could be tested by others. Their results were reproducible. Their ideas were explained in clear and concise terms that could be comprehended by others. Their ideas were scrutinized and shown to be valid. Their ideas led to predictions which were subsequently confirmed. If the Intelligent Design crowd is right, they should present their evidence to the public. No amount of editorial bias or black helicopters of prejudiced editors—real or imagined—could stand in their way if they could prove that they were correct. To date, Intelligent Design has been soundly refuted because they can't even present a hypothesis that can be tested, let alone collect data to substantiate their claims. They just can't do it.

Bottom Line of Intelligent Design

"Intelligent Design" rests upon two scientific-sounding principles. First, many features or processes in the universe are "irreducibly complex" (e.g. blood clotting), which means that they must have been assembled at the same time rather than being formed by an evolutionary process that required a multitude of small changes that accumulated over incredibly long periods of time. Second, other features or processes in nature, particularly all living organisms, contain "complex specified information" (e.g. DNA) that must have been the handiwork of a mysterious intelligent designer. This stuff sounds cool, but it is not science. ID is a belief system, plain and simple. Nonetheless, Intelligent Design is here to stay. There will always be an unlikely event, a mysterious phenomenon, a fine-tuned physical constant, or a missing fossil that provides enough wiggle room for Intelligent Design folks to claim that God slipped in a supernatural event without leaving a clue behind. Therefore Intelligent Design will always claim to have grounds for stating that they are right. Not scientific grounds, but philosophical, logical, emotional, spiritual, or moral grounds. But Intelligent Design is not a wise foundation for your faith. ID is not testable, falsifiable, or supported by observations. It is a well-intentioned but misguided effort to refute science with Bible-based pseudo-science. It has no place in public or private school classrooms because it is not science, and folks are starting to figure it out. For example, my home state of Pennsylvania was in the national spotlight concerning this issue in late 2005. U.S. District Judge John E. Jones stopped Intelligent Design in its tracks in the Dover Area school district, which had required ninth-graders to hear a scientific-sounding statement about Intelligent Design before they studied evolution. Jones deemed ID a sham, saying in his decision[11] that "The district's purpose was to advance creationism, an inherently religious view, both by introducing it directly under the label ID and by disparaging the scientific theory of evolution so that creationism would gain credence by default." That's the ID strategy in a nutshell, and Jones' assertion that ID has "utterly no place" in science classes serves as a wake up call for other school districts to be on the watch for crafty creationists.

References
1. S. Jay Olshansky, Bruce A. Carnes, Robert N. Butler; If Humans Were Built to Last, Scientific American, 13(2),2003, Special Edition, New Look at Human Evolution, 94-100
2. James D. Watson with Andrew Berry; DNA—The Secret of Life, Alfred A. Knopf, New York, 2003, 202-203
3. Jocelyn Selim; "Useless Body Parts" Discover, June 2004, 42-45
4. Charles Darwin; The Descent of Man, Great Minds Series, Prometheus Books, Amherst, NY, 5-26
5. Jocelyn Selim; "Useless Body Parts" Discover, June 2004, 42-45
6. Jerry Coyne; Creationism by Stealth, a Review of: Jonathan Wells—Icons of Evolution: Science or Myth?, Nature 410 (2001) 745-746
7. Matt Ridley, Genome—The Autobiography of a Species in 23 Chapters, Harper Perennial, 1999, 21
8. Steven Jay Gould; The Panda's Thumb—More Reflections in Natural History, W W Norton and Company, 1980, 19-26
9. G.L. Schroeder; The Science of God; Simon and Schuster; New York, NY; 1997; 27-29
10. Hugh Ross; The Genesis Question—Scientific Advances and the Accuracy of Genesis; Navpress 1998, Colorado Springs, CO; 40-42
11. Peter D. Ward, Donald Brownlee; Rare Earth—Why Complex Life Is Uncommon in the Universe, Copernicus, Springer-Verlag New York, Inc., New York, NY, 2000, 157-189
12. Alan H. Guth; The Inflationary Universe—The Quest for a New Theory of Cosmic Origins, Helix Books, Perseus Books, Addison-Wesley, Reading MA, 1997, 1-2
13. Alan H. Guth;, The Inflationary Universe—The Quest for a New Theory of Cosmic Origins, Helix Books, Perseus Books, Addison-Wesley, Reading MA, 1997, 185-186
14. Tim Appenzelle; Search for Other Earths, National Geographic, Dec. 2004, 68-95
15. Daniel R. Altschuler; Children of the Stars—Our Origin, Evolution and Destiny; 2002; Cambridge University Press; New York, NY; 11-48
16. Leonard Susskind, The Cosmic Landscape—String Theory and the Illusion of Intelligent Design, Little, Brown and Company, New York, NY, 2006, 8-15, 293—324
17. Michael J. Behe; Darwin's Black Box—The Biochemical Challenge to Evolution; Touchstone, New York, NY, 1996
18. Michael J. Behe; Darwin's Black Box—The Biochemical Challenge to Evolution; Touchstone, New York, NY, 1996, 51-73
19. Michael J. Behe; Darwin's Black Box—The Biochemical Challenge to Evolution; Touchstone, New York, NY, 1996, 74-97
20. Michael J. Behe; Darwin's Black Box—The Biochemical Challenge to Evolution; Touchstone, New York, NY, 1996, 98-116
21. Michael J. Behe; Darwin's Black Box—The Biochemical Challenge to Evolution; Touchstone, New York, NY, 1996.117-139
22. Michael J. Behe; Darwin's Black Box—The Biochemical Challenge to Evolution; Touchstone, New York, NY, 1996, 140-161
23. Michael J. Behe; Darwin's Black Box—The Biochemical Challenge to Evolution; Touchstone, New York, NY, 1996, 160
24. Richard Dawkins; The Blind Watchmaker—Why the Evidence of Evolution Reveals a Universe without Design, W W Norton and Company, New York, 1996
25. Kenneth Miller; Finding Darwin's God—A Scientist's Search for Common Ground Between God and Evolution; 1999, Cliff Street Books, Harper Collins; New York, NY
26. Kenneth Miller; Finding Darwin's God—A Scientist's Search for Common Ground Between God and Evolution; 1999, Cliff Street Books, Harper Collins; New York, NY, 138-139
27. Kenneth Miller; Finding Darwin's God—A Scientist's Search for Common Ground Between God and Evolution; 1999, Cliff Street Books, Harper Collins; New York, NY, 141-160
28. James D. Watson with Andrew Berry; DNA—The Secret of Life, Alfred A. Knopf, New York, 2003, 204
29. Jonathan Wells; Icons of Evolution, Science or Myth, Why Much of What We Teach About Evolution is Wrong, Regnery Publishing, Washington D.C., 2000
30. www.tparents.org/Library/Unification/Talks/Wells/DARWIN.htm
31. Bob Larson; Larson's New Book of Cults, Tyndale House Publishers Inc., Wheaton, IL, 1989, 437-445
32. Jerry Coyne; Creationism by Stealth, a Review of: Jonathan Wells—Icons of Evolution: Science or Myth?, Nature 410 (2001) 745-746
33. William Dembski; The Design Inference—Eliminating Chance Through Small Probabilities, 1998
34. William Dembski; Intelligent Design—The Bridge Between Science and Theology, 1999
35. Frederick Crews; Saving Us From Darwin, in The Best American Science and Nature Writings, Natalie Angier, editor, Houghton Mifflin Company, New York, 2002, 41-43
36. Michael Ruse; Darwin and Design—Does Evolution Have a Purpose?, Harvard University Press, Cambridge, MA, 2003, 313-336
37. Mark Perakh; Unintelligent Design, Prometheus Books, Amherst New York, 2004, 19-110
38. Jonathan Wells; Icons of Evolution, Science or Myth, Why Much of What We Teach About Evolution is Wrong, Regnery Publishing, Washington D.C., 2000

39. Richard Dawkins; The Ancestor's Tale—A Pilgrimage to the Dawn of Evolution, Houghton Mifflin Company, Boston, MA, 2004, 551

40. Mark Perakh, Unintelligent Design, Prometheus Books, Amherst New York, 2004

41. In the United States District Court for the Middle District of Pennsylvania, Tammy Kitzmiller, et al. Plaintiffs v. Dover Area School District, et al., Defendants, Case No. 04cv2688, Memorandum Opinion, Judge Jones, Dec. 20, 2005

Appendix E.
SCUMBAGs

Those who respect *Scientists Constantly Unraveling Mysteries* and also have enough faith to *Believe in Almighty God* are SCUMBAGs in my book! The SCUMBAG perspective is, in the words of H. J. Van Till, "a vision that recognizes the entire universe as a creation that has, by God's unbounded generosity and unfathomable creativity, been given all the capabilities for self-organization and transformation necessary to make possible something as inhumanly incomprehensible as unbroken evolutionary development."[1] SCUMBAGs think that the ability to create a self-sustaining universe from scratch reflects God's brilliance and creativity. They consider every aspect of creation to be a reflection of God's glory, yet the SCUMBAG neither needs, desires, nor expects scientists to affirm the existence of God. SCUMBAGs readily concede that the scriptures do not provide enough information to define scientific processes or delineate chronologies, and they do not presume that God secretly guided the progress of natural processes. SCUMBAGs explicitly reject creationist attempts to circumvent the scientific process by deducing scientific principles out of Genesis because they take God seriously when He says that we have no spiritual insight into the mechanisms of creation, as illustrated by Job 38 and

39, which are provided in Appendix F. This is not to say that SCUMBAGs do not believe in supernatural events. SCUMBAGs tend to restrict their faith in the miracles to those events that are plainly presented as supernatural acts in the Bible, such as the virgin birth, healing ministry, atoning death, resurrection and ascension of Christ.

SCUMBAGs trust in God and accept the findings of science. They have no problem with God creating a universe in which natural mechanisms result in the formation of the universe, galaxies, planets, oceans, clouds, fish, trees or humans. SCUMBAGs don't panic at the thought of every feature of the universe ultimately being attributed to impersonal, natural phenomena littered with random events, mass extinctions, ecological disasters, pain and death. Although it may offend those who think that God is a dainty Creator who couldn't let poor little puppies struggle to survive, SCUMBAGs think that there is nothing biblically repulsive about God creating a universe in which life could emerge under the constraints of the laws of nature. SCUMBAGs actually are impressed with God when His wondrous creation emerges under the guidance of natural forces; after all it's His universe and His natural forces! SCUMBAGs realize that a "perfect God" can establish a universe filled with features that atheists gleefully consider "imperfect". SCUMBAGs have a line they will not cross concerning their loyalty to science, however. They refuse to condone the biased efforts of atheistic scientists who dismiss the existence of God under the guise of intellectualism. Therefore SCUMBAGs embrace solid science while dismissing the religious, social, political, and politically correct views espoused by some scientists.

There are two species of SCUMBAG. Liberal SCUMBAGs regard the early chapters of Genesis as a collection of divinely inspired myths, allegories or spiritual teachings laden with faith-building themes. Kenneth Miller's outstanding work, *Finding Darwin's God*, makes an eloquent case for liberal theistic evolution . Kenneth Miller asserts that it is unreasonable to extract scientific information or natural history from portions of the Bible intended to nourish our souls. He argues that banking on the inability of the scientific community to explain the history and mechanisms of the evolution of life on Earth is an ill-advised, illogical and unbiblical basis for one's faith. Kenneth Miller encourages us to recognize evolution as an enduring signature of His creativity[3]. Keith Miller (no relation to Ken) recently edited a compilation of essays emphasizing that the evolution of the universe, Earth, and life reflect God's sovereignty and genius[4]. Richard Colling's recent book, *Random Designer*[5], also gives free reign to the creative genius of God, suggesting that all of the workings of nature, even evolution, are expressions of His brilliance. Liberal SCUMBAGs respect the Genesis story but clearly considers it to be symbolic in nature. In particular, Adam represents mankind; he certainly was not an actual person.

Conservative SCUMBAGs (that's me!) are in agreement with their liberal counterparts concerning science, but differ somewhat when it comes to the interpretation of some portions of Genesis. Conservatives believe that some portions of the early chapters of Genesis are Holy Spirit-inspired visions of actual events. No information on the duration or sequence or mechanisms of origins is provided, however, because the story unfolds in a poetic (rather than chronological) order. The events described in Genesis One may contain divinely inspired glimpses of the sun, moon, Earth, stars, clouds, land, waters, plants and animals given from the perspective of a hypothetical spectator—a tour guide—on Earth's surface during creation[6]; a perspective that is consistent with all of the other descriptions of nature found in the Bible that are expressed from the viewpoint of an Earth-bound spectator. For example, when the Bible says that the land rose out of the waters, it may actually correlate to the continents emerging out of the oceans. These brief observations cannot be used to establish historical timelines, derive scientific theories, prove that the Bible confirms science, or demonstrate that science confirms that Bible. These scriptures may simply contain a fascinating view of an evolving creation. The use of 24 hour-creation days is no problem for the SCUMBAG because the creation week simply provides a literary lattice upon which the descriptions are arranged. Conservative SCUMBAGs also acknowledge that other portions of Genesis may indeed have symbolic, rather than literal, meaning.

References
1. H.J. Van Till; Theistic Evolution; in Three Views on Creation and Evolution, J.P. Moreland and J.M. Reynolds, General Editors, 1999, Zondervan Publishing House, Grand Rapids Michigan,173
2. Kenneth Miller; Finding Darwin's God—A Scientist's Search for Common Ground between God and Evolution; 1999, Cliff Street Books, Harper Collins; New York, NY
3. Kenneth Miller; Finding Darwin's God—A Scientist's Search for Common Ground between God and Evolution; 1999, Cliff Street Books, Harper Collins; New York, NY, 255–259
4. Keith Miller, editor, Perspectives on an Evolving Creation, Eerdsman, Grand Rapids, MI, 2003
5. Richard G. Colling, Random Designer—Created from Chaos to Connect with the Creator, Browning Press, Bourbonnais, Illinois, 2004
6. Appendix G

Appendix F.
God's Blackout on Science

God has strong feelings about those who claim to have spiritual insight into the detailed methods of how to create a universe or a planet or a species, and He shared these sentiments with Job in chapters 38 and 39. Take a look.

Job 38: 1-41 Then the LORD answered Job out of the storm. He said: "Who is this that darkens my counsel with words without knowledge? Brace yourself like a man; I will question you, and you shall answer me. Where were you when I laid the earth's foundation? Tell me, if you understand. Who marked off its dimensions? Surely you know! Who stretched a measuring line across it? On what were its footings set, or who laid its cornerstone-while the morning stars sang together and all the angels shouted for joy? Who shut up the sea behind doors when it burst forth from the womb, when I made the clouds its garment and wrapped it in thick darkness, when I fixed limits for it and set its doors and bars in place, when I said, 'This far you may come and no farther; here is where your proud waves halt'? Have you ever given orders to the morning, or shown the dawn its place, that it might take the earth by the edges and shake the wicked out of it? The earth takes shape like clay under a seal; its features stand out like those of a garment. The wicked are denied their light, and their upraised arm is broken. Have you journeyed to the springs of the sea or walked in the recesses of the deep? Have the gates of death been shown to you? Have you seen the gates of the shadow of death? Have you comprehended the vast expanses of the earth? Tell me, if you know all this. What is the way to the abode of light? And where does darkness reside? Can you take them to their places? Do you know the paths to their dwellings? Surely you know, for you were already born! You have lived so many years! Have you entered the storehouses of the snow or seen the storehouses of the hail, which I reserve for times of trouble, for days of war and battle? What is the way to the place where the lightning is dispersed, or the place where the east winds are scattered over the earth. Who cuts a channel for the torrents of rain, and a path for the thunderstorm, to water a land where no man lives, a desert with no one in it, to satisfy a desolate wasteland and make it sprout with grass? Does the rain have a father? Who fathers the drops of dew? From whose womb comes the ice? Who gives birth to the frost when the waters from the heavens become hard as stone, when the surface of the deep is frozen? Can you bind the beautiful Pleiades? Can you loose the cords of Orion? Can you bring forth the constellations in their seasons or lead out the Bear with its cubs? Do you know the laws of the heavens? Can you set up God's dominion over the earth? Can you raise your voice to the clouds and cover yourself with a flood of water? Do you send the lightning bolts on their way? Do they report to you, 'Here we are'? Who endowed the heart with wisdom or gave understanding to the mind? Who has the wisdom to count the clouds? Who can tip over the water jars of the heavens when the dust becomes hard and the clods of earth stick together? Do you hunt the prey for the lioness and satisfy the hunger of the lions when they crouch in their dens or lie in wait in a thicket? Who provides food for the raven when its young cry out to God and wander about for lack of food?

Job 39: 1-30 Do you know when the mountain goats give birth? Do you watch when the doe bears her fawn? Do you count the months till they bear? Do you know the time they give birth? They crouch down and bring forth their young; their labor pains are ended. Their young thrive and grow strong in the wilds; they leave and do not return. Who let the wild donkey go free? Who untied his ropes? I gave him the wasteland as his home, the salt flats as his habitat. He laughs at the commotion in the town; he does not hear a driver's shout. He ranges the hills for his pasture and searches for any green thing. Will the wild ox consent to serve you? Will he stay by your manger at night? Can you hold him to the furrow with a harness?

Will he till the valleys behind you? Will you rely on him for his great strength? Will you leave your heavy work to him? Can you trust him to bring in your grain and gather it to your threshing floor? The wings of the ostrich flap joyfully, but they cannot compare with the pinions and feathers of the stork. She lays her eggs on the ground and lets them warm in the sand, unmindful that a foot may crush them, that some wild animal may trample them. She treats her young harshly, as if they were not hers; she cares not that her labor was in vain, for God did not endow her with wisdom or give her a share of good sense. Yet when she spreads her feathers to run, she laughs at horse and rider. Do you give the horse his strength or clothe his neck with a flowing mane? Do you make him leap like a locust, striking terror with his proud snorting? He paws fiercely, rejoicing in his strength, and charges into the fray. He laughs at fear, afraid of nothing; he does not shy away from the sword. The quiver rattles against his side, along with the flashing spear and lance. In frenzied excitement he eats up the ground; he cannot stand still when the trumpet sounds. At the blast of the trumpet he snorts, 'Aha!' He catches the scent of battle from afar, the shout of commanders and the battle cry. Does the hawk take flight by your wisdom and spread his wings toward the south? Does the eagle soar at your command and build his nest on high? He dwells on a cliff and stays there at night; a rocky crag is his stronghold. From there he seeks out his food; his eyes detect it from afar. His young ones feast on blood, and where the slain are, there is he."

I'll never know how anyone can read those two chapters and still claim to have spiritual insight into how or when God created anything, or how He established the laws that govern their very existence and sway their behavior. Of course God is aware of everything, including every single form of life on Earth, *Luke 12:6-7 Are not five sparrows sold for two pennies? Yet not one of them is forgotten by God. Indeed, the very hairs of your head are all numbered. Don't be afraid; you are worth more than many sparrows.* But neither these verses nor any other portion of scripture contain divine instructions on making stuff, or how nature functions and changes over unimaginably long periods of time. These two chapters of Job demonstrate that the history and processes of creation are a biblical mystery, which is the fundamental reason that creationist explanations of our origins are so consistently and demonstrably wrong.

Appendix G.
Genesis Observer

I am convinced that the author of Genesis One was inspired by God to describe creation events as if a person was there to watch them. The record of events in Genesis One seems to make sense when we realize that the observer was positioned on the Earth's surface, rather than orbiting the planet or roaming the heavens[1,2]. Although the Bible never explicitly declares that God's creative acts should be correlated to when they become visible rather than to when they actually occurred[3], this vantage point is implicit in the second verse of the Bible, where the Spirit of God is reported to be moving over the ocean waves, *Genesis 1:2 and the Spirit of God was hovering over the waters.* It is also a common biblical perspective. God's creation is always described from the only perspective known to the authors of scripture; a person with an Earthbound frame of reference. I call this hypothetical ancient reporter the Genesis Observer.

The Genesis Observer recorded a few observations, not reams of data.

Although the poetic description of the sun's movements in Psalm 19 is perfectly accurate, one cannot deduce the physics of the solar system from these verses. *Psalm 19:4-6 In the heavens he has pitched a tent for the sun, which is like a bridegroom coming forth from his pavilion, like a champion rejoicing to run his course. It rises at one end of the heavens and makes its circuit to the other; nothing is hidden from its heat.* The same principle applies to Genesis One; there are only a few observations concerning the Earth and its life, but they were not intended to provide a database for the derivation of scientific theories of our origins.

The Genesis Observer wrote a short story.

The Bible is meant to lead us into truth, not a coma, therefore the Genesis Observer limited himself to a single page of notes. It appears that God favored beautiful prose rather than technical jargon to describe His acts. Perhaps He knew that more people would read it that way.

The Genesis Observer emphasized man.

God knows that our interest in our origins are very intense, therefore man is presented as the pinnacle of creation. I find it amusing that so many scientists criticize Genesis for presenting man as God's crowning achievement when there are tens of millions of other species, while nearly every scientific book on the story of life leads up to the climatic few chapters at the end of the book on— you guessed it—human evolution! Even atheists know that the way to get people to read books is to make it interesting to the reader, and human readers like human topics.

The Genesis Observer correlated creation to a six-day effort, followed by a seventh day of rest.

Some would argue that there is no biblical basis to preclude the six days of creation from covering billions of years[4]. But why would God inspire the author of Genesis to present the story in terms of six days if it actually took 14 billion years? Why wouldn't God simply use the Hebrew words that corresponded to long periods of time[5] rather than six days marked by morning and evening if creation did indeed take a long, long time? Perhaps the sole reason was the elegant literary pattern that is so neatly established by the use of six periods of time, such as days.

Problem	Preparation	Population
Genesis 1:2	Days 1–3	Days 4–6
Darkness	1a creation of light (day)	4a creation of sun
	1b separation from darkness (night)	4b creation of moon, stars
Watery abyss	2a creation of firmament	5a creation of birds
	2b separation of waters above from waters below	5b creation of fish
Formless Earth	3a separation of earth from sea	6a creation of land animals
	3b creation of vegetation	6b creation of humans
"without *form* and *void*"	Formlessness is formed	Void is filled

But why days? Why not six hours or six months or six years or six centuries? Perhaps the fifth commandment provides a clue. *Exodus 2:8-11 Remember the Sabbath day by keeping it holy. Six days you shall labor and do all your work, but the seventh day is a Sabbath to the LORD your God. On it you shall not do any work, neither you, nor your son or daughter, nor your manservant or maidservant, nor your animals, nor the alien within your gates. For in six days the LORD made the heavens and the earth, the sea, and all that is in them, but he rested on the seventh day. Therefore the LORD blessed the Sabbath day and made it holy.*

Creationists insist that the six day work week and subsequent day of rest was literal, therefore our week is patterned in the same way. Maybe it's the other way around! Perhaps God wanted to establish a simple pattern for man to follow and used the literary pattern of the creation story to set the example. Just as He established the Earth in six days and rested on the seventh, so should we work six days and honor the Lord on the seventh. Maybe God knew that keeping the Sabbath was more important to our spiritual health than understanding the actual chronology of creation. Therefore He may have expressed His efforts as six days of work followed by a day of rest, providing a practical pattern for His followers. After all, it is a bit unreasonable to expect us to work for 14 billion years before getting a day off.

The Genesis Observer did not reveal how God made anything!

God imposed a blackout on revelations describing the processes through which He made the universe, Earth, or the life it supports. Therefore the Genesis Observer simply described what he saw, not how it came to be.

References
1. Hugh Ross; The Genesis Question—Scientific Advances and the Accuracy of Genesis; Navpress 1998, Colorado Springs, CO; 20-26
2. Hugh Ross; The Fingerprint of God; 1989; Whitaker House; New Kensington, PA; 165-169
3. Meredith G. Kline, Space and Time in the Genesis Cosmogony, Perspectives on Science and Christian Faith, 48 (1996) 2-15
4. Appendix B
5. Mark Perakh, Unintelligent Design, Prometheus Books, Amherst New York, 2004, 173-191

Appendix H. What Do You Want On Your Tombstone?

Making a Good First Impression

Fossils are lifeless testaments that are invaluable tools for tracing the history of life on Earth[1,2]. "Fossils are remains or traces of organisms that lived during past geologic times and were buried in rocks that accumulated in the earth's outer portion, or crust."[3] They are lasting impressions of organisms that died a long time ago. The fossil record is more of a survey than a census because most dead plants and animals weren't in the right place at the right time to be fossilized when they died. Many of those that were likely to become fossilized were devoured, displaced or disrupted upon their demise. Further, most fossils that did form have not been found because they are hidden within inaccessible rocks or are buried at unknown locations. To make matters worse, many fossils are incomplete because they retain only a portion of the organism's body structure. Nevertheless, this planet has fostered such a prolific amount of diverse life that a massive amount of fossil evidence has been accumulated; enough to paint a rich mosaic of the history of life on Earth[4,5]. The most familiar fossils are found in sedimentary rocks. Animal fossils typically look like an X-ray, providing images of

221

bones, teeth or shells, while plant fossils may appear as intricate impressions. Most of these fossils originated when plants or animals died and were slowly buried by sediments in a stream. The soft tissues gradually decayed, but the stiffer components would have retained their form[6]. The rigid parts of the remains and entombing sediments hardened under increasing pressure from continued deposition of sediments above them. Eventually, the accumulated sediments would form a rock, with the fossil trapped within. Fossil molds occur when the dearly departed came to rest in sediment that became firm around it before the corpse decayed; therefore a void in the solid rock was formed when decomposition eventually occurred. Fossil casts were made when such molds were filled with clay particles that later solidified.

The processes required to form sedimentary rocks and their fossilized inhabitants are slow with respect to our lifetime, but rapid with respect to the age of the planet. The age of a fossil can be accurately estimated if the age of the rock that contains it can be determined by radiometric dating[7]. Fossils are composed of sediments that rarely contain crystals bearing radioactive minerals, though. The lack of datable fossils in sedimentary rocks doesn't pose a problem in dating a fossil because igneous rocks that are just above, below, or within the sedimentary layer can be easily dated[8, 9]. Therefore the appearance of fossils in sedimentary rocks describes the forms of the organisms that passed away, while the interspersed igneous rocks reveal when they died. Fossils are nature's tombstones.

There are many other ways that a plant or animal can make its mark on the geologic record. Fates that can yield a fossil include freezing to death, drying up and shriveling in the desert, getting stuck in sticky stuff like tar or sap, or getting buried rapidly by the remains of other plants. Fossils have also formed when dissolved minerals in water that seeped into soft decaying spaces precipitated between the hard structures of the dead critter. Animals that walked on moist ground or crawled along the ocean floor have left behind fossilized tracks. Remnants of indigestible meals swallowed by burrowing invertebrates can form fossils, as can the just-swallowed meal of an animal that died immediately after dining! Much to the delight of my youngest children, you can even uncover fossilized dung and vomit[10]. Although disgusting in nature, such fossils provide direct evidence of the decedent's diet. For example, the absence of Pebbles Flintstone and Bam-Bam Rubble bones in fossilized Dino-poop tells us that that T. Rex did not eat humans, as some creationists would have you believe. A 130 million year old fossil of a two-foot long mammal was found with a ripped up five-inch dinosaur fossil located where the mammal's stomach would have been; proving that this mammal's last meal was a baby dinosaur[11]!

A Brief History of Life

The fossil record tells us much about the history of life on Earth[12]. The earliest known forms of life were single-celled bacteria, which were rod-like in shape and lacked a nucleus (prokaryotes). About 3 ½ billion years ago, bacteria alone inhabited the Earth. One and a half billion years went by before single-celled organisms with a nucleus (eukaryotes) appeared, whose origin has been traced to the mutually beneficially union of two or more bacterial cells. One and a half billion years passed before the next major advancement occurred in the form of multi-cellular eukaryotic organisms. The nature of these Ediacarian fossils (named after the Ediacara Hills of Australia where they were discovered) remains puzzling because some think that they were similar to lichens, while others think these animals became extinct. Some paleontologists note that they resemble more complex organisms that were soon to appear in the Cambrian Period[13].

Soon thereafter, roughly 540 million years ago, a proliferation of large and complex life, including corals, brachiopods, mollusks and trilobites, joined their single-celled peers in the waters. This outburst of life is referred to as the Cambrian Explosion, in recognition of Cambria (the Roman name for Wales), where these fossils were first examined. The Cambrian Explosion of life took roughly 10 million years to become fully established, leaving behind an abundance of marine invertebrate fossils that marked a rapid diversification of life on Earth. All of the major types of body architectures, or phyla, made their debut during the Cambrian Explosion (with a single exception—the bryozoans)[14]. For example, chordates appeared with features that you and I share (that's right, you are a chordate), including symmetric left and right sides, a stiff back with a nerve cord running parallel to it, and a digestive system that starts at one end and finishes at the other.

Some of the major events found on the timeline of life since the Cambrian Explosion[15] include the appearance of plants 500 million years ago, the movement of insects and other invertebrates onto the land 450 million years ago followed by four-limbed vertebrates 360 million years ago. Three hundred twenty million years ago amphibians were slinking about. Two notable groups of animals, dinosaurs and mammals, appeared 225 million years ago. Sixty five million years ago the dinosaurs and more than half of the other species on the planet succumbed to a tremendous environmental shock caused by a comet or meteor roughly 6-10 miles in diameter impacting the Earth at 25,000 miles per hour[16]. The mammals rapidly diversified thereafter. About 5 million years ago, human-like animals appeared, and human fossils 100,000-150,000 years old have been found that are virtually indistinguishable from the bones that you carry around each day in your flabby sack of flesh. Descriptions of the multitude of species that have inhabited this planet during the last three and a half billion years are detailed in many texts (e.g. *The Book of Life*[17]).

The fossil record provides a glimpse of more than the history of life on Earth, though. It also allows us to understand *why* the forms of life on Earth changed[18]. This is possible because the geologic record contains both fossils and evidence of environmental changes that were occurring at the same time. Combining the fossil information with the environmental information reveals a recurrent three-step theme; (1) long periods of ecologic stability characterized by insignificant changes in plant and animals species were interrupted by (2) environmental disruptions caused by natural forces, such as climate change or meteor impacts, that induced mass extinctions, followed by (3) the rapid emergence of a multitude of new species that were significantly different from their predecessors.

Noah Way

The nearly four billion year old history of life on Earth found in the fossil record is a thorn in the side of Young Earth Creationists. It is not surprising, therefore, that they have identified a catastrophe of biblical proportions that rapidly deposited the entire fossil record several thousand years ago; Noah's flood. Although geologists disproved Flood Geology in the early 1800's, long before

Darwin came along, creationists resurrect Flood Geology on occasion in the hopes that no one will remember its prior demise. The exaggeration of the extent and effects of Noah's flood demonstrates how creationists spin the scriptures to promote their agenda.

References
1. Kenneth Miller; Finding Darwin's God—A Scientist's Search for Common Ground Between God and Evolution; 1999, Cliff Street Books, Harper Collins; New York, NY; 31-48
2. Niles Eldredge; The Triumph of Evolution and the Failure of Creationism; Henry Holt and Company; 2000; New York, NY; 32-61
3. Patricia Vickers Rich, Thomas Hewitt Rich, Mildred Adams Fenton, Carroll Lane Fenton, The Fossil Book—A Record of Prehistoric Life, Dover Publications Inc. Mineola, New York, 1996, 2
4. Richard Fortey; Fossils—the Key to the Past, Third Edition, Smithsonian Institution Press, Washington, D.C. in Association with the Natural History Museum, London, 2002
5. Peter Andrews, John Barber, Michael Benton, Marianne Collins, Christine Janis, Ely Kish, Akio Morishima, J. John Sepkoski, Jr., Christopher Stringer, Jean-Paul Tibbles; The Book of Life—An Illustrated History of the Evolution of Life on Earth, general editor Stephen Jay Gould, W.W. Norton and Co., New York, NY, 2001
6. Peter Andrews, John Barber, Michael Benton, Marianne Collins, Christine Janis, Ely Kish, Akio Morishima, J. John Sepkoski, Jr., Christopher Stringer, Jean-Paul Tibbles; The Book of Life—An Illustrated History of the Evolution of Life on Earth, general editor Stephen Jay Gould, W.W. Norton and Co., New York, NY, 2001, 33-35
7. Patricia Vickers Rich, Thomas Hewitt Rich, Mildred Adams Fenton, Carroll Lane Fenton; The Fossil Book—A Record of Prehistoric Life, Dover Publications Inc. Mineola, New York, 1996, 40-44
8. Donald R. Prothero, Robert H. Dott, Jr.; Evolution of the Earth, Seventh Edition, McGraw Hill Higher Education, 2004, 86-99
9. Ernst Mayr, What Evolution Is, Basic Books, New York, NY, 2001, 19
10. Patricia Vickers Rich, Thomas Hewitt Rich, Mildred Adams Fenton, Carroll Lane Fenton; The Fossil Book—A Record of Prehistoric Life, Dover Publications Inc. Mineola, New York, 1996, 3-11
11. Associated Press, Wed. Jan. 12, 2005, "Discovery Proves Mammal Ate Dinosaur" on www.foxnews.com, "Fossil shows baby dinosaur in mammal's belly" on www.cnn.com
12. Niles Eldredge; The Triumph of Evolution and the Failure of Creationism; Henry Holt and Company; 2000; New York, NY; 32-61
13. Niles Eldredge; The Triumph of Evolution and the Failure of Creationism; Henry Holt and Company; 2000; New York, NY; 32-36
14. Carl Zimmer; Evolution—The Triumph of an Idea, HarperCollins Publishers, 2001, Introduction by Stephen Jay Gould, 128-129
15. Carl Zimmer; Evolution—The Triumph of an Idea, HarperCollins Publishers, 2001, Introduction by Stephen Jay Gould, 70-71
16. Peter D. Ward, Donald Brownlee; Rare Earth—Why Complex Life Is Uncommon in the Universe, Copernicus, Springer-Verlag New York, Inc., New York, NY, 2000, 157-189
17. Peter Andrews, John Barber, Michael Benton, Marianne Collins, Christine Janis, Ely Kish, Akio Morishima, J. John Sepkoski Jr., Christopher Stringer, Jean-Paul Tibbles; The Book of Life—An Illustrated History of Life on Earth, W.W. Norton and Company, general editor Stephen Jay Gould, New York, NY, 2001
18. Niles Eldredge; The Triumph of Evolution and the Failure of Creationism; Henry Holt and Company; 2000; New York, NY; 47-56
19. Appendix C

Appendix I.
The Process of Evolution

Stephen Jay Gould's recent one-paragraph summary of the evolutionary process is a testimony to its elegance. "Public difficulty in grasping the Darwinian theory of natural selection cannot be attributed to any conceptual complexity—for no great theory ever boasted such a simple structure of three undeniable facts and an almost syllogistic inference therefrom…First, that all organisms produce more offspring than can possibly survive; second, that all organisms within a species vary, one from the other; third, that at least some of this variation is inherited by offspring. From these facts, we infer the principle of natural selection; since only some offspring can survive, on average the survivors will be those variants that, by good fortune, are better adapted to changing local environments. Since these offspring will inherit the favorable variations of their parents, organisms of the next generation will, on average, become better adapted to local conditions."[1]

David Quammen introduced his recent National Geographic article with a concise two-paragraph summary that links microevolution and macroevolution[2]. "The gist of the concept is that small, random, heritable differences among individuals result in different chances of survival and reproduction—success for some, death without offspring for others—and that this natural culling leads to significant changes in shape, size, strength, armament, color, biochemistry and behavior among the descendents. Excess population growth drives the competitive struggle. Because less successful competitors produce fewer surviving offspring, the useless or negative variations tend to disappear, whereas the useful variations tend to be perpetuated and gradually magnified throughout a population.

"So much for one part of the evolutionary process, known as anagenesis, during which a single species is transformed. But there's also a second part, known as speciation. Genetic changes sometimes accumulate within an isolated segment of a species, but not throughout the whole, as that isolated population adapts to its local conditions. Gradually it goes its own way, seizing a new ecological niche. At a certain point is becomes irreversibly distinct—that is, so different that its members can't interbreed with the rest. Two species now exist where formerly there was one. Darwin called that splitting-and-specializing phenomenon the "principle of divergence." It was an important part of his theory, explaining the overall diversity of life as well as the adaptation of the individual species."

Need a bit more detail than that? Niles Eldredge's five-paragraph summation of how evolution may work ties together microevolution and macroevolution as influenced by a wide range of events, from subtle evolutionary changes to traumatic extinction and speciation events induced by global mass extinctions[3]. (For the sake of clarity and brevity, Eldredge's references to detailed examples in his book have been removed from the following excerpt from *The Triumph of Evolution and the Failure of Creationism*.)

"On the smallest scales, with little or no environmental disruption and little ecological perturbation, local populations of different species within local ecosystems undergo normal processes of mutation and natural selection, but selection will be for the most part for the status quo. However, different populations of the same species living in adjacent ecosystems will undergo slightly different mutational and selection histories, and in this way genetic diversity within a species as a whole may increase through time.

"Ecological disruptions of local ecosystems (e.g., damage by fires, storms, oil spills) kills off many individuals within local populations and triggers the normal processes of ecological succession, with pioneer species dominating early assemblages, and species characteristic of later (mature) stages coming in later. Ecosystems are reassembled through recruitment from outlying populations, adaptations already in place are utilized, and little if any evolutionary change occurs.

"Longer-term ecological disruption (as, for example, when glaciers invade temperature zones from higher latitudes) disrupt ecosystems even further; in response, species engage in habitat tracking, collapsing toward the Tropics in search of suitable (recognizable) habitat. Yet even in these times of great environmental change, ecosystem disruption, and displacement of species, natural selection remains dominantly stabilizing as long as species can continue to identify and occupy suitable habitat...

"Only when environmental stress reaches a threshold—when ecological systems are so severely stressed that they can no longer survive—and when habitat tracking is not an option for many species, does extinction begin to claim many regionally distributed species, clearing the way for rapid speciation events in many separate lineages...According to the fossil record, most evolutionary change in the history of life occurs in conjunction with these physically induced episodes of ecological stress and extinction. Here, natural selection becomes strongly directional, as new species, with new adaptations, develop rapidly.

"Finally, at the grander geographic scales—up to and including the entire Earth—environmental disruption is so severe, and extinction occurs on such grand scale, that entire large-class arrays of species—taxa such as families, orders and classes—may go extinct, triggering...the rapid diversification of other lineages, which in many cases are clearly ecological replacements for the lineages that had succumbed to extinction..."

Eldredge acknowledges the lack of scientific unanimity on the details and the on-going debate over a multitude of issues, but reminds us that science has reached a clear consensus—life has evolved and continues to evolve[4]. The process of evolution is the best scientific model that explains the changes of life on Earth[5].

Not a Know-It-All

There are many questions that evolution can explain only in part, or cannot yet explain at all, or may never be able to explain. How did life begin? Why are proteins composed solely of left-handed amino acids? What is the exact relationship of every species to every other species in the tree of life? What is the exact sequence of steps by which complex organs evolved? What are the precise mechanisms by which species have originated? Why did the Cambrian Explosion occur when it did, and why did so many body architectures emerge at that time? Exactly how many genes are in iguana DNA? What are all of the functions of every gene in the genome? Carl Zimmer's recent Discover cover story on human evolution was presented in terms of the big questions that remain unanswered, *Great Mysteries of Human Evolution—New Discoveries Rewrite the Book on Who We Are and Where We Came From*[6]. Who was the first hominid? Why do we walk upright? Why are our brains so big? Why aren't our heads getting bigger (ask your wife this question as your next baby comes barreling down her birth canal, she'll clue you in)? When did we first use tools? How did we get modern minds? What genes make us human? Have we stopped evolving? Evolutionists are well aware of the unsolved mysteries of life and the incomplete nature of evolutionary science. Stephen Jay Gould, for example, in his role as general editor of a book on evolution, entitled his introduction *A Flawed Work in Progress*[7]. While most scientists remain convinced that our closest relatives are chimps, Jeffrey Schwartz maintains that orangutans may be our closest cousins[8]. After all, orangutans not only resemble humans with respect to bones, teeth, brain asymmetries, and behavior, but they also have hairlines, grins, and long-term male-female relationships!

The responsibility of science is to identify and solve—even in part—these and other mysteries of life. They are chipping away at these problems, and it may take decades or centuries to resolve the remaining issues. Profoundly difficult problems, like the origin of life, may never be fully understood. Other puzzles, like the left-handedness of proteins, may be a bit easier to handle in that mineral surfaces[9] and an amino acid (serine)[10] possess properties that may have favored the selection of left-handed amino acids over right-handed ones. Some issues seem to be more contentious than others. For example, sociobiologists have made tremendous strides in explaining the influence of evolution on social behavior of animals and people[11], but not all scientists agree on how evolution has shaped human behavior. Despite these disputes, evolution remains the best idea for explaining the history and processes of life because it is supported by a preponderance of the evidence. No other idea is even close to providing such a comprehensive and testable explanation of life. Evolution has triumphed over its rivals and critics because it fits the scientific data concerning life's history and provides an explanation of how these changes occurred.

Intelligent Design advocates will encourage you to place your faith in the continued inability of scientists to resolve these issues. These Intelligent Design proponents have decided that inexplicable miracles are responsible for many of the changes found in our fossil and genetic records. Case closed. You should be reluctant to take their bait. The church has a long and pathetic history of pronouncing natural mysteries to be supernatural wonders, only to be embarrassed thereafter when the natural causes are revealed. Creationists don't even realize it, but their alleged biblical prohibition on the evolution of life has already become the next great example of well-intentioned but misguided attempts to deduce science from scripture. There simply is nothing ungodly or unintelligent about creating a universe in which life evolved under the scrutiny of the laws of nature.

References

1. Peter Andrews, John Barber, Michael Benton, Marianne Collins, Christine Janis, Ely Kish, Akio Morishima, J. John Sepkoski, Jr., Christopher Stringer, Jean-Paul Tibbles; The Book of Life—An Illustrated History of the Evolution of Life on Earth, general editor Stephen Jay Gould, W.W. Norton and Co., New York, NY, 2001, Introduction by Stephen Jay Gould, xii
2. David Quammen, Was Darwin Wrong? No., National Geographic, Nov. 2004, 2-35
3. Niles Eldredge; The Triumph of Evolution and the Failure of Creationism; Henry Holt and Company; 2000; New York, NY, 87-88
4. Niles Eldredge; The Triumph of Evolution and the Failure of Creationism; Henry Holt and Company; 2000; New York, NY, 88-89
5. Appendix Q
6. Carl Zimmer, Great Mysteries of Human Evolution—New Discoveries Rewrite the Book on Who We Are and Where We Came From, Discover 24(9), September 2003, 34-43
7. Peter Andrews, John Barber, Michael Benton, Marianne Collins, Christine Janis, Ely Kish, Akio Morishima, J. John Sepkoski, Jr., Christopher Stringer, Jean-Paul Tibbles, The Book of Life—An Illustrated History of the Evolution of Life on Earth, general editor Stephen Jay Gould, W.W. Norton and Co., New York, NY,2001, 1-5
8. Jeffrey Schwartz, The Red Ape—Orangutans and Human Origins, revised and Updated, Westview Press, 2005
9. Robert M. Hazen, "Life's Rocky Start," from Scientific American, in The Best American Science and Nature Writings, Natalie Angier, editor, Houghton Mifflin Company, New York, 2002, 137-147
10. Serine Flavors the Primordial Soup, edited by William G. Schilz and Melissa Braddock, Chemical and Engineering News of the Week, C&EN, August 11, 2003, 5
11. John Alcock, The Triumph of Sociobiology, Oxford University Press, 2001

Appendix J. What Some Famous Evolutionists Think of God, Faith, Christians and the Bible

Criticisms of the Genesis account may be no more than short and sweet dismissals of the first chapters of the Bible. For example, Linda Gamlin begins her illustrated and informative book on evolution by describing a multitude of creation myths, including the seemingly contradictory versions found in Genesis One and in the subsequent chapters involving the Garden of Eden. Her message is clear; the Bible is just like any other creation legend, and "religious authorities" realize that these stories should be viewed as "valuable lessons on how people should live, rather than as factual accounts of how life on Earth actually began"[1].

Some of the most prominent evolutionists of our time have taken great pleasure in drawing more caustic atheistic or anti-Christian conclusions from their studies of evolutionary theory. Kenneth Miller, an evolutionist who is also Christian, has documented statements from evolutionists that clearly reveal their skepticism of the existence of God, the legitimacy of spirituality, the integrity of God's word, and the divine purpose of life[2]. A quick look at quotes from some distinguished scientists (many of which have been previously highlighted in Miller's text) is illuminating because it demonstrates that some scientists relish the opportunity to rip into the Bible, faith and Christianity.

Richard Dawkins, a brilliant zoologist and author of several exceptional books on evolution[3-5] pulls no punches while expressing his contempt for religion. Frankly, I find such honest contempt refreshing compared to the patronization of spirituality offered up by many of his peers. Many of Dawkins' objections concerning those who have used the Bible to achieve selfish goals are obviously correct, and some of his criticisms of Catholicism date back to the Reformation. Dawkins has nothing but animosity for any organized religion, however, not just Catholicism. Responding to those who question the motives behind such disdain, he replies in blunt tones, "I am often asked why I am so hostile to 'organized religion'. My first response is that I am not exactly friendly toward disorganized religion either. As a lover of truth, I am suspicious of strongly held beliefs that are unsupported by evidence: fairies, unicorns, werewolves, any of the infinite set of conceivable and unfalsifiable beliefs epitomized by Bertrand Russell's hypothetical teapot orbiting the sun. The reason organized religion merits outright hostility is that, unlike belief in Russell's teapot, religion is a powerful, influential, tax-exempt and systematically passed on to children too young to defend themselves[6]." In other words, Christ is no more credible than Tinkerbell, which is why Christian parents brainwash their children at such an early age. Even missionaries earn no respect from Dawkins, who attributes the fruits of their labor to scientific gadgets, "Admittedly, religious missionaries have successfully claimed converts in great numbers all over the undeveloped world. But they succeed not because of the merits of their religion but because of the science-based technology for which it is pardonably, but wrongly, given credit.[7]". Maybe Dawkins is right. Perhaps St. Paul was passing out penicillin pills on his missionary journeys back in the first century between his stonings and shipwrecks. Maybe I should start mailing generators, toasters, PCs and chainsaws to the missionaries that my church supports. Dawkins simply refuses to acknowledge or debate the scriptural, prophetic, historical evidence concerning Christ, choosing instead to present the gospel in terms of offensive attributes of people contaminated with faith. In describing a mind infected with religion, Dawkins tells us[8] that the symptoms of the virus include holding "a conviction that doesn't seem to owe anything to evidence or reason", making "a positive virtue of faith's being strong and unshakable, in spite of not being based upon evidence", believing that "it is a virtue to not solve mysteries", finding "himself behaving intolerantly towards vectors of rival faiths", acknowledging that "the beliefs you hold so passionately would have been a completely different and largely contradictory set of convictions, if only you had happened to be born in a different place", attributing your conversion to a belief other than that of your parents (a rare disorder) to "a particularly potent infective agent, a John Wesley, a Jim Jones, a St. Paul", or admitting that emotional religious experiences are "startlingly similar to those more ordinarily associated with sexual love". Dawkins simply doesn't think much of faith, either[9]. "Faith is such a successful brainwasher in its own favour, especially a brainwasher of children, that it is hard to break its hold. But what, after all, is faith? It is a state of mind that leads people to believe something—it doesn't matter what—in the total absence of supporting evidence. If there were good supporting evidence then faith would be superfluous, for the evidence would compel us to believe it anyway." It appears that atheism can impart a healthy brainwashing as well, because Dawkins' explanation of faith is sheer nonsense. Christianity is built upon the foundation of Christ's miracles, teachings, sinless walk, atoning death, resurrection and ascension, coupled with the transformed lives of the disciples, the baptism of the Holy Spirit at Pentecost, and the explosive growth of the early church. Christ Himself voiced frustration after His resurrection that people were so slow to believe despite the scores of prophecies[10, 11] that verified His identity as the Son of God. *Luke 24:25-27 He said to them, "How foolish you are, and how slow of heart to believe all that the prophets have spoken! Did not the Christ have to suffer these things and then enter his glory?" And beginning with Moses and all the Prophets, he explained to them what was said in all the Scriptures concerning himself.* Thomas was presented with indisputable physical evidence of Christ's resurrection, but he still had to demonstrate his faith in Christ's authority and salvation, and did so by proclaiming *John 28:20 Thomas said to him, "My Lord and my God!"* No matter, though, because Dawkins has set his sights higher than debunking the faith of mere mortals. After patiently explaining the scientific rationale for evolution while pointing out the errors of creationist (which is fine with me), Dawkins reached grandiose spiritual conclusions concerning the moral fabric of the universe[12], declaring "The universe that we observe has precisely the properties we should expect if there is, at bottom, no design, no purpose, no evil and no good, nothing but blind, pitiful indifference." Speaking of the improbability that a fully formed organ such as the eye could spontaneously appear as a fully functional organ, Dawkins couldn't resist the temptation to eradicate a fully functional God as well[13], saying "The same applies to the odds against the spontaneous existence of any fully fashioned, perfect and whole beings, including—I see no way of avoiding the conclusion—deities." A little advice for those contemplating writing weekly fund-raising letters for creationists: include a quote from Dawkins in every issue—you'll be set for the next ten years!

Stephen Jay Gould, a brilliant evolutionist and prolific author who died in 2003, wrote an eloquent book that seemed to embrace religion and science in non-overlapping roles[14], but let his true colors show when he referred to the embracing love of God[15, 16] as "just a story we tell ourselves". Gould clearly sought to deflate our spiritual delusions of grandeur[17], stating "Evolution substituted a naturalistic explanation of cold comfort for our former conviction that a benevolent deity fashioned us in his own image to have dominion over the entire earth and all other creatures—and that all but the first five days of earthly history have been graced by our ruling presence. In evolutionary terms, however, humans represent but one tiny twig on an enormous and luxuriantly branching tree of life…" In addition to assuming that believers are not only insignificant in the grand scheme of life and naïve enough to assume that the Earth was made in six 24-hour days, Gould also assured us that there was no significance attached to our appearance[18], "For our favored and well tested theory, Darwinian natural selection, offers no solace or support for these traditional hopes about human necessity or cosmic importance."

William Provine, an eminent biologist at Cornell University, has succinctly dismissed the notions of life after death and moral absolutes. He concluded that "Modern science directly implies that there are no inherent moral or ethical laws...We must conclude that when we die, we die, and that is the end of us...There is no way that the evolutionary process as currently conceived can produce a being that is truly free to make moral choices."[19]

Richard Lewontin is a renowned evolutionary biologist and an avid believer in materialism that has no room or need for the Almighty[20,21], saying "Moreover, that materialism is absolute, for we cannot allow a Divine Foot in the door." Neither does he condone the notion of truth revealed by the God of the Bible as long as he and his buddies are around to lead the public to the god of science[22,23], proclaiming "The primary problem is not to provide the public with the knowledge of how far it is to the nearest star and what genes are made of...Rather, the problem is to get them to reject irrational and supernatural explanations of the world, and demons that exist only in their imaginations, and to accept a social and intellectual apparatus, Science, as the begetter of truth." According to Lewontin, even Jesus couldn't get it right when He explained the power of spiritual truth[24,25]! *John 8:31-32 To the Jews who had believed him, Jesus said, "If you hold to my teaching, you are really my disciples. Then you will know the truth, and the truth will set you free."* Lewontin's commentary on these verses is truly enlightening, "It is not the truth that sets you free. It is your possession of the power to discover the truth."

Edward Wilson, a Pulitzer Prize winning Harvard University biologist who has studied the biological foundation of social behavior in animals, has determined that[26] "...the final decisive edge enjoyed by scientific naturalism will come from its capacity to explain traditional religion, its chief competitor, as a wholly material phenomenon." Wilson considers the emergence of God in the human society as an evolutionary event that any behavioral scientist, even one from another planet, would recognize because our worship of God bears an uncanny resemblance to monkeys deferring to a dominant male monkey[27,28], "Behavioral scientists from another planet would notice immediately the semiotic resemblance between animal submission behavior on one hand and human obeisance to religious and civil authority on the other. They would point out the most elaborate rites of obeisance are directed at the gods, the hyper-dominant if invisible members of the human group." Wilson has also assured us that the conquest of religion by science is already complete[29], "Material reality discovered by science already possesses more content and grandeur than all religious cosmologies combined."

Other evolutionists have a slightly different conviction concerning the foundation of all religions; a fear of death. In their outstanding book on human longevity, Olshansky and Carnes conclude that the teachings of modern religion concerning eternal life and paradise are no more than a modest innovation on ancient Asian legends of long life that attempted to soothe the universal human fear of aging and death[30], saying "The notion that paradise is not only real but is also accessible to everyone is a common theme among these early legends. Later, the major religions modified this theme to incorporate a paradise that was accessible only after death, and even then one that was restricted to those whose lives had been governed by the values of their religion".

Even proponents of evolution that believe in a personal God are targeted as creationists in evolutionist's clothing. Frederick Crews' essay on creationist attempts to save us from Darwinism[31] asserts that the God of Christianity could not have used mutation and selection as a tool in fashioning life, as asserted by Kenneth Miller in his book *Finding Darwin's God*. Crews said that[32] "The God who entrusted his will entirely to mutation and selection can hardly be the one who, as Miller alleges, presented the Hebrews with an ethical guidebook, 'knowing exactly what they would understand'; who transformed himself into a man so as to settle accounts in his ledger of human sin; who 'has a plan for each of us'; and who has endowed us with 'immortal souls.' As a fruit of a keen scientific mind, *Finding Darwin's God* appears to offer the strongest corroboration yet of William Provine's infamous rule, if you want to marry Christian doctrine with modern evolutionary biology, 'you have to check your brains at the church-house door.'". Crews closes his essay with a pathetic misrepresentation of the Bible's teaching on man's responsibilities on Earth and relationship with God coupled with an unabashed tree-hugging session[33], declaring "Today, when we have burst from six million to six billion exploiters of a biosphere whose resilience can no longer be assumed, the time has run out for telling ourselves that we are the darlings of a deity who placed nature here for our convenience. We are the most resourceful, but also the most dangerous and disruptive, animals in this corner of the universe. A Darwinian understanding of how we got that way could be the first step toward a wider ethics commensurate with our real transgressions, not against God but against Earth itself and its myriad forms of life."

Steven Pinker, a cognitive scientist, also has an explanation for the illusion of God. Apparently He is nothing more than a problem-solving mental package shaped by natural selection that served our backward ancestors well. Unfortunately, we are stuck with this antiquated "God module" that tends to make us believe in the Almighty. Fortunately for us, Pinker has lifted himself above these cloaks of evolutionary clutter and has enlightened us by explaining[34, 35] "why a mind would evolve to find comfort in beliefs it can plainly see are false."

Some scientists aren't bashful about bashing the scriptures as well! After all, if God does not exist, how can the Bible be His Word? Richard Dawkins sweeps away the Bible's integrity by explaining that the virgin birth of Christ was cooked up to fulfill a mistranslated prophecy, as any "Christian scholar" knows[36]. Dawkins has also made a silly criticism of one of Christ's promises[37], "Faith cannot move mountains (though countless generations of children are solemnly told the contrary and believe it)." Does Dawkins really think that Christ was talking about plate tectonics when He made the following statement, *Matthew 17:20...I tell you the truth, if you have faith as small as a mustard seed, you can say to this mountain, 'Move from here to there' and it will move. Nothing will be impossible for you.* I wonder if he also thinks that Christians should glow in the dark because Jesus told His disciples *Matthew 5:14 You are the light of the world.*

Dawkins is not alone in his smug refutations and distortions of the Bible. Jonathan Marks informs us[38] that the genealogical connection between humans and apes threatens some because it "seems to go against the biblical narrative—but so do a lot of things", such as the English and Spanish languages not originating at the foot of the Tower of Babel. He also explains that Jesus could not have been threatened by Herod's massacre of the infants because the census of Quirinius, which motivated Joseph and Mary's return to Bethlehem, occurred ten years after Herod the Great had died. Marks also informs us that a "reasonably sophisticated audience" appreciates that the Exodus narrative is just another myth that was established to justify the priestly caste of the male descendents of Aaron[39]".

Stephen Jay Gould, in his role as editor of an outstanding text on the history of life on Earth entitled *The Book of Life*, wasted no time in mocking the Book of Life described in the Book of Revelation. In the introduction to this text[40], Gould provides us with yet another inspiring atheistic devotional, "...following the completion of the blessed millennium (the 1,000-year future reign of Christ, not the secular stretch that we have just entered in the year 2000), the "*dead shall be raised incorruptible*"—to appear before God's throne in a Last Judgment that shall allocate the good guys to heaven and relegate the less worthy to the fiery inferno where, in compensation, they may at least enjoy the eternal company of history's truly interesting characters. God, we are further told, will make his judgment by reading our deeds from an opened book that just happens to bear the same title as this work—so I feel especially wary about the reissue of this volume. Indeed, I'd better watch out, and neither shout nor pout, for you never know who might be coming to town." Gould revealed his contempt for Christianity by christening a new edition of a wonderful book that celebrated four billion years of life on Earth by mocking the Bible on page one.

While Mark Parehk makes it clear that he can neither prove nor disprove the existence of a supernatural God, he does find flaws and inconsistencies in the allegedly historic events of the trial and crucifixion of Jesus[41]. Immediately after accusing Christians[42] of believing the gospels only because "of the indoctrination received in their childhood", Parehk presents remarkable insights into the innermost thoughts of people he never met based on his assumption, or perhaps childhood indoctrination, that they certainly would be really nice and polite to Jesus and never break a law, "The Pharisees who controlled the Sanhedrin had no reason to take Jesus' activities seriously[43]." "The case against Jesus was not serious enough to merit at the supreme court of the land[44]." "It is implausible that they [the Sanhedrin] would transfer Yeshua [Jesus], a Jew, to the Roman authorities for punishment[45]." "It is hard to believe that the elders of the Sanhedrin would conduct any business on the evening of that day, since, according to Jewish law, the Sabbath begins on Friday evening[46]." And my favorite, "Even if Yeshua were found guilty by the Sanhedrin, they would do everything possible to shield him from the Romans, and if they chose to punish him, it would be done by their own means. These means would never include death on a cross[47]."

Let's see if I can put all of these spiritual insights of famous evolutionists together for you dummy Christians in a short atheistic evolutionist creed.

"There is no God. He is no more than a mirage that numbs our fear, pain, loneliness, grief, guilt, stupidity and shallowness. He is an obsolete problem-solving mental package. He is the Great Invisible Monkey that we fear and revere! He is a way for religious power brokers to justify their existence. He is the symptom of a powerful mind virus from a home infected with religion; the indelible image from our early childhood brainwashing! He is a way to clear our conscience as we exploit the planet. The incredibly large number of galaxies in the universe and species on Earth proves that God could not exist, let alone care for us. After all, no decent deity would permit cute guppies to struggle for survival. God is just a state of mind that leads us to believe anything as long as we have no supporting evidence! Even the gospel of Christ is preposterous because the Pharisees were really a bunch of good old boys that would have actually protected Jesus from the Romans rather than handing him over to be crucified!"

This appendix contains just a small sampling of quotes that reveal the disdain that many popular scientists harbor toward any and all things religious. Michael Ruse's new book provides another collection of quotes from Dawkins, Coyne, Gould and Wilson that will irritate Christian believers to no end[48]. Can anyone seriously wonder why so many Christians—not just creationists—instantly equate evolution with atheism? It seems that notable scientists from every branch of science feel compelled to tell us their own special reasons that God does not exist, with each painting his viewpoint as the only conclusion that anyone with half a brain would reach. Perhaps if scientific organizations like the AAAS would hammer the anti-Christian bias of these researchers as vigorously as they expose creationist pseudo-science, the American public would not be so reluctant to accept the overwhelming body of evidence that substantiates the history and process of evolution.

I Assume I Am Right

All of these outstanding scientists have made significant contributions to our understanding of the evolution of life. They routinely clean the clocks of creationist critics when it comes to the history and processes of evolution. But there is no need to be intimidated by their attempts to exert their influence in the spiritual arena. These folks cannot detect God with the tools of their trade. They refuse to even consider the thought of God revealing Himself through the Word of God, the person of Christ or the Holy Spirit. They simply assume that a Creator cannot exist and then massage their research findings until they confirm their atheistic bias. As a result, their grandiose spiritual insights are not quite as impressive or persuasive as their well-documented scientific studies of the history and process of evolution. For example, some biologists who have studied the social behavior of animals may tell us that humans were the first animals imaginative enough to invent God. So what? I think that humans were the first critters smart enough to realize that He exists. Scientists may inform us that humans were so afraid of death that they resorted to inventing a God who dispenses eternal life. Big deal! It is perfectly natural to fear death because we know in our spirit that we will stand before God when we die. Cosmologists may tell us that the universe has been swirling about for billions of years without the need for an infinitely lazy or useless Creator. Really? I think scientists envy a God capable of Big Banging a universe into existence with both hands tied behind His back while they struggle to repair their garbage disposals. Religious authorities may argue that human spirituality is our feeble intellect's way of accounting for the origins of nature. Why would that be? I think that God created everything in accordance with the laws of nature and we can't help but marvel at His glorious creation. Evolutionists may teach us that God is our imagination's pathetic means of dealing with grief, loneliness and despair. That's funny; I seem to notice that atheists seem to have their own share of human misery because they refuse to accept the grace of God. Scientists may warn us that sin is a concept employed by the intellectually challenged to explain their shortcomings. Well, if these geniuses are so darn smart, why are their personal lives and family affairs as messed up as those of the idiot believers that they criticize?

Save the Baby, Dump the Bathwater

There is no reason to shy away from the idea that we are an evolutionary and spiritual triumph. Creating a universe in which life
could evolve should be considered a stroke of God's genius rather
than a sign that He is out to lunch. Nonetheless, if you spend any
amount of time exploring the creation vs. evolution debate in a
bookstore or on the Internet, you will encounter other proofs that
God does not exist authored by intelligent, well-regarded, scientists. You shouldn't get too bent out of shape, though; intellectual
attacks on God are nothing new. The Apostle Paul faced skeptic
scholars thousands of years ago, and concluded, *1 Corinthians 1:17-
24 For Christ did not send me to baptize, but to preach the gospel—not
with words of human wisdom, lest the cross of Christ be emptied of its
power. For the message of the cross is foolishness to those who are perish-
ing, but to us who are being saved it is the power of God. For it is written: "I will destroy the wisdom of the wise; the intelligence of the intelligent I will frustrate." Where is the wise man? Where is the scholar? Where
is the philosopher of this age? Has not God made foolish the wisdom of
the world? For since in the wisdom of God the world through its wisdom
did not know him, God was pleased through the foolishness of what was
preached to save those who believe. Jews demand miraculous signs and
Greeks look for wisdom, but we preach Christ crucified: a stumbling block
to Jews and foolishness to Gentiles, but to those whom God has called, both
Jews and Greeks, Christ the power of God and the wisdom of God. Or, if
you prefer, the Reader's Digest version; Psalm 14:1…The fool says in his
heart, "There is no God."…*

But don't be so naïve as to think that all scientists are proponents of atheism or that the science of an unbeliever is wrong
because he has made a spiritual error or holds an offensive political view. The *historical* and *mechanistic* aspects of evolution are hard
science even though the *philosophical* and *spiritual* claims that some
skeptics associate with evolution are hardly science. Creationists
advise us to shun anything even remotely associated with evolution
as a result, as if we had no ability to discern between scientific
information and spiritual nonsense. I find it a bit hypocritical that
the same creationists who encourage Christians to maintain confidence in the Bible while setting aside the moral, intellectual and
doctrinal failures of some preachers will discourage Christians

from recognizing sound evolutionary science while setting aside the spiritual biases of individual researchers. Face it, just because someone has atheistic tendencies does not mean that they cannot excel in science. When I was naked, sweating, delirious, and screaming in the midst of my first kidney stone attack (yes, it was a very ugly event), I wanted the very best health care professionals in the ER to greet my ambulance! I didn't care if they were Castro-loving, God-hating, dope-smoking, tree-hugging atheists; I just wanted a really good doctor to get that boulder out of my ureter. Likewise, you just can't deny that arrogant, atheistic, sin-stained, anti-Christian evolutionists may also be incredibly brilliant scientists who excel in their explorations of the history and process of evolution.

References
1. Linda Gamlin; Evolution, Doring Kindersly, New York, 2000, 6
2. Kenneth Miller; Finding Darwin's God—A Scientist's Search for Common Ground Between God and Evolution; 1999, Cliff Street Books, Harper Collins; New York, NY; 165-191, 269-285
3. Richard Dawkins; The Selfish Gene, Oxford University Press, New York, NY, 1989 (first edition 1976)
4. Richard Dawkins; The Blind Watchmaker—Why the Evidence of Evolution Reveals a Universe Without Design, W.W. Norton and Company, 1996 (first edition1986)
5. Richard Dawkins; The Extended Phenotype—The Long Reach of the Gene, 1999 (first edition 1982)
6. Richard Dawkins; A Devil's Chaplain—Reflections on Hope, Lies, Science and Love, Houghton Mifflin, 2003, 117-118
7. Richard Dawkins; A Devil's Chaplain—Reflections on Hope, Lies, Science and Love, Houghton Mifflin, 2003, 15
8. Richard Dawkins; A Devil's Chaplain—Reflections on Hope, Lies, Science and Love, Houghton Mifflin, 2003, 137-144
9. Richard Dawkins; The Selfish Gene, Oxford University Press, 1989, New York, 330
10. Josh McDowell; Evidence That Demands a Verdict—Vol. 1, Campus Crusade for Christ, 1973
11. Josh McDowell; The New Evidence That Demands a Verdict, Thomas Nelson Publishers, Nashville
12. Richard Dawkins; River Out of Eden; HarperCollins 1995; New York, NY; 132-133
13. Richard Dawkins; The Blind Watchmaker—Why the Evidence of Evolution Reveals a Universe Without Design, W.W. Norton and Company, 1996 (first edition1986), 317
14. Stephen Jay Gould; Rocks of Ages—Science and Religion in the Fullness of Life; Ballantine Books, 1999; 1-10
15. Kenneth Miller; Finding Darwin's God—A Scientist's Search for Common Ground Between God and Evolution; 1999, Cliff Street Books, Harper Collins; New York, NY, 170
16. Transcript of the program CBS Sunday Morning on Nov. 29, 1998. The interviewer was Rita Braver.
17. Stephen Jay Gould, in the Introduction to: Carl Zimmer, Evolution—The Triumph of an Idea, Harper Collins Publishers, 2001, New York, xi
18. Stephen Jay Gould, in the Introduction to: Carl Zimmer, Evolution—The Triumph of an Idea, Harper Collins Publishers, 2001, New York, xii
19. W. Provine; Evolution and the Foundation of Ethics; MBL Science 3; 1988; 25-29
20. Richard Lewontin; Billions and Billions of Demons, New York Review of Books, January 9, 1997, 28-32
21. Phillip E. Johnson; Reflection 2, in Three Views on Creation and Evolution, J.P. Moreland and J.M. Reynolds, General Editors, 1999, Zondervan Publishing House, Grand Rapids Michigan, 267-271
22. Richard Lewontin; Billions and Billions of Demons, New York Review of Books, January 9, 1997, 28-32
23. Phillip E. Johnson; Reflection 2, in Three Views on Creation and Evolution, J.P. Moreland and J.M. Reynolds, General Editors, 1999, Zondervan Publishing House, Grand Rapids Michigan, 267-271
24. Richard Lewontin; Billions and Billions of Demons, New York Review of Books, January 9, 1997, 28-32
25. Phillip E. Johnson; Reflection 2, in Three Views on Creation and Evolution, J.P. Moreland and J.M. Reynolds, General Editors, 1999, Zondervan Publishing House, Grand Rapids Michigan, 267-271
26. Edward O. Wilson; On Human Nature, Harvard University Press, 1978, 192
27. I. Barbour; When Science Meets Religion, Enemies, Strangers or Partners; Harper Collins, 2000, 154-156
28. Edwin O. Wilson, Consilience—The Unity of Knowledge, Knopf, New York, 1998, 259
29. Edwin O. Wilson, Consilience—The Unity of Knowledge, Knopf, New York, 1998, 265
30. S. Jay Olshansky and Bruce A. Carnes, The Quest for Immortality—Science at the Frontiers of Aging, W.W. Norton and Company, New York, 2001, 46
31. Frederick C. Crews, Saving Us from Darwin, New York Review of Books, October 4 and 18, 2001; The Best American Science and Nature Writings, Natalie Angier, editor, Houghton Mifflin Company, New York, 2002, 34-57
32. Frederick Crews; Saving Us From Darwin, in The Best American Science and Nature Writings, Natalie Angier, editor, Houghton Mifflin Company, New York, 2002, 53
33. Frederick C. Crews; Saving Us from Darwin, The Best American Science and Nature Writings, Natalie Angier, editor, Houghton Mifflin Company, New York, 2002, 57
34. Steven Pinker; How the Mind Works, W.W. Norton, New York, 1997, 30,555
35. Kenneth Miller; Finding Darwin's God—A Scientist's Search for Common Ground Between God and Evolution; 1999, Cliff Street Books, Harper Collins; New York, NY; 165-191, 285
36. Richard Dawkins; The Selfish Gene, Oxford University Press, 1989, New York, 270
37. Richard Dawkins; The Selfish Gene, Oxford University Press, 1989, New York, 330
38. Jonathan Marks; What It Means to be 98% Chimpanzee—Apes, People and Their Genes, University of California Press, Berkeley, CA, 2002, 254-255
39. Jonathan Marks; What It Means to be 98% Chimpanzee—Apes, People and Their Genes, University of California Press, Berkeley, CA, 2002, 246-247
40. Peter Andrews, John Barber, Michael Benton, Marianne Collins, Christine Janis, Ely Kish, Akio Morishima, J. John Sepkoski, Jr., Christopher Stringer, Jean-Paul Tibbles; The Book of Life—An Illustrated History of the Evolution of Life on Earth, general editor Stephen Jay Gould, W.W. Norton and Co., New York, NY, 2001, 1
41. Mark Perakh, Unintelligent Design, Prometheus Books, Amherst New York, 2004,237-241
42. Mark Perakh, Unintelligent Design, Prometheus Books, Amherst New York, 2004, 239
43. Mark Perakh, Unintelligent Design, Prometheus Books, Amherst New York, 2004,239

44. Mark Perakh, Unintelligent Design, Prometheus Books, Amherst New York, 2004,239
45. Mark Perakh, Unintelligent Design, Prometheus Books, Amherst New York, 2004,240
46. Mark Perakh, Unintelligent Design, Prometheus Books, Amherst New York, 2004,240
47. Mark Perakh, Unintelligent Design, Prometheus Books, Amherst New York, 2004,240
48. Michael Ruse; The Evolution-Creation Struggle, Harvard University Press, Cambridge, MA, 2005, 201-213

Appendix K.
A Better Big Bang

When first proposed, the Big Bang model represented a grand achievement for describing the early moments of the universe, but it was not the complete package. For example, the expansion of the universe was correlated to its original density. This density value was seemingly unconstrained to any particular value and was therefore treated as a free parameter—a fudge factor of sorts. As it turns out, if the original density value had been a bit larger, the universe would have collapsed upon itself before galaxies could have formed. A bit smaller and the universe would have expanded too quickly for galaxies to ever form. But our Baby Bear universe was just right! It seemingly had the perfect density when it started out because we live on a pleasant planet in a stable solar system in a slowly swirling galaxy. Just one second after the Big Bang, the density of the universe was within 0.0000000000001% of the perfect value[1]! This fortuitous tuning of an adjustable parameter has been cited as a classic example of supernatural Intelligent Design because the odds of it happening randomly were incomprehensibly small, and only God was around to do the adjusting[2].

This apparent "tuning" of the Big Bang also puzzled Alan Guth. Rather than chalking it up to God adjusting the density button on

His universal remote control, Guth realized that the original Big Bang model of the universe was correct—but incomplete. He then revolutionized our understanding of the earliest moments of the universe by describing a remarkably fast burst of expansion, which he coined "inflation", that occurred right after the Big Bang. About 10^{-37} seconds after the Big Bang, the universe began to double in size every 10^{-37} seconds while its density remained constant. During this inflationary expansion, the universe expanded at a rate that exceeded the speed of light! (No, this is not a violation of the speed-of-light speed limit associated with the theory of relativity because the universe itself was expanding faster than the speed of light, not objects traveling within the universe.) The universe was emerging out of what we non-physicist folk call "nothing." After 100 dou-blings, 10^{-35} seconds had elapsed and the vast universe that we can detect today was only 1 meter in radius^3. The expansion rate then smoothly and quickly slowed to the value predicted by the original Big Bang model. A startling consequence of this inflation was that the original density of the universe did not have to be adjusted or tuned at all; the inflationary expansion actually drove the density of the universe to the perfect value regardless of its value prior to infla-tion[4,5]! In other words, there was no need for the intelligent design of an adjustable parameter after all—the forces of nature pushed the expansion to the perfect value!

Does this mean that God does not exist or that the Bible is a myth, especially because Guth considers Genesis to be no more than a "story we were told when we were young."?[6]. Not at all! I believe that it demonstrates that God is a lot brighter than most of us dare to imagine. Guth himself noted that Andrei Linde, an influ-ential cosmologist who ironed out a few of the loose ends of the inflationary model while developing a new inflationary universe scenario[7,8], ascribed the genesis of the universe to God's use of an elegant and natural inflationary expansion. Linde said "I just had the feeling that it was impossible for God not to use such a good possibility to simplify His work, the creation of the universe."[9,10]. I like Linde's perspective; a really intelligent God might actually look for an elegant and simple way to make a universe rather than a convoluted, complex, smoke-and-mirrors scheme. (Believers need to be cautious about trumpeting quotes of physicists attributing something to "God" with no further clarification of that term;

"God" oftentimes means something quite different than the God of the Bible in such contexts.)

How Can Nothing Produce Something?

About 14 billion years ago, the universe emerged out of nothingness. There were no stars, no planets, and no pizzas. There wasn't even empty space. But our intuition and the laws of nature tell us that energy cannot just appear. The total energy of the universe must be conserved, according to the First Law of Thermodynamics, and if the universe was originally nothing then the total mass and energy in the universe today should still be zero. (Remember that mass can be considered as condensed energy via Einstein's famous equation, $E=mc^2$, where c is a very large constant, the speed of light.) But the universe is bursting with energy, such as the solar radiation that bathes our planet, and it is sprinkled with mass, including planets, comets, stars, and pizza. How could all of this mass and energy come from nothing? Isn't that a violation of the First Law of Thermodynamics? Don't we need a making-something-out-of-nothing miracle to get the ball rolling?

No! Another less familiar form of energy, gravitational potential energy, must be accounted for[11]. Unlike mass and energy, energy stored in a gravitational field is considered negative[12] because energy is released when a gravitational field is formed. This unusual feature allows the "negative" amount of energy in a gravitational field to cancel out "positive" amount of energy and mass, yielding a total energy of zero. Therefore the universe could have emerged from what most of us call "nothing" *without violating the laws of nature*. This led Guth to conclude, "Conceivably, everything can be created from nothing."[13] From Guth's perspective, the universe can be considered as the "ultimate free lunch"[14]; a description that drives creationists bonkers.

Why Did the Big Bang Go Bang?

Although the moment of creation did not have to violate the laws of nature, there is no generally accepted or experimentally verified scientific explanation of the event itself. This remains one of the great mysteries of nature. The first notable proposal to sort out the physics of the moment of creation was championed by Edward Tryon in 1973, who suggested that the universe emerged out of "nothing" as the product of an incredibly small yet powerful event called a vacuum fluctuation[15]. Physicists, the ultimate geeks, have shown us that nothing is actually something when it comes to vacuum fluctuations. In the realm of the tiniest sub-atomic particles, probability is the rule of law. Unlike bricks, whose position and velocity can be readily ascertained, inherent uncertainties are associated with the position or velocity of such miniscule particles. Even their very existence is uncertain, because they can literally emerge out of nothing for a fleeting moment and then disappear again! For example, these fugitives may be an electron and its anti-particle, the positron. They may hang around for only a billionth of a trillionth of a second while separated by a millionth of a millionth of a meter before disappearing into nothingness[16]. The brief appearance of such incredibly small particles has even been measured indirectly, but how could a vast and ancient universe arise from such a subatomic percolation? As it turns out, the lifetime of that which emerges out of nothing gets longer as the particles get smaller. To create something really substantial like a universe that can exist for billions of years, the mass would have to be 10^{-65} grams, a mass which is 10^{38} times smaller than the mass of a single electron. Even if this "solution" to the question of what happened at the very moment of the Big Bang has merit, it only pushes the mystery of creation back even further. If indeed the universe emerged as a fluctuation out of a seething broth of nothingness, where did the nothingness and its pop-up particles come from?

In 1982 Alexander Vilenkin combined the concept from general relativity that the geometry of space is deformable with the concept of quantum mechanics and suggested that a tiny system can suddenly make a discontinuous transition from one state to another as long as the conservation laws are not broken. He suggested that the universe emerged out of a nothing that really was nothing (no matter, no space, and no time) by instantaneously transforming itself into a subatomic universe. Vilenkin then invoked Guth's inflationary expansion to explain how such a small universe could quickly grow to its vast proportions[17].

Stephen Hawking and James Hartle have painted another picture of the beginning of the universe. In their model, "nothingness" is not imposed on the origination of the universe because the universe is "something", and the constraint of a prior condition of "nothingness" may be unnecessary. As time is reversed there is neither an eternal past nor a creation moment. At times less than 10^{-43} second, the fabric of the universe was "dissolving into quantum ambiguity[18]". The universe "would neither be created nor destroyed. It would just BE.[19]"

Don't Get Strung Out

The Big Bang model may be a great model of the early universe, but it is not the ultimate model of the universe's origin. While the Big Bang model points to a somewhat discomforting origination from an infinitely dense, infinitely hot and infinitely small point, "string theory"[20,21] models elementary particles as infinitely thin one-dimensional loops that cannot be smaller than 10^{-34} meters. According to string theory, nothing—including the universe at the moment of Big Bang—can be smaller than this irreducible quantum length. The consequences of this model indicate that the Big Bang marked the transition from a pre-Big Bang era in which the "universe could have begun almost empty and built up to the bang, or it might have even gone through a cycle of death and rebirth."[20] In other words, our observable universe may have had an origin at the Big Bang, but it may have been *preceded* by another universe. How can anyone hope to know if the string theory is more accurate than the Big Bang? Is it just a metaphysical mystery without a hard, scientific basis? Hardly! The great theoretical promise of the string theory model is its potential to reconcile relativity with quantum mechanics at the moment of creation. What about experimental proof? The events that preceded the Big Bang may have left a discernible impression in the cosmic background radiation temperature and may have also produced a random background of gravitational waves. If either of these effects can be experimentally gleaned in the future, it will provide a direct indication of the merits of the String Theory. Don't hold your breath, though. No one is capable of discerning these traces experimentally. It is likely to be a long, long, long time before this ever happens, *if* it ever happens!

Portrait or Landscape?

Recently, Leonard Susskind[22] has shown how string theory can lead to a natural explanation for the seemingly miraculous set of finely tuned parameters that have enabled intelligent life (that's you, dummy!) to form. These "just right" values seem to scream of Intelligent Design, because if they were "off" by just a tad, life could not have formed anywhere in the known universe. Is there any other option other than "dumb luck" or an "Intelligent Designer" to explain our existence in a human-friendly universe? Yes, says Susskind! He explains that M-theory (the newest and coolest version of string theory) does not point to a single set of laws of physics. It actually provides a launching pad for 10^{500} different sets of laws representing 10^{500} opportunities for life nestled within 10^{500} other "pocket universes" in a vast megaverse. This number is so incredibly large that having "just right" or "fine-tuned" parameters in at least one universe seems to be more inevitable than immaculate! Even the incredible precision of the cosmological constant, the hallmark of Intelligent Design, doesn't seem so remarkable in this context. Susskind calls this smorgasbord of environments in distinct universes as the "Landscape". If he is right, then string theory yields every possible type of universe, and it should surprise no one that there is at least one human-friendly universe (ours)! This Anthropic Principle (the idea that the universe must be fine-tuned for human development because otherwise we wouldn't be thinking about this stuff) is commonly refuted as creationist nonsense by most scientists, but not Susskind! He views string theory as the pathway to 10^{500} different universes. From this perspective, it may be an inevitable result (rather than dumb luck) that the parameters of physics would be right for life in at least one of them—ours!

No Way!

If you are like me, you may want to believe that a supernatural act caused the Big Bang because it is so much easier to believe in a miracle than to understand what these crazy cosmologists are talking about! Maybe God sneezed and sprayed out a universe! Unfortunately, the Bible tells us nothing about how He made the heavens, other than providing imagery that He indeed did it, such as the following verses. *Psalm 33:6 By the word of the LORD were the heavens made, their starry host by the breath of his mouth. Jeremiah 32:17 Ah, Sovereign LORD, you have made the heavens and the earth by your great power and outstretched arm. Nothing is too hard for you.* But what if God said "Bang"? What if He simply let nature take its course? There is no reason to presume that the creation of the universe was not influenced by the wiles of random events or manifested in the Big Bang or rapidly expanded by inflation or briefly muddled in quantum ambiguity! Who (other than creationists desperate to prove God exists or atheists anxious to prove that He doesn't) honestly thinks that they have the authority to tell God what rules He must have followed when He created the universe? I know that the thought of God using chance events to bring forth something marvelous is repulsive to some Protestant theologians[23], but unless they discover the secret eleventh commandment found in II Shenanigans 4:14, "Thou shalt not indulge in quantum physics", I would suggest they get over it. Richard Colling is right, God is a lot smarter than we think[24]. I seriously doubt if His best ideas resemble the step-by-step instruction sheets stuffed inside of bicycle boxes that creationists consider to be the hallmarks of creative design. Stephen Hawking is right when he encourages scientists to forge a scientific understanding of the very moment of creation[25]. They may not be successful, but there is nothing evil, unspiritual, or threatening about their efforts.

Even if scientists unravel all of the mysteries of the early universe and iron out all of the wrinkles of the Big Bang model, an even deeper mystery awaits their attention. As phrased by Guth in the closing sentence of his book on the inflationary universe, "What is it that determined the laws of physics?"[26] Perhaps some of you would feel more comfortable if that question was modified to read, "*Who* is it that determined the laws of physics?" But the Bible says nothing about the origin of the laws of physics, either, so why ascribe them to the supernatural? God may have had an even better idea rooted in a mysterious natural phenomenon. And what if someone, somewhere, someday is bright enough to figure out the perfect model of the universe? What if science one day provides a clue as to why the universe exists at all? Will God be out of business? Stephen Hawking has suggested another possibility, "However, if we do discover a complete theory, it should in time be understandable in broad principle by everyone, not just a few scientists. If we find the answer to that, it would be the ultimate triumph of human reason. For then we would know the mind of God."[27] What if Leonard Susskind is right? What if there are an almost infinite number of universes? Who are we to think that each one does not belong to God and may be yet another reflection of His glory—even if they are void of life?

Therefore before joining the ranks of those who consider investigations of the universe's origin to be offensive, ungodly or dangerous, perhaps you should ask yourself a few questions, such as "Is my faith in God so weak that I must attempt to refute cosmologists' understanding of the first 10^{-30} second of the universe's existence, even if I have absolutely no idea what they are talking about?", or "Should my faith rest in the inability of scientists to understand events that occurred during the Planck era[28], the first 10^{-43th} second after the Big Bang, when the known forces of nature (the strong nuclear force that hold atomic nuclei together, the weak force that controls radioactive decay, the gravitational force that pulls objects together and the electromagnetic force) were unified in a single force?"

Just let the scientists explore. They are only figuring out what happened when God made our universe, even if they never realize or acknowledge it.

References
1. Alan H. Guth; The Inflationary Universe—The Quest for a New Theory of Cosmic Origins, Helix Books, Perseus Books, Addison-Wesley, Reading MA, 1997, 17-31
2. G.L. Schroeder; The Science of God; Simon and Schuster; New York, NY; 1997; 26
3. Alan H. Guth; The Inflationary Universe—The Quest for a New Theory of Cosmic Origins, Helix Books, Perseus Books, Addison-Wesley, Reading MA, 1997, 185
4. Alan H. Guth; The Inflationary Universe—The Quest for a New Theory of Cosmic Origins, Helix Books, Perseus Books, Addison-Wesly, Reading MA, 1997, 167-187
5. Brad Lemley; Guth's Grand Guess; Discover, April 2002, 32-39
6. Brad Lemley; Guth's Grand Guess; Discover Magazine, April 2002, 32-39
7. Andrei Linde; A New Inflationary Universe Scenario—A Possible Solution of the Horizon, Flatness, Homogeneity, Isotropy, and Primordial Monopole Problem, Physics Letters, 108B, 389-392 (1982)
8. Alan H. Guth; The Inflationary Universe, Addison-Wesley, Reading, Massachusetts, 1997, 201-212
9. Alan H. Guth; The Inflationary Universe, Addison-Wesley, Reading, Massachusetts, 1997,206
10. Alan Wrightman and Roberta Brawer; Origins—The Lives and Worlds of Modern Cosmologists, Harvard University Press, Cambridge, Massachusetts, 1990
11. Alan H. Guth; The Inflationary Universe—The Quest for a New Theory of Cosmic Origins, Helix Books, Perseus Books, Addison-Wesly, Reading MA, 1997, 9-12
12. Alan H. Guth; The Inflationary Universe—The Quest for a New Theory of Cosmic Origins, Helix Books, Perseus Books, Addison-Wesly, Reading MA, 1997, 289-293
13. Alan H. Guth; The Inflationary Universe—The Quest for a New Theory of Cosmic Origins, Helix Books, Perseus Books, Addison-Wesly, Reading MA, 1997, 15
14. Alan H. Guth; The Inflationary Universe—The Quest for a New Theory of Cosmic Origins, Helix Books, Perseus Books, Addison-Wesly, Reading MA, 1997, 15
15. .Alan H. Guth; The Inflationary Universe—The Quest for a New Theory of Cosmic Origins, Helix Books, Perseus Books, Addison-Wesly, Reading MA, 1997, 271-276
16. .Alan H. Guth; The Inflationary Universe—The Quest for a New Theory of Cosmic Origins, Helix Books, Perseus Books, Addison-Wesly, Reading MA, 1997, 272
17. Alan H. Guth; The Inflationary Universe—The Quest for a New Theory of Cosmic Origins, Helix Books, Perseus Books, Addison-Wesly, Reading MA, 1997, 273-275
18. Alan H. Guth; The Inflationary Universe—The Quest for a New Theory of Cosmic Origins, Helix Books, Perseus Books, Addison-Wesly, Reading MA, 1997, 275
19. Stephen W. Hawking; A Brief History of Time—From the Big Bang to Black Holes, Bantam Books, New York, 1988, 136
20. Gabriele Veneziano; The Myth of the Beginning of Time, Scientific American, My 2004, 54-65
21. Maurizio Gasperini, Gabriele Veneziano; The Pre-Big Bang Scenario in String Cosmology, Physics Reports 373 (1-2) 1-212, January 2003
22. Leonard Susskind, The Cosmic Landscape—String Theory and the Illusion of Intelligent Design, Little, Brown and Company, New York, NY, 2006
23. R.C. Sproul; Not a Chance—The Myth of Chance in Modern Science and Cosmology, Baker Books, Grand Rapids, Michigan, 1994
24. Richard G. Colling; Random Designer—Created from Chaos to Connect with the Creator, Browning Press, Bourbonnais, Illinois, 2004, 108
25. Stephen Hawking; The Universe in a Nutshell, Bantam Books, New York, NY, 2001, 7
26. Alan H. Guth; The Inflationary Universe—The Quest for a New Theory of Cosmic Origins, Helix Books, Perseus Books, Addison-Wesly, Reading MA, 1997, 276
27. Stephen Hawking; The Theory of Everything, New Millenium Press, Beverly Hills, CA, 2002,167
28. Neil deGrasse Tyson and Donald Goldsmith, Origins—Fourteen Billion Years of Cosmic Evolution, W. W. Norton & Company, New York, NY, 2004, 25-29

Appendix L.
How Life on Earth May Have Formed from Stuff on Earth

No one yet knows how life on Earth began, but there are a few ideas being kicked around based on the composition of living organisms.

The Ingredients

Six Pack of Elements

All life, from bacteria to babies, is based almost entirely on six elements: carbon, hydrogen, oxygen, nitrogen, sulfur, and phosphorus. Although hydrogen was formed early in the history of the universe, the other heavier atoms were formed in the furnaces of supernova explosions—gigantic explosions that marked the death of stars. Life could not have formed until these atoms were first manufactured and then accumulated in the young Earth[1-3]. Although carbon, hydrogen, oxygen and nitrogen constitute 99.9% of living organisms, the relatively small contributions of sulfur and phosphorus are critical. For example, the molecules of heredity, DNA and RNA, are linked together by chemical groups containing phosphorus.

Liquid Water

All life requires and retains water. Bacteria, for example, are 75% water and the first life was probably just as soggy. Even my own kids were sloshing about in a small, warm, salty, ocean for nine months before they were born! This proliferation of liquid water in living systems is undoubtedly a testament to the aqueous environs in which life first formed[47]. Ice is too cold and rigid to foster life, and steam is not dense enough to dissolve large molecules, therefore life probably did not form until liquid water was available on Earth's surface. Liquid water would have been a strong enough solvent to dissolve compounds while also being fluid enough to facilitate the movement of dissolved molecules, enabling them to interact with one another.

Amino Acids and Proteins

There are 20 standard amino acids found in living organisms. Each one is composed of carbon, hydrogen, oxygen and nitrogen, although two also contain sulfur. Each amino acid has an amine group on one end, an acid on the other, and a small chemical structure in between that makes it unique. Each amino acid is available in two, mirror-image configurations—left-handed and right-handed—that have the same composition but a non-superimposable arrangement (just like your left and right hands). Amino acids can react with one another to make long molecules referred to as proteins, while simultaneously forming water. Proteins contain only left-handed amino acids that are joined together in a characteristic order, but it takes more than the correct composition to make the protein useful. Its potency is also attributed to its folded architecture because, just like a key, a protein becomes useless when it unfolds or gets bent out of shape. Thousands of different proteins play a multitude of roles in your body. They are the working machinery of each cell. They serve as the structural framework of hair, fingernails, skin and corneas. They are the UPS of your metabolism, carrying oxygen in the blood and transporting sugar into cells. Some proteins, referred to as enzymes, act as catalysts that make the reactions of life happen quickly at body temperature.

Sugars and Carbohydrates

Sugars are made of carbon, hydrogen and oxygen. Glucose and fructose are examples of simple sugars. Table sugar, sucrose, is a disaccharide composed of glucose and fructose. Long polymeric forms of sugar are referred to as carbohydrates. Starch, for example, contains hundreds of simple sugars. Animals use sugars for energy, while plants manufacture very long sugar molecules, such as cellulose, that provide structural support.

Lipids and Membranes

Lipids, such as waxes, fats, oils and cholesterol, are easily distinguishable from the other building blocks of life because they do not mix with water. Therefore lipids are found in cell membranes because it easier for them to surround the water-rich interior of the cell than to dissolve in it. Cell membranes hold a cell together and act as the border patrol, protecting the cell's interior from unwelcome intruders while permitting welcome guests to enter and exit. The nuclear membrane within a cell separates the nucleus from the surrounding fluid in the cytoplasm.

Nucleotides and Nucleic Acids

A nucleotide is a sugar with a phosphoric acid on one side and one of five organic bases, referred to as C, U, T, G and A, on the other. Nucleotides can link up to form nucleic acids—long chains of sugar and phosphate linkages with the organic bases dangling off to the side. DNA, which contains the sugar deoxyribose, is concentrated in the nucleus of a cell. It is made of two nucleic acids wrapped around each other in a right-handed, double-helical geometry resembling a twisted ladder. The rungs of the DNA ladder are composed of a pair of bases, one extending from each of the helical backbones. Only four organic bases occur the DNA molecule, C, G, A and T. C joins with G while A pairs up with T. Let's imagine that we can climb the helical DNA ladder within a human cell to appreciate the role of DNA. There are four types of rungs that you may encounter as you look at each rung from left-to-right; C-G, G-C, A-T, and T-A. A sequence of three rungs, or codon, has enough information to define one of the natural amino acids[5, 6]. As you continue climbing, you should memorize the sequence of amino acids because you will be using that information to make a protein. Unfortunately, this task is complicated in human DNA because a great number of extraneous rungs are scattered throughout the protein-encoding rungs[7]. When you finally reach the codon that signals you to stop, it indicates that you have just climbed the thousands of rungs that constitute a single gene, the segment of DNA that encodes at least one protein. As you continue climbing, you will find that the genes are separated by substantial segments of seemingly irrelevant repeating sequences[8] and important DNA segments that can turn a gene on or off[9]. Eventually you will reach the end of the last gene on the DNA ladder, indicating that you have traversed an entire chromosome. Had you been climbing a small human chromosome, such as number 20, you would have counted 66 million base pairs, only 1.5% of which were responsible for encoding 747 genes[10]. Having decoded one chromosome is noteworthy, but there are 23 pairs of chromosomes in most human cells, one pair from Dad and the other from Mom. The human genome, one set of 23 chromosomes[11], is composed of three billion base pairs that were first thought to encode 35,000 or so genes[12], but more recent estimates of the number of protein-encoding genes being closer to 20,000[13].

The other molecule of heredity is RNA, which appears in the form of a single strand. The nucleotides that constitute RNA are a sugar (ribose), phosphoric acid and the bases C, G, U and A. RNA serves to carry out the instructions found in the DNA[14]. For example, enzymes and three forms of RNA accomplish the manufacture of proteins from the information in the chromosomes during several steps. First, the DNA ladder splits along the joined base pairs. Roving nucleotides in the cell nucleus match up with the exposed protein-encoding base codons, assembling a strand of mRNA. C and A in the exposed strand of unwinding DNA match with G and U, respectively, in mRNA. After the DNA information is downloaded, the mRNA moves from the nucleus to the portion of the cell outside of the nucleus (the cytoplasm). Ribosomes (themselves composed of rRNA) read the mRNA codon data, and tRNA molecules deliver the appropriate amino acid to the growing protein chain of amino acid links. When the "stop" triplet is reached, the folded chain of amino acids is complete and a protein has been produced.

The Hardest Part is Getting Started

How did these molecules of life form in the first place? How did life of Earth begin? Researchers continue to postulate scenarios that could have yielded the monomers and polymers of life[15]. Most scientists are convinced that the reactions yielding the building blocks of life occurred in the ocean waters before life emerged. Methods of forming these compounds at conditions reminiscent of the early Earth have been proposed and demonstrated by numerous investigators, as recently summarized by Stanley Miller and Antonio Lazcano[16]. In the early 1950's, Stanley Miller mixed several gases (methane, ammonia, water and hydrogen) thought to have been prevalent in the Earth's atmosphere in a piece of glassware that housed a small puddle and two electrodes. Electric discharges between the electrodes provided the energy that encouraged the gases to react. No guppies, bacteria, or sea monkeys appeared, but a mixture of compounds that included some amino acids did[17]! A flurry of experiments followed, each seeking to determine if other building blocks of life could form by letting chemistry take its course. Sparks, radiation, heat and pressure were used to simulate ancient solar radiation, lightning and shock waves that were available as energy sources billions of years ago. Variations in ingredients, temperature and pressure were used to reflect different models of the Earth's evolving atmosphere and ocean. The result? Rather than the handful of amino acids identified by Miller, nearly all of the naturally occurring amino acids have shown up. Further, in 1960 John Oro pioneered the abiotic (not made by a living organism) synthesis of A (adenine), one of the organic bases found in the nucleotides that join to form DNA and RNA[18]. The manufacture of other bases followed. Chemical pathways for the production of ribose, another component of nucleic acid, have also been identified. The brew was probably even peppered with abiotic organic compounds tucked away inside of comets, dust, asteroids and carbon-containing meteorites that impacted the Earth[19].

Recently, extreme conditions have been considered as the birthplace of life. The waters of the early Earth passed through the porous ocean floor and were heated under pressure by underlying magma bodies and then emerged from vertical openings on the ocean floor[20]. Although the small building blocks of life may have formed in this manner, there is no evidence that simply zapping or heating an aqueous solution can crank out the large polymers of life.

Who Was First?

Which macromolecule of life formed first anyway? It is difficult to imagine that life began with DNA because DNA requires proteins to assemble it. Likewise it is hard to imagine that life started with proteins because they cannot duplicate information without DNA. Therefore Francis Crick (who along with James Watson discovered the shape of DNA) proposed that RNA preceded both proteins and DNA in the "RNA world" because of the ability of RNA to both retain information and act as a modest catalyst. If RNA was able to somehow catalyze its own replication, then neither proteins nor DNA may have been required to get life rolling[21]. This replicator could have started the chain of events[22], leading from the RNA world to the RNA-protein world to the DNA-RNA-protein world that characterizes life as we know it[23]. This early role of RNA in the replication of genetic information may also explain why the information in DNA passes through an RNA intermediate during its replication rather than proceeding through a more efficient pathway; the RNA intermediate may be a remnant of evolutionary history of life[24].

It's a Dirty Job, But Someone Has to Do It

Although no one yet knows how a biomolecule like RNA could have formed, scientists are investigating the formation of the polymers of life[25]. The chemistry must include energy and water. Although water is a good solvent, it also inhibits water-producing reactions such as the formation of proteins, carbohydrates, and nucleic acids. Although the presence of a reactive group on the nucleotide may have helped things along, such activated nucleotides would have probably been inadequate for generating large polymers. Therefore many researchers think that the formation of RNA was facilitated by the catalytic surfaces of clay that were in contact with water and the building blocks of life. The role of numerous minerals in the emergence of life may have been critical because of their capability to confine, constrain, select and arrange molecules[26].

For example, hydrothermal vents along oceanic ridge crest present an opportunity for catalytic clays and minerals to react with a number of gases thought to be present in the Earth's early history[27]. In fact, some think that the role of minerals was so critical that first forms of life were not made of organic (carbon-based) compounds at all, but rather silicon-based self-replicating compounds that were capable of forming long molecules. These crystalline silicate minerals, which are found in clays, mud, and rocks, may have served as scaffolds that help to sustain organic compounds. Eventually, the organic self-replicating compounds may have become self-replicating RNA, making their inorganic predecessors obsolete[28, 29].

Those exploring these ideas on the origin on life are intimately aware of the challenges that face them. It may take them years, decades, centuries, or millennia to figure out how life began, and there is also a chance that they may never succeed. Even if they are forever stumped, that does not mean that the origin of life was miraculous! It may simply be too hard to figure out. But there is no reason for them to give up, and there is no reason to build your faith on a gut feeling that they will fail.

References
1. J. William Schopf; The What, When and How of Life's Beginnings, in Life's Origin—The Beginnings of Biological Evolution, edited by J. William Schopf, University of California Press, Berkeley, California, 2002, 1–4
2. John Oro; Historical Understanding of Life's Beginnings, in Life's Origin—The Beginnings of Biological Evolution, edited by J. William Schopf, University of California Press, Berkeley, California, 2002 27–29
3. Alan W. Schwartz, Sherwood Chang; From Big Bang to Primordial Planet: Setting the Stage for the Origin of Life, in Life's Origin—The Beginnings of Biological Evolution, edited by J. William Schopf, University of California Press, Berkeley, California, 2002, 46–50
4. J. William Schopf, When Did Life Begin? in Life's Origin—The Beginnings of Biological Evolution, edited by J. William Schopf, University of California Press, Berkeley, California, 2002, 159
5. Lynn Helena Caporale; Darwin in the Genome—Molecular Strategies in Biological Evolution, McGraw-Hill, New York, 2003, 30
6. James D. Watson with Andrew Berry; DNA—The Secret of Life, Alfred A. Knopf, New York, 2003, 75
7. James D. Watson with Andrew Berry; DNA—The Secret of Life, Alfred A. Knopf, New York, 2003, 108–109, 207
8. James D. Watson with Andrew Berry; DNA—The Secret of Life, Alfred A. Knopf, New York, 2003, 203
9. James D. Watson with Andrew Berry; DNA—The Secret of Life, Alfred A. Knopf, New York, 2003, 179
10. James D. Watson with Andrew Berry; DNA—The Secret of Life, Alfred A. Knopf, New York, 2003, 207
11. James D. Watson with Andrew Berry; DNA—The Secret of Life, Aldrew A. Knopf, New York, 2003, 164–165
12. James D. Watson with Andrew Berry; DNA—The Secret of Life, Alfred A. Knopf, New York, 2003, 195–217
13. International Human Genome Sequencing Consortium, Finishing the euchromatic sequence of the human genome, Nature, 2004, Oct. 21;431(7011): 931–945
14. James D. Watson with Andrew Berry; DNA—The Secret of Life, Alfred A. Knopf, New York, 2003, 76–78
15. J. William Schopf; When Did Life Begin? in Life's Origin—The Beginnings of Biological Evolution, edited by J. William Schopf, University of California Press, Berkeley, California, 2002, 158
16. Stanley L. Miller, Antonio Lazcano; Formation of the Building Blocks of Life, in Life's Origin—The Beginnings of Biological Evolution, edited by J. William Schopf; University of California Press, Berkeley, California, 2002, 78–112
17. Stanley L. Miller; A Production of Amino Acids Under Possible Primitive Earth Conditions, Science 1953 117:528
18. John Oro; Synthesis of Adenine from Ammonium cyanide, Biochemical and Biophysical Research Communications, 2;407–412
19. Stanley L. Miller, Antonio Lazcano; Formation of the Building Blocks of Life, in Life's Origin—The Beginnings of Biological Evolution, edited by J. William Schopf, University of California Press, Berkeley, California, 2002, 103–105
20. Jon Erickson; Plate Tectonics—Unraveling the Mysteries of the Earth, Revised Edition 2001, Checkmark Books, New York, 184,186
21. James D. Watson with Andrew Berry; DNA—The Secret of Life, Alfred A. Knopf, New York, 2003, 83–85
22. Richard Dawkins; The Selfish Gene, Oxford University Press, 1989, New York, 12–20
23. Leslie E. Orgel.; The Origin of Biologic Information, in Life's Origin—The Beginnings of Biological Evolution, edited by J. William Schopf, University of California Press, Berkeley, California, 2002, 140–157
24. James D. Watson with Andrew Berry; DNA—The Secret of Life, Alfred A. Knopf, New York, 2003, 83, 85
25. James P. Ferris; From Building Blocks to the Polymers of Life, in Life's Origin—The Beginnings of Biological Evolution, edited by J. William Schopf, University of California Press, Berkeley, California, 2002, 113–139
26. Robert M. Hazen; Life's Rocky Start, from Scientific American, in The Best American Science and Nature Writings, Natalie Angier, editor, Houghton Mifflin Company, New York, 2002, 137–147
27. Stanley L. Miller, Antonio Lazcano; Formation of the Building Blocks of Life, in Life's Origin—The Beginnings of Biological Evolution, edited by J. William Schopf, University of California Press, Berkeley, California, 2002, 100–102
28. Richard Dawkins; The Blind Watchmaker—Why the Evidence of Evolution Reveals a Universe Without Design, W.W. Norton and Company, 1996 (first edition1986), 139–166
29. Leslie E. Orgel; The Origin of Biologic Information, in Life's Origin—The Beginnings of Biological Evolution, edited by J. William Schopf, University of California Press, Berkeley, California, 2002, 151–154

Appendix M.
Embarrassaurous Yecs

Dinosaurs appear in the fossil record before birds and then shared the stage with our flying feathered friends long before mammals and mankind showed up. Young Earth Creationists are constrained to lump the dinosaurs into the same time period as mammals and man, however, because they were all supposedly made within the 144-hour creation week. Therefore creationists scour the Bible hoping to glean the slightest hint of these massive reptiles. What does the Bible say about dinosaurs? Nothing! Adam and Eve didn't ride them, Noah didn't fill his ark with them, and Moses did not have Aaron sacrifice them. The Bible has no mention of dinosaurs and people hanging out together because they died out about 65 million years ago. The absence of human remains in fossilized dinosaur dung is another indication that dinosaurs did not terrorize man. The lack of T-Rex bones in excavations of human archeological sites and the absence of T-Rex images on cave drawings also indicate that early man did not hunt dinosaurs! Lack of evidence has never stopped pseudo-science, though. Therefore creationists have developed a suite of Bible verses and scientific evidence that allegedly support the co-existence of man and dinosaur.

Exhibit A is the Bible's description of the Behemoth-saurus.

Job 40:15-24 "Look at the behemoth, which I made along with you and which feeds on grass like an ox. What strength he has in his loins, what power in the muscles of his belly! His tail sways like a cedar; the sinews of his thighs are close-knit. His bones are tubes of bronze, his limbs like rods of iron. He ranks first among the works of God, yet his Maker can approach him with his sword. The hills bring him their produce, and all the wild animals play nearby. Under the lotus plants he lies, hidden among the reeds in the marsh. The lotuses conceal him in their shadow; the poplars by the stream surround him. When the river rages, he is not alarmed; he is secure, though the Jordan should surge against his mouth. Can anyone capture him by the eyes, or trap him and pierce his nose?

Next is Exhibit B, the leviathan-asaurus.

Job 41:1-34 "Can you pull in the leviathan with a fishhook or tie down his tongue with a rope? Can you put a cord through his nose or pierce his jaw with a hook? Will he keep begging you for mercy? Will he speak to you with gentle words? Will he make an agreement with you for you to take him as your slave for life? Can you make a pet of him like a bird or put him on a leash for your girls? Will traders barter for him? Will they divide him up among the merchants? Can you fill his hide with harpoons or his head with fishing spears? If you lay a hand on him, you will remember the struggle and never do it again! Any hope of subduing him is false; the mere sight of him is overpowering. No one is fierce enough to rouse him. Who then is able to stand against me? Who has a claim against me that I must pay? Everything under heaven belongs to me. I will not fail to speak of his limbs, his strength and his graceful form. Who can strip off his outer coat? Who would approach him with a bridle? Who dares open the doors of his mouth, ringed about with his fearsome teeth? His back has rows of shields tightly sealed together; each is so close to the next that no air can pass between. They are joined fast to one another; they cling together and cannot be parted. His snorting throws out flashes of light; his eyes are like the rays of dawn. Firebrands stream from his mouth; sparks of fire shoot out. Smoke pours from his nostrils as from a boiling pot over a fire of reeds. His breath sets coals ablaze, and flames dart from his mouth. Strength resides in his neck; dismay goes before him. The folds of his flesh are tightly joined; they are firm and immovable. His chest is hard as rock, hard as a lower millstone. When he rises up, the mighty are terrified; they retreat before his thrash-

*ing. The sword that reaches him has no effect, nor does the spear or the
dart or the javelin. Iron he treats like straw and bronze like rotten wood.
Arrows do not make him flee; slingstones are like chaff to him. A club
seems to him but a piece of straw; he laughs at the rattling of the lance.
His undersides are jagged potsherds, leaving a trail in the mud like a
threshing sledge. He makes the depths churn like a boiling caldron and
stirs up the sea like a pot of ointment. Behind him he leaves a glisten-
ing wake; one would think the deep had white hair. Nothing on earth is
his equal—a creature without fear. He looks down on all that are
haughty; he is king over all that are proud."*

Creationists conveniently abandon their demands for literal
renderings of the scriptures when it comes to these two beasts. The
behemoth had bones of bronze and limbs of iron. The leviathan
had flashes of light bursting out of his nostrils, fire spewing out of
his mouth and a belly composed of broken pottery. These accounts
are figurative descriptions of two contemporary animals. The behemoth may be an elephant or hippo, while the leviathan may be a
crocodile[1,2]. Job 40 and 41 describe animals found in a local zoo,
not Jurassic Park.

Exhibit C is the dragon legend. Some creationists correlate these
tales to ancient accounts of close encounters with bad-breathed
dinosaurs!

Exhibit D, the dinosaur-adorned flag of Wales, reflects the
proud heritage of men in kilts clobbering evil dinosaurs!

Exhibit E is a fossil exhibiting human and dinosaur footprints.
Apparently early humans and dinosaurs jogged together in Texas!
Something was strange about these human footprints, though.
Upon closer examination, most of them were actually found to be
dinosaur prints, with a few chiseled frauds and erosional features
thrown in for good measure[3]. Old Earth Creationists that reject a
Young Earth timeline routinely expose the fallacies of these footprints[4], and even most die-hard Young Earth creationists have
backed away from this alleged fossil evidence[5].

Exhibit F is a dinosaur carving on the wall of the Bernifal
cave in France. Jack Cuozzo presents a photo of this carving
along with his hand-drawn sketch that makes it oh-so-obvious
that this is an artistic rendering of a dinosaur battling a mam-
moth. I'm not so sure. In Pittsburgh, we have annual sightings of

the Virgin Mary on windows, walls, pizza and refrigerators that bear a stronger resemblance to a woman than this lumpy bumpy wall does to a dinosaur[6].

References
1. Kenneth Miller; Finding Darwin's God—A Scientist's Search for Common Ground Between God and Evolution; 1999, Cliff Street Books, Harper Collins; New York, NY, 94-95
2. Hugh Ross; The Genesis Question—Scientific Advances and the Accuracy of Genesis; Navpress 1998, Colorado Springs, CO; 48
3. Robert T. Pennock; Tower of Babel—The Evidence Against the New Creationism, MIT Press, Massachusetts Institute of Technology, 2000, 216-221
4. Hugh Ross; Creation and Time—A Biblical and Scientific Perspective on the Creation-Date Controversy; NavPress Publishing Group, Colorado Springs, CO, 1994, 114-116
5. Robert T. Pennock; Tower of Babel—The Evidence Against the New Creationism, MIT Press, Massachusetts Institute of Technology, 2000, 220-221
6. Jack Couzzo; Buried Alive—The Startling Truth About Neanderthal Man, Master Books, Green Forest, AR, 132-134

Appendix N. The Fossil Record of Human Evolution

Richard Dawkins has provided a guide leading us back over three billion years to the ancestors of all life on Earth[1], while Robert Boyd and Joan Silk have provided an overview of human evolution that stretches back to small mammals resembling shrews that lived 65,000,000—55,000,000 years ago[2]. Let's look only at the past 55 million years or so in this appendix.

55,000,000—34,000,000 years ago the first primates that had modern features appeared sporting grasping hands and feet, fingernails, hind-limb-dominated postures and relatively large brains[3]. Roughly 36,000,000—33,000,000 years ago, primates in Africa that possessed several dental and cranial characteristics of contemporary monkeys appeared[4].

27,000,000—17,000,000 years ago hominoids appeared. These animals were the first that shared features with modern apes and humans, such as the lack of a tail and forward facing eyes[5]. 15,000,000—10,000,000 ago these nimble, tree-dwelling animals developed thicker enameled teeth and larger jaws and flourished and expanded into Eurasia[6].

Currently, there is relatively little fossil information dating to the period between 10,000,000—5,000,000 years ago[7], but a

well-publicized recent find in Chad[8] has uncovered 6,000,000—
7,000,000 year old fossils, including a nearly complete cranium that
was much more human-like than ape-like in appearance[9]. 5,000,000
years ago hominids, animals that had characteristics more similar to
you than an ape, appeared. They walked upright and had jaws holding an arch of thickly enameled teeth[10].

The fossil record corresponding to the last 5,000,000 years is
particularly informative, and it tells a tale of numerous species,
some of which existed at the same time, and a progressive evolution characterized in general by an increase in body size and brain
size[11-13]. Figure 1, adapted from Tattersall's figure in the book by
Tattersall and Schwartz entitled *Extinct Humans*[11], illustrates the tiny
twigs on the evolutionary tree of life that represent a simplification
of *one of many* postulated relationships between these species.

Determining the best way to classify these fossils is no easy task,
and demonstrating the evolutionary relationship between them is
even harder. There are many different trees that have been proposed
to explain human evolution, and there is a good deal of debate over
this matter. But that does not mean—as creationists imply—that
these are not actual fossils, or that there is no relationship between
these fossils, or that humans did not evolve. Like it or not, humans
did evolve, and the details of the process will continue to become
clearer with each fossil find. Keeping in mind that there are many
options other than the one shown in Figure 1, which was based on
several proposed trees of human evolution[14-17], let's take a look at our
ancestors and relatives that lived during the past four and a half million years.

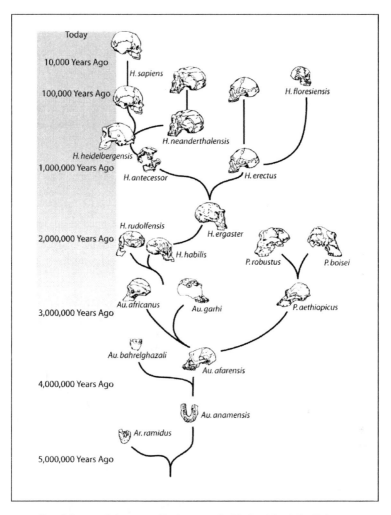

Figure 1. Human evolutionary tree with a best guess simplification of the relationship between species indicated by lines. The figure is adapted from that of Tattersall and Schwartz (Extinct Humans; Westview Press; Boulder Colorado; 2001, 244), with additional data on *H. floresiensis* from Wong (The Littlest Human, Scientific American, Feb. 2005, 64-65). Other hypothesized relationships can be found in many places, such as Kate Wong's article and a beautifully illustrated book entitled The Book of Life (The Book of Life—An Illustrated History of the Evolution of Life on Earth, general editor Stephen Jay Gould, W.W. Norton and Co., New York, NY, 2001, 230—231).

Ardipithecus ramidus fossils date back to about 4,400,000 years, and contain both hominid and apelike features[18]. 4,000,000 year old fossils of *Australopithecus anamensis* have been found. This species was similar enough to the later species *Australopithecus afarensis* to be

considered its ancestor, yet different enough in several cranial and
dental features such as small ear holes and the shape of the dental
arcade to be considered a different species[19].The oldest well-known
hominid fossils date back to 3,500,000 years ago and are classified
as *Australopithecus afarensis*; short, small-brained, bipedal, creatures that
exhibited no known tool making or hunting skills[20]. A hominid jaw
found in Chad dates to over 3,000,000 years, and has been designated as *Australopithecus bahrelghazali*[21,22]. Several species of hominids
lived between 3,000,000 and 2,500,000 years ago, including
Australopithecus aethiopicus, Australopithecus robustus, and *Australopithecus
boisei*[23]. These three species have also been classified as *Paranthropus*
rather than *Australopithecus*, and are not considered to be descendants of modern humans[24]. The other two species associated with
this period, *Australopithecus garhi* and *Australopithecus africanus*, may
have paved the way between *Australopithecus afarensis* and the bigger
brained *Homo* hominids that were to follow[25, 26]. For example,
Australopithecus africanus was similar to *Australopithecus afarensis* in
many aspects, but this species also resembled modern humans in
that they had a shorter face, a less protruding nose[27].

A notable change in the human fossil record appears roughly
2,000,000 years ago; our ancestors started to become big-headed!
Fossils in the genus referred to as *Australopithecus* had brain sizes of
just under 4/10-liter to about 6/10-liter, while modern humans
have a biggie-sized cranial capacity of 1.4 liters. The transition
began to occur roughly 2,000,000 years ago with the appearance
of various hominids referred to as the *Homo* genus[28, 29]. The earliest
human species in the *Homo* genus, *Homo habilis* and *Homo rudolfen-
sis*, were similar to *Australopithecus*, but had more humanlike teeth,
brains that could exceed the 6/10-liter size, a smaller and less protruding face, a more rounded skull, smaller jaw muscles, and a
propensity for making very simple stone tools[30]. Between 1,800,000
and 1,700,000 years ago, *Homo ergaster* showed up[31] exhibiting some
traits of the earlier species of *Homo*, some features of modern man
including a smaller face, smaller teeth, and an inner ear system, and
some unique features, such as a ridge along the top of the skull
from front to back and a horizontal ridge along the back of the
skull. *Homo ergaster* had left life in the trees behind, produced an
improved set of stone tools, had probably learned to start fires and
hunt large game. The brain size had increased to about 1-liter, and

the height of adults had increased to about 5 or 6 feet. About 1,600,000 years ago, some of the *Homo ergaster* species moved out of Africa into neighboring continents and may have subsequently evolved into *Homo erectus*, which had a big browridge and a long, thick-walled, 1000 cc skull with a bulging ridge on the back. Recently, a down-sized ancestor of *Homo erectus* was found on the island of Flores, located between Asia and Australia[32-34]. Classified as *Homo floresiensis* but nicknamed "hobbits", these 3 ½' tall adult humans lived until at least 18,000 years ago and possibly until 12,000 years ago when a volcanic eruption may have done them in! Although they lived at the same time as *Homo sapiens* in the region, but it is not yet known if these two species interacted.

Although *Homo erectus* may not be in the direct lineage of modern humans, *Homo antecessor*, which dates back 800,000 years ago is also thought to have descended from *Homo ergaster* and may be a predecessor to modern *Homo sapiens*[35]. Subsequently, several species dating between roughly 600,000 and 200,000 years ago have been lumped into *Homo heidelbergensis*, which packed a 1.2-liter, well-rounded cranium. *Homo heidelbergensis* is thought to have yielded two familiar species[36], *Homo sapiens* (you) and *Homo neanderthalensis* (your Neanderthal in-laws!).

The Neanderthals made their debut 200,000—300,000 years ago, with the earliest fossils being most similar to *Homo heidelbergensis*. Neanderthals dominated Europe and western Asia during the warm period between Ice Ages that started 130,000 years ago and lasted 50,000 years. They had very large brains, ranging in size from 1.25 to 1.75 liters! Their jaw was much larger, their face was bigger, their skull was longer and more rounded, their muscles were stronger, the roots of their teeth were more massive and their brow was more protrusive than the comparable features of *Homo sapiens*[37]. As card-carrying members of the Old Stone Age Local 306, the Neanderthals were known to wield stone tools that had been carefully chipped into shape. They may have hunted large game such as red deer, bison, sheep and goats. Neanderthals probably lived short, difficult lives, but at least they had a chance for a decent burial. It is difficult to determine whether these graves simply provided a means of getting rid of a decomposing body, or whether they also carried some social or religious meaning[38]. About 30,000 years ago, though, there were none left to bury; the Neanderthals were extinct.

Anatomically modern *Homo sapiens* with a skeleton just like yours showed up more than 100,000 years ago[39] in the Middle East and Africa, and the earliest fossils of *Homo sapiens* recently found in Ethiopia date back 160,000 years[40]. Relative to their extinct human predecessors, *Homo sapiens* have a small face with a protruding chin, a rounded skull, longer limbs and thinner-walled bones. Although their body was just like yours, the earliest *Homo sapiens* did not exhibit our cultures, traditions, technologies, symbolic behavior, social organization or religious expression at this time. They were proficient manufacturers, as evidenced by the trinkets and carefully crafted bone tools, stone lamps, and bone needles found near burial sites. Both *Homo sapiens* and *Homo neanderthalensis* lived in the Middle East roughly 90,000—60,000 years ago. This region may have served as a boundary between the two species, with the Neanderthals living there at different times during this era.

A dramatic change in human history occurred 45,000—35,000 years ago in North Africa, Europe, Northern Asia and Australia[41]. Prior to this event, termed the Great Leap Forward by Jared Diamond, man-made artifacts had shown little advancement for a million years[42]. Suddenly—on a geologic time scale—*Homo sapiens* made more intricate tools, including blades, spear-throwers, bows, arrows, and scrapers, from stone, bone and antler. These tools were so popular that the requisite raw materials such as flint were transported great distances from their source to the sites where they were made and used. The dead were buried with artifacts of their life such as clothes, tools, necklaces and art. Wondrous sculptures and spectacular paintings and engravings of human and animal forms have been found on cave walls. The artistry even conveys the movements and habits of the animals. Sophisticated shelters were constructed within small villages where small groups lived. Early appliances included pits dug into permafrost that served as heaters and fire-fueled lamps, stoves and hearths. They creatively used every scrap of animal remains. For example, humans living in colder climates ate the meat, built structural supports from bones, wrapped themselves or their homes with fur, and burned bones in hearths. Political correctness had not yet evolved, so men were out hunting while women were assigned the more mundane gathering chores, and at the end of the day everyone sat down and discussed their adventures over a shared dinner. Burials were common and elaborate, with care taken to provide the deceased with objects, perhaps being construed as useful items for the afterlife (I have always wondered if the burial of such items was early evidence of a gene on the Y-chromosome that compels men to throw things out). Simple instruments have been recovered, as have plaques inscribed with symbols. The cause of these remarkable changes has not been ascertained, although it has been attributed to both cultural and biological changes.

Somewhere along the line of human history, our unique capacity for language developed. It is difficult to say when our ancestors first used language. Some think that skulls dating back millions of years could have housed brains capable of the processing language, while others associate the human cultural revolution 40,000 years ago with the first emergence of speech[43]. Although the timing of the origin of language is uncertain, its unique place in the realm of humanity is not. Language is one of the most striking physical attributes that *Homo sapiens* possess[44], and regardless of when it originated, it was undoubtedly in use 40,000 years ago.

The emergence of *Homo sapiens* in Europe 40,000 years ago coincides with the demise of the Neanderthal. During a period of time that lasted about 13,000 years, both species inhabited Europe. Although no one can now state unequivocally why the Neanderthals became extinct, competition for the resources of this region may have been a significant contributor to their disappearance[45]. *Homo sapiens* managed to spread from Africa to all of the continents during the last 100,000 years, especially during the last 50,000 years. The late entrance into North America and South America was probably facilitated by a land bridge between Siberia into Alaska roughly 11,000—12,000 years ago.

Modern human civilization is typically lumped into the last ten millennia. About 10,000 years ago, the New Stone Age began. The agricultural revolution was advancing in the Fertile Crescent bound by the Tigris and Euphrates as the last Ice Age was receding[46]. Intricate stone tools were being fashioned by grinding and polishing. Humans apparently began to shift from a pattern of hunting and gathering to more organized production of plants and animals. Groups of humans began to settle into villages as opposed to constantly wandering. Human skills and handiwork began to become more sophisticated. Baskets were being woven from reeds and pottery was being formed. 9,000 years ago agriculture had taken root, and the production of food supplies to settled groups of people enabled societies to expand, villages to become more populous, classes of society to form, and monuments to be built. Temples and shrines were built 8,000 years ago in the center of villages in Mesopotamia. Five thousand years ago, the first form of writing, Cuneiform, was being used to record accounts of historical events. 5,000 years ago metal was being crafted, marking the beginning of the Bronze Age. 4,000 years ago, the Iron Age began. Not long thereafter, the Book of Genesis was written. 2,000 years ago the Christian Age began, 1,000 years ago the Middle Ages began, and right now you are a part of a several hundred-year old Modern Age that has seen a spectacular rapid rise in the number of humans on this planet[47].

So there you have it. A long history of our ancestors has been uncovered that stretches back millions of years. Our heritage has not been a linear progression of one species after another. Like every other species of life, human evolution is best described as a richly branching family tree in which many species have existed, some at the very same time. The human fossil record is one of the best examples of evolution—macroevolution—that has been found. Creationist attempts to discredit its message are utterly impotent. Niles Eldredge's expose of the creationists' critiques of the human fossil record[48] is summarized in a pointed statement within his closing paragraph on the subject, "That the best creationists can do with the human fossil record is to call the most recent fossils fully human, the earliest mere apes, and those in the middle—the intermediates, if you will—outright fakes is pathetic.[49]". Eldredge is absolutely correct. More sophisticated critiques offered up by Intelligent Design advocates are just as bad because they can do no more than point to uncertainties of how these species are related to one another[50]—a matter of scientific debate that evolutionists not only acknowledge but also examine in painstaking detail. As science slowly gains a clearer perspective on human evolution with each newly discovered human fossil[51-53], Intelligent Design advocates can only resort to digging up decades-old stories of fossil frauds in a futile attempt to paint any scientist that "believes" in evolution as untrustworthy.

References

1. Richard Dawkins; The Ancestor's Tale—A Pilgrimage to the Dawn of Evolution, Houghton Mifflin Company, Boston, MA, 2004
2. Robert Boyd, Joan B. Silk; How Humans Evolved, 2nd Edition, W.W. Norton & Company, New York, 2000, 297,306
3. Robert Boyd, Joan B. Silk; How Humans Evolved, 2nd Edition, W.W. Norton & Company, New York, 2000, 306–307
4. Robert Boyd, Joan B. Silk; How Humans Evolved, 2nd Edition, W.W. Norton & Company, New York, 2000, 310
5. Robert Boyd, Joan B. Silk; How Humans Evolved, 2nd Edition, W.W. Norton & Company, New York, 2000, 318
6. Robert Boyd, Joan B. Silk; How Humans Evolved, 2nd Edition, W.W. Norton & Company, New York, 2000, 319
7. Robert Boyd, Joan B. Silk; How Humans Evolved, 2nd Edition, W.W. Norton & Company, New York, 2000, 326
8. USA Today, July 11, 2002, Skull Alters Notions of Human Origins, 1, Tim Friend; Fossil Discovery Shakes Human Family Tree, 5D
9. M. Brunet, F. Guy, D. Pilbeam, H. Mackaye, A. Likius, D. Ahounta, A. Beauvilain, C. Blondel, H. Bocherens, J. Boisserie, L.De Bonis, Y. Coppens, J. Dejax, C. Denys, P. Duringer, V. Eisenmann, G. Fanone, P. Fronty, D. Geraads, T. Lehmann, F. Lihoreau, A. Louchart, A. Mahamat, G. Merceron, G. Mouchelin, O. Otero, P. Campomanes, M. De Leon, J. Rage, M. Sapanet, M. Schuster, J. Sudre, P. Tassy, X. Valentin, P. Vignaud, L. Viriot, A. Zazzo, C. Zollikofer; Nature. 418(6894):145–151, July 11, 2002
10. Robert Boyd, Joan B. Silk;, How Humans Evolved, 2nd Edition, W.W. Norton & Company, New York, 2000, 327
11. I. Tattersall, J. Schwartz; Extinct Humans; Westview Press; Boulder Colorado; 2001, 223–247
12. Robert Boyd, Joan B. Silk; How Humans Evolved, 2nd Edition, W.W. Norton & Company, New York, 2000, 326–514
13. Niles Eldredge; The Triumph of Evolution and the Failure of Creationism; Henry Holt and Company; 2000; New York, NY, 55–60
14. Kate Wong; The Littlest Human, Scientific American, Feb. 2005, 56–65
15. Robert Boyd, Joan B. Silk; How Humans Evolved, 2nd Edition, W.W. Norton & Company, New York, 2000, 341–343
16. Peter Andrews, John Barber, Michael Benton, Marianne Collins, Christine Janis, Ely Kish, Akio Morishima, J. John Sepkoski, Jr., Christopher Stringer, Jean-Paul Tibbles; The Book of Life—An Illustrated History of the Evolution of Life on Earth, general editor Stephen Jay Gould, W.W. Norton and Co., New York, NY,2001, Introduction by Stephen Jay Gould, 2–3, 186
17. I. Tattersall, J. Schwartz; Extinct Humans; Westview Press; Boulder Colorado; 2001, 102,126, 244
18. Robert Boyd, Joan B. Silk; How Humans Evolved, 2nd Edition, W.W. Norton & Company, New York, 2000, 341–343
19. Robert Boyd, Joan B. Silk; How Humans Evolved, 2nd Edition, W.W. Norton & Company, New York, 2000, 340–341
20. Robert Boyd, Joan B. Silk; How Humans Evolved, 2nd Edition, W.W. Norton & Company, New York, 2000, 326–340
21. I. Tattersall, J. Schwartz; Extinct Humans; Westview Press; Boulder Colorado; 2001, 102,126,244
22. Ian Tattersall; Becoming Human—Evolution and Human Uniqueness, 1998, A Harvest Book, Hartcourt Brace and Company, 185
23. Robert Boyd, Joan B. Silk; How Humans Evolved, 2nd Edition, W.W. Norton & Company, New York, 2000, 343–360
24. I. Tattersall, J. Schwartz; Extinct Humans; Westview Press; Boulder Colorado; 2001, 244
25. Robert Boyd, Joan B. Silk; How Humans Evolved, 2nd Edition, W.W. Norton & Company, New York, 2000, 347–349
26. I. Tattersall, J. Schwartz; Extinct Humans; Westview Press; Boulder Colorado; 2001, 244
27. Robert Boyd, Joan B. Silk; How Humans Evolved, 2nd Edition, W.W. Norton & Company, New York, 2000, 343–346,349
28. Kenneth Miller; Finding Darwin's God—A Scientist's Search for Common Ground Between God and Evolution; 1999, Cliff Street Books, Harper Collins; New York, NY, 46–47
29. Niles Eldredge; The Triumph of Evolution and the Failure of Creationism; Henry Holt and Company; 2000; New York, NY, 55–60
30. Robert Boyd, Joan B. Silk; How Humans Evolved, 2nd Edition, W.W. Norton & Company, New York, 2000, 361–369
31. Robert Boyd, Joan B. Silk; How Humans Evolved, 2nd Edition, W.W. Norton & Company, New York, 2000, 408–429
32. P.Brown, T. Sutikna, M.J. Morwood, R.P. Soejono, Jatmiko, E. Wayhu Saptomo, Rokus Awe Due; A new, small-bodied Hominin from the late Pleistocene of Flores, Indonesia Nature 431, 1055—1061 (28 October 2004); doi:10.1038/nature02999
33. M.J. Morwood, R.P. Soejono, R.G.Roberts, T. Sutikna, C.S.M. Turney, K.E. Westaway, W.J. Rink, J. X. Zhao, G.D. Van den Bergh, Rokus Awe Due, D. R. Hobbs, M.W. Moore, M.I. Bird, L.K. Fifield; Archaeology and age of a new hominin from Flores in eastern Indonesia, Nature 431, 1087—1091 (28 October 2004); doi:10.1038/nature02956
34. Kate Wong; The Littlest Human, Scientific American, Feb. 2005, 56–65
35. Robert Boyd, Joan B. Silk; How Humans Evolved, 2nd Edition, W.W. Norton & Company, New York, 2000, 436–437
36. I. Tattersall, J. Schwartz; Extinct Humans; Westview Press; Boulder Colorado; 2001, 164
37. Robert Boyd, Joan B. Silk; How Humans Evolved, 2nd Edition, W.W. Norton & Company, New York, 2000, 436–441
38. Robert Boyd, Joan B. Silk; How Humans Evolved, 2nd Edition, W.W. Norton & Company, New York, 2000, 442–450
39. Robert Boyd, Joan B. Silk; How Humans Evolved, 2nd Edition, W.W. Norton & Company, New York, 2000, 452–455
40. T.D White, B. Asfaw, D. DeGusta, H. Gilbert, G. Richards, G. Suwa, F. Howell, Pleistocene Homo sapiens from Middle Awash, Ethiopia, Nature, June 12, 2003, 742–747
41. Robert Boyd, Joan B. Silk; How Humans Evolved, 2nd Edition, W.W. Norton & Company, New York, 2000, 455–471
42. Richard Dawkins; The Ancestor's Tale—A Pilgrimage to the Dawn of Evolution, Houghton Mifflin Company, Boston, MA, 2004, 35–36

43. Robert Boyd, Joan B. Silk; How Humans Evolved, 2nd Edition, W.W. Norton & Company, New York, 2000, 489-514
44. Tattersall, I.; Becoming Human—Evolution and Human Uniqueness; Harcourt Brace, Orlando Florida, 1999,166
45. I. Tattersall, J. Schwartz; Extinct Humans; Westview Press; Boulder Colorado; 2001, 219-221
46. Richard Dawkins; The Ancestor's Tale—A Pilgrimage to the Dawn of Evolution, Houghton Mifflin Company, Boston, MA, 2004, 26-34
47. Stephen Hawking; The Universe in a Nutshell, Bantam Books, New York, NY, 2001, 156
48. Niles Eldredge; The Triumph of Evolution and the Failure of Creationism; Henry Holt and Company; 2000; New York, NY, 126-129
49. Niles Eldredge; The Triumph of Evolution and the Failure of Creationism; Henry Holt and Company; 2000; New York, NY, 128
50. Jonathan Wells; Icons of Evolution, Science or Myth, Why Much of What We Teach About Evolution is Wroing, Regnery Publishing, Washington D.C., 2000, 209-228
51. Jeffrey H. Schwartz, Ian Tattersall; The Human Fossil Record, Volume 1, Terminology and Craniodental Morphology of Genus Homo (Europe), Wiley-Liss, New York, NY, 2002
52. Jeffrey H. Schwartz, Ian Tatterasall; The Human Fossil Record, Volume 2, Craniodental Morphology of Genus Homo (Africa and Asia), Wiley-Liss, New York, NY, 2003
53. Ralph L. Holloway, Douglas C. Broadfield, Michael S. Yuan, Jeffrey H. Schwartz; The Human Fossil Record, Volume 3, Brain Endocasts: The Paleoneurological Evidence, Wiley-Liss, New York, NY, 2004

Appendix O.
Meet My Old Man

Getting a Date for Adam

Genesis genealogies can tell us approximately how long ago Adam lived.

Genesis 5:4-32 After Seth was born, Adam lived 800 years and had other sons and daughters. Altogether, Adam lived 930 years, and then he died. When Seth had lived 105 years, he became the father of Enosh. And after he became the father of Enosh, Seth lived 807 years and had other sons and daughters. Altogether, Seth lived 912 years, and then he died. When Enosh had lived 90 years, he became the father of Kenan. And after he became the father of Kenan, Enosh lived 815 years and had other sons and daughters. Altogether, Enosh lived 905 years, and then he died. When Kenan had lived 70 years, he became the father of Mahalalel. And after he became the father of Mahalalel, Kenan lived 840 years and had other sons and daughters. Altogether, Kenan lived 910 years, and then he died. When Mahalalel had lived 65 years, he became the father of Jared. And after he became the father of Jared, Mahalalel lived 830 years and had other sons and daughters. Altogether, Mahalalel lived 895 years, and then he died. When Jared had lived 162 years, he became the father of Enoch. And after he became the father of Enoch, Jared lived 800 years and had other sons and daughters. Altogether, Jared lived 962 years, and then he died. When Enoch had lived 65 years, he became the father of Methuselah. And after he became the father of Methuselah, Enoch walked with God 300 years and had other sons and daughters. Altogether, Enoch lived 365 years. Enoch walked with God; then he was no more, because God took him away. When Methuselah had lived 187 years, he became the father of Lamech. And after he became the father of Lamech, Methuselah lived 782 years and had other sons and daughters. Altogether, Methuselah lived 969 years, and then he died. When Lamech had lived 182 years, he had a son. He named him Noah and said, "He will comfort us in the labor and painful toil of our hands caused by the ground the LORD has cursed." After Noah was born, Lamech lived 595 years and had other sons and daughters. Altogether, Lamech lived 777 years, and then he died. After Noah was 500 years old, he became the father of Shem, Ham and Japheth.

To bridge the timeline between Noah and Abram (Abraham), we need to skip ahead a few chapters to Genesis 11.

Genesis 11:10-26 This is the account of Shem. Two years after the flood, when Shem was 100 years old, he became the father of Arphaxad. And after he became the father of Arphaxad, Shem lived 500 years and had other sons and daughters. When Arphaxad had lived 35 years, he became the father of Shelah. And after he became the father of Shelah, Arphaxad lived 403 years and had other sons and daughters. When Shelah had lived 30 years, he became the father of Eber. And after he became the father of Eber, Shelah lived 403 years and had other sons and daughters. When Eber had lived 34 years, he became the father of Peleg. And after he became the father of Peleg, Eber lived 430 years and had other sons and daughters. When Peleg had lived 30 years, he became the father of Reu. And after he became the father of Reu, Peleg lived 209 years and had other sons and daughters. When Reu had lived 32 years, he became the father of Serug. And after he became the father of Serug, Reu lived 207 years and had other sons and daughters. When Serug had lived 30 years, he became the father of Nahor. And after he became the father of Nahor, Serug lived 200 years and had other sons and daughters. When Nahor had lived 29 years, he became the father of Terah. And after he became the father of Terah, Nahor lived 119 years and had other sons and daughters. After Terah had lived 70 years, he became the father of Abram, Nahor and Haran.

These scriptures, along with an estimate of when Abram was born, combine to provide us with an estimate of roughly 4000 BC for Adam's advent if one assumes that the genealogies are complete.

Old Timers Disease

But did those guys in the lineage of Adam to Abraham *really* father children at the age of about 100 and then go on to live to an age of nearly 1000? Methuselah holds the longevity record, racking up 969 years. Many believe that prior to the flood, God announced the end of the near-millennial lifespan and phased in a term limit of 120-years. *Genesis 6:3 Then the LORD said, "My Spirit will not contend with man forever, for he is mortal; his days will be a hundred and twenty years."* (Others view the 120-year time period of Genesis 6:3 as a countdown until the flood rather than a reduced lifespan.) Ten generations after Noah, Abraham considered living to 100 to be remarkable and fathering children at 100 to be miraculous. Moses was well aware of the brevity of our life, as he lamented in a psalm. *Psalm 90:10 The length of our days is seventy years—or eighty, if we have the strength; yet their span is but trouble and sorrow, for they quickly pass, and we fly away.* What explanations have been offered up for a 1000-year lifespan?

Old Age was the Norm

One creationist strategy for explaining the long lifespans between Adam and Abraham is to consider them as the norm, and our short contemporary longevity as the aberration. Hugh Ross implies that a large dose of extraterrestrial radiation from the Vela supernova 20,000—30,000 years ago[1] may have been responsible for our shortened lifespan. Of course, Ross offers no proof, just a good dose of imagination.

Gerald Schroeder suggests that a 10-fold slowing of man's metabolism may have occurred in early biblical history. Schroeder cites progeria, a disease that causes teenagers to die with the body of an old person, as evidence that dramatic changes in the human lifespan are not beyond the realm of possibilities[2]. Once again, it's a case of science by suggestion.

Young Earth Creationists attribute the reduction in the human life span to the climatic and dietary changes associated with the effects of Noah's flood. Creationists support their doctrine with ancient legends of the Akkadian, Sumerian and Babylonian cultures where kings were known to have lived thousands of years[3]. I never will understand why creationists believe that citing legends constitutes a persuasive scientific argument; such a strategy only reinforces the skeptics' notions that the Bible is also a compilation of legends.

M & M's

There are many other ways to explain these long lives, and they can be classified as M-words.

One can simply accept these ages as *mysteries* or *miracles* that tell us only that these fellows lived a long time. In other words, the Bible doesn't give an explanation—so don't try to make one up! This is a simple approach, but these ages are presented in a routine manner that makes them seem rather mundane, unlike most biblical miracles that are clearly celebrated as supernatural interventions of an all-powerful God.

Some have suggested that the years were actually *months*. Although this is a convenient way to reduce the lifespan to a reasonable number, it has embarrassing implications concerning youthful sexual activity. For example, Mahalalel could have died at an age of 895 months (rather than 895 years), or 74 ½ years. That sounds reasonable, but Mahalalel would have been only 65 months old (5 ½ years) when he fathered Jared! Wow! And I thought my kids were out of control!

Some view these lifespans as a way of accounting for the length of *multiple missing man dynasties*[4] rather than the age of single individual. Consider the Adam-Seth-Enosh connection. *Genesis 5:1-11 This is the written account of Adam's line. When God created man, he made him in the likeness of God. He created them male and female and blessed them. And when they were created, he called them "man." When Adam had lived 130 years, he had a son in his own likeness, in his own image; and he named him Seth. After Seth was born, Adam lived 800 years and had other sons and daughters. Altogether, Adam lived 930 years, and then he died. When Seth had lived 105 years, he became the father of Enosh. And after he became the father of Enosh, Seth lived 807 years and had other sons and daughters. Altogether, Seth lived 912 years, and then he died. When Enosh had lived 90 years, he became the father of Kenan. And after he became the father of Kenan, Enosh lived 815 years and had other sons and daughters. Altogether, Enosh lived 905 years, and then he died.* Perhaps that means that Adam and his direct line were at the head of affairs for 930 years. Afterward the family line of Seth has pre-eminence for 912 years. This was followed by the family of Enoch for 905 years. This perspective not only reduces the lifespan to an unspecified length, but it also increases the length of time to Adam's origination to 10,000 B.C. or so. But this view has serious problems. Consider Enosh. He was born only 235 years (130 + 105) after Adam showed up, yet somehow someone kept such good records that they figured out that his descendents were put in charge 1842 years later (930 + 912). This gap between the birth of the heir and the time when his descendents took over the family continues to increase with later generations! Further, it is a bit tenuous to say that the death of a person actually corresponds to the end of their family reign rather than their personal demise. Consider Noah. Numerous Old Testament books speak of Noah, and in the New Testament Jesus, Peter, Luke and the author of the Book of Hebrews speak of Noah as if he were a real person rather than a symbolic figure. Noah's life is fairly well chronicled in Genesis, where he is found fathering children at 500, entering the ark at 600, disembarking at 601, living 350 more years after the flood during which time he was planting vineyards, and then dying at a ripe old age of 950. It seems that these milestones are tied to the one man Noah rather than Noah, his sons, grandsons, great-grandsons, great-great-grandsons, etc.

Die Hard

Scientists involved in the study of aging[5] commonly use another M-word to explain 900-year lifespans; *myth*. Their skepticism of the literal rendering of these passages is understandable. People die of "old age" all the time[6] and most of us hope to be one of them. Passing 70 is no big deal, yet the 100-year barrier is very difficult to break and it is incredibly rare that anyone lives beyond the age of 120 anywhere in the world today.

There is no secret death gene that executes you suddenly at a pre-determined age; the exact date of your demise is not encoded in your DNA. Neither is there a biological clock in your thyroid that kills you when it strikes midnight. Nor does your body wear out exactly like a car; your cells contain DNA blueprints for new cells but your Chrysler cannot reproduce its transmission[7]. Therefore the durability of the patriarchs cannot be simply attributed to a longer genetic warranty, a slower biological clock, or a lifestyle and environment that lessened the rate at which they broke down. Further, there is no fossil evidence that humans have ever lived 900 years. *Homo sapiens* date back about 150,000 years, and fossil evidence indicates that the average life expectancy for our species was probably 20[8]. Hardly any of our *Homo sapiens* ancestors collected Social Security because only a small proportion survived 60 years. Our Neanderthal cousins had an even rougher time of it, rarely making it to 45[9].

Although the mysteries associated with aging and death still abound, scientists have begun to develop an understanding of why we live as long as we do[10,11]. First, you have your parents to blame. Although you may never obtain a cash windfall from Mom and Pop, your have already received their genetic heritage. Each of your parents, in turn, received genetic information for their traits from their parents. For a moment, let's put aside whose nose you have and consider how the inheritance of traits has influenced lifespan[12,13]. It is quite unlikely that any of your direct ancestors died before puberty; if they had, you wouldn't be here[14]! Your ancestors were a long and glorious line of winners, at least in the respect that they lived long enough to pass on their genes to the next generation[15]. Therefore genes promoting good health through adolescence must be favored by natural selection. If lethal genes (those which result in conditions that lead to death) and semi-lethal genes (those which are so debilitating that they can make a person susceptible to death) are expressed during childhood, they are not likely to be common in subsequent generations because those who die before having children cannot pass these devastating genes to another generation[16]. Genes associated with detrimental effects that become evident *after* the childbearing years are more likely to be passed on to the next generation because those children will have already been born before the parents face those painful consequences. Because genes can have multiple functions in life, the very same genetic package that natural selection favored in the early years of life may wreak havoc in old age! Although our genes favor good health throughout youth and the childbearing ages, degrading health and death may follow at their command. Therefore the health struggles we face in our 80's and 90's are simply the price we pay for living so well during our teens and 20's! The difficulties of old age and the near certainty of death after a century are the prices we pay for enjoying a virile, healthy youth.

But you shouldn't complain because modern man actually has it quite good. Most people did not live much beyond the age of 45 during the period of human history between 100 and 100,000 years ago. Antibiotics, refrigeration, wastewater treatment, food distribution, water purification, medicines, heating, and air conditioning are but a few of the technological advances that have propelled the average life expectancy from 45 to 78 during the past 100 years. This statistic is primarily a reflection of the drastic decrease in infant mortality rather than a remarkable extension of the upper limits of old age, though, and the "rise in life expectancy has slowed to a crawl"[17].

Although scientists today squabble over whether the longest human lifespan will remain at about 120 or may one day reach 150, all of them agree that there is no evidence of a 10-fold longer lifespan during the time of the biblical patriarchs, or any other time for that matter. If our bodies were built for thriving in old age, we would be better equipped to handle longevity, with less brittle bones, bent backs, and bulging bladders[18]. The evidence indicates that the human body has been optimized to maintain health until Mom and Dad crank out the next generation; after that it's all downhill. Nonetheless, the long life enjoyed today exceeds that of any era of human history.

How does all of this relate to Methuselah's longevity? There is simply no scientific evidence for the incredible longevity of the patriarchs. If you believe that the patriarchs did indeed live hundreds of years, perhaps you should simply consider it a matter of faith or a mystery or miracle that happened for this small group of folks, rather than a scientific fact that applied to all humans who lived at that time.

References
1. Hugh Ross; The Genesis Question—Scientific Advances and the Accuracy of Genesis; Navpress 1998, Colorado Springs, CO; 115–122
2. G.L. Schroeder; The Science of God; Simon and Schuster; New York, NY; 1997; 202–203
3. Hugh Ross; The Genesis Question—Scientific Advances and the Accuracy of Genesis; Navpress 1998, Colorado Springs, CO; 114–115
4. Gleason L. Archer; A Survey of Old Testament Introduction, Moody Press, Chicago, Il, 1994, 210–212
5. S. Jay Olshansky, Bruce A. Carnes; The Quest for Immortality—Science at the Frontiers of Aging, W.W. Norton and Company, New York, 2001, 32–34, 40, 43–45
6. Sherwin B. Nuland; How We Die—Reflections of Life's Final Chapter, Vintage Books edition, 1995, New York, 43–63
7. S. Jay Olshansky, Bruce A. Carnes; The Quest for Immortality—Science at the Frontiers of Aging, W.W. Norton and Company, New York, 2001, 564
8. S. Jay Olshansky, Bruce A. Carnes; The Quest for Immortality—Science at the Frontiers of Aging, W.W. Norton and Company, New York, 2001, 115
9. Robert Boyd, Joan B. Silk; How Humans Evolved, 2nd Edition, W.W. Norton & Company, New York, 2000, 553
10. Robert Boyd, Joan B. Silk; How Humans Evolved, 2nd Edition, W.W. Norton & Company, New York, 2000, 553–580
11. S. Jay Olshansky, Bruce A. Carnes; The Quest for Immortality—Science at the Frontiers of Aging, W.W. Norton and Company, New York, 2001, 50–136
12. S. Jay Olshansky, Bruce A. Carnes; The Quest for Immortality—Science at the Frontiers of Aging, W.W. Norton and Company, New York, 2001, 50–105
13. Robert Boyd, Joan B. Silk; How Humans Evolved, 2nd Edition, W.W. Norton & Company, New York, 2000, 553–580
14. Richard Dawkins; The Selfish Gene, Oxford University Press edition, Oxford, 1989 (first printing 1976),40
15. Kenneth Miller; Finding Darwin's God—A Scientist's Search for Common Ground Between God and Evolution; 1999, Cliff Street Books, Harper Collins; New York, NY
16. Richard Dawkins; The Selfish Gene, Oxford University Press edition, Oxford, 1989 (first printing 1976), 40–41
17. S. Jay Olshansky and Bruce A. Carnes, The Quest for Immortality—Science at the Frontiers of Aging, W.W. Norton and Company, New York, 2001, 76–79, 85–88
18. S. Jay Olshansky, Bruce A. Carnes, Robert N. Butler, If Humans Were Built to Last, Scientific American, 13(2), 2003, Special Edition, New Look at Human Evolution, 94–100

Appendix P. Biblical Objections Concerning Adam Not Being the First and Only Human

It is certainly reasonable to have a religious belief that Adam and Eve were the first and only man and woman on Earth based solely on the information provided in Bible. I don't have a problem with folks who read Genesis and come away thinking that Adam and Eve were literally the only people on the face of this planet. My contention is that this perspective is not the *only* biblical option one can maintain for those who believe that Adam and Eve were real people.

Genesis One does not necessarily refer to the creation of only Adam and Eve.

Although many believe that the "man" of Genesis One speaks only of Adam and Eve, there are other viewpoints. Some think that Genesis One speaks of creation of mankind in general, while Genesis Two speaks of Adam and Eve in particular. Others believe Genesis One focuses on the physical body, while Genesis Two explains the

spiritual nature. It has also been suggested that Adam and Eve
were symbolic of the population of mankind rather than two specific individuals.

Genesis Five does not necessarily teach that "man" created on Day Six was the one man, Adam.

The fifth chapter of Genesis reiterates that God created "man" or
"them" as "male and female" before speaking of the individual
named Adam. *Genesis 5:1-3 This is the written account of Adam's line.
When God created man, he made him in the likeness of God. He created
them male and female and blessed them. And when they were created, he
called them "man."When Adam had lived 130 years, he had a son in his
own likeness, in his own image; and he named him Seth.* The King James
Version provides a slightly different translation, using the name
Adam rather than the term "man" in one place, *Genesis 5:1-3 This
is the book of the generations of Adam. In the day that God created man,
in the likeness of God made he him; Male and female created he them; and
blessed them, and called their name Adam, in the day when they were created. And Adam lived an hundred and thirty years, and begat a son in his
own likeness, after his image; and called his name Seth:* Nonetheless,
when this verse says that God "called their name Adam", the words
"their", "them" and "male and female" may indicate a generic reference to mankind. The individual who, at the age of 130, fathered
Seth was certainly the individual named Adam.

The Bible does not state that all men and women were biological descendants of Adam.

That may be a reasonable deduction to make based on the scriptures,
but it is not the *only* reasonable one. Creationists vehemently defend
Adam's pole position in the human family tree. The first verse that is
commonly cited for Adam's universal fatherhood is from the Old
Testament. *Malachi 2:10 Have we not all one Father? Did not one God
create us? Why do we profane the covenant of our fathers by breaking faith
with one another?* The NIV translation uses the upper case "F" for
Father, making it a reference to God and irrelevant to the ancestry
of Adam. The King James Version renders it a small "f" in apparent
reference to Adam. *Malachi 2:10 Have we not all one father? hath not*

one God created us? why do we deal treacherously every man against his brother, by profaning the covenant of our fathers? Even if the reference is to Adam, the "we" Malachi spoke of may have been referring to the Jews that received this message—not all of the people on Earth. Either way, one cannot cite this verse as indisputable biblical "proof" that Adam was the genetic forefather of all humanity.

The second verse often cited to prove that Adam and Eve are the biological parents of all humans is tucked away in the Garden of Eden. *Genesis 3:20 Adam named his wife Eve, because she would become the mother of all the living.* Could a reasonable person read this verse and believe that all people descended from Adam and Eve? Of course! But do you really think that the only possible frame of reference for the term "all" was in regards to the planet's human population? How about "all" people in their locality, or "all" of the people in their immediate family, or "all" of the people in the region where the author of Genesis lived?

The third verse used to place Adam at the base of our family tree is found in the New Testament. The Apostle Paul spoke of our relation one to another as he was preaching to a crowd in Athens. *Acts 17:22-27 Paul then stood up in the meeting of the Areopagus and said: "Men of Athens! I see that in every way you are very religious. For as I walked around and looked carefully at your objects of worship, I even found an altar with this inscription: TO AN UNKNOWN GOD. Now what you worship as something unknown I am going to proclaim to you. The God who made the world and everything in it is the Lord of heaven and earth and does not live in temples built by hands. And he is not served by human hands, as if he needed anything, because he himself gives all men life and breath and everything else. From one man he made every nation of men, that they should inhabit the whole earth; and he determined the times set for them and the exact places where they should live. God did this so that men would seek him and perhaps reach out for him and find him, though he is not far from each one of us.* Paul, speaking only 2000 years ago, stated that "every nation of men" was made from "one man", the same term used in the International Standard Version, which would certainly seem to point to Adam. This is consistent with the New Revised Standard translation, which reads "one ancestor". The King James Version, New King James Version and Darby's New Translation, however, use the phrase "one blood", which would mean that the inhabitants of all nations share a common human nature, but not a necessarily a common ancestor. The New English Bible uses one "stock", which could simply refer to our shared human nature. The American Standard Version and the Revised Standard Version read "one"; which could refer to any of the above. Although Acts 17:26 has been interpreted by some as an indication that Adam is the common biological ancestor of mankind, it may only imply that all people share the same inherently sinful human nature.

A fourth verse can be offered up as evidence of the literal manufacture of Adam and Eve in the Garden of Eden, *1 Timothy 2:11-13 A woman should learn in quietness and full submission. I do not permit a woman to teach or to have authority over a man; she must be silent. For Adam was formed first, then Eve.* Paul is making an argument to Timothy, a young spiritual overseer of an early church, based on the order of creation of man and woman presented in the Garden of Eden. But the lesson Paul draws from the creation story of Adam and Eve is the same whether they were just two of the people, the only two people, or mythic representatives of mankind.

Appendix Q. The Strengths of the Theory of Evolution

Let's explore the scientific appeal of the process of evolution by reviewing its strength—this mechanism correlates the scientific evidence of the history of evolution. It is the model that best fits that data. It is the best explanation of how life on Earth has changed during the past four billion years and continues to change today.

The simplest life was first.

The oldest fossils are the pre-Cambrian single-celled bacteria without nuclei that lived nearly four billion years ago. These are the "simplest" life forms we know of, and it makes sense that they would precede more complicated organisms[1]. Even though the mysterious origins of these little critters may never be substantiated, one would expect the smallest, simplest life to appear early if life evolved through a natural process.

There is a commonality of "ingredients" that points back to a common ancestor[2].

If life developed by mutations and variations from a common ancient ancestor, one would expect that the basic building blocks of life would be present in all life. Indeed, all living organisms contain water, DNA, RNA, and proteins contained within at least one membrane-encapsulated cell. This suggests that all life descended from a common ancestor with the same components.

There is an order to life in the fossil record, trending from a few small simple life forms to many large and complex life forms[3].

Single-celled bacteria without nuclei were followed by single-celled bacteria with nuclei. Subsequently, multi-celled life appeared and were followed by the incredibly large and complex life of the Cambrian Explosion, followed a rich half billion years of complexity and diversity.

There is a diversity of life.

Evolutionary paths that are pressured by environmental forces and guided by natural selection provide for a diversity of distinct life forms[4]. The vast menu of changing habitats on this planet has favored the evolution of life that is well suited for their niche, ranging from mountains and deserts to your intestinal tract and backyard[5].

There is a grouping of common characteristics that reflects how these diverse organisms are related[6].

If contemporary life evolved from a richly branching tree of life, then a relatively few types of organisms should share a great number of characteristics with relatives that originated recently. There should also be an ever-widening circle of relatives with fewer commonalities, culminating in a grouping of all life forms characterized by a small but complex set of common features. Niles Eldredge makes effective use of a dog species, *Canis familiaris*, as an example. Because there are dogs, there should be species that remind you of dogs but are not quite dogs! These closest relatives include coyotes and wolves. More distant relatives include the fox and several extinct animals that share some peculiar features of the middle ear. This group of animals falls within the Family canidae, which share common other similarities with raccoons and weasels, particularly in the ear region. All of these beasts, from dogs to weasels, share some scissor-like dental features with an even broader grouping of animals, such as cats, civets and seals. All of these animals, from dogs to seals, belong to the Order Carnivora. Carnivores have three middle-ear bones, mammary glands, and placental development of fetuses, just like an even larger group of animals (including humans) referred to as mammals. Mammals, in turn, are related to birds and reptiles in that the females produce an amniotic egg. All of these amniotic animals are similar to amphibians such as frogs and salamanders in that they have four appendages. What do all of these animals, from dogs to salamanders, have in common with fish? They have all considered vertebrates because that all have a backbone. Vertebrates are related to fungi, plants and amoeba in that they are composed of eukaryotic cells (cells with a nucleus). Finally, how is eukaryotic life related to the lowly bacteria and blue-green algae composed of cells lacking a nucleus? They all contain living micro-machines built from RNA, DNA and proteins. This grouping is referred to as the Linnaean hierarchy, and it reserves a place for everything that has life.

Animals of isolated geographical location are most similar to those of the most nearby continental mass[7].

If life from a continent's coastal area traveled to an isolated, off-shore island, the island life that evolved would be similar to life that evolved on that same nearby continent. Darwin, for example, observed the similarity between the life on Galapagos Islands and the life on the nearby coast of South America. Similarly, the forms of life on the Cape de Verde islands are similar to those found in the neighboring portions of the nearest continent, Africa.

Living animals and the fossils of similar extinct animals are found in the same locality[8].

If life developed by gradual changes over eras of time, one would expect that the ancestors of a modern species would have lived in the same part of the world. Modern animals are indeed roaming over the graveyards of their deceased and fossilized predecessors.

There are fossil records of major transitions.

There are indeed very few vivid fossils that exemplify major transitions in the fossil record because the time required for such changes to occur is thought to be small relative to the gaps of the fossil record. Nonetheless, there are numerous examples of macro-evolution that illustrate what evolution predicts; a set of changes that define a group of organisms will not happen simultaneously because some ancestral features will be retained while new ones are added.

There is a classic set of transitory fossils between 60,000,000-year old horse-like animals that resembled the rhinoceros to the modern day Black Beauty[9]. Creationists have frequently borne false witness against their neighbor scientists on this topic by accurately reporting that paleontologists do not think that these fossils represent a monotonic transition from the rhino to the horse, but then falsely asserting that paleontologists therefore do not believe in evolutionary transitions reflected by these fossils[10]. That isn't true. Evolution used to be thought of as gradualism; a slow, straightforward, linear progression of one species into another. Stasis reflects the abrupt change in species followed by long intervals of stability. Although there is a difference between the rates of change associated with gradualism and stasis (with most evolutionists currently favoring stasis), neither side ever doubted the existence of transitional fossils or the evolutionary progression from one species to another. Further, it is often difficult to ascertain if a transitional species was an intermediate form that gave rise to other species or became extinct. It is frequently the case that two scientists may not agree on the exact placement of a fossil within the branched evolutionary tree of life, but both certainly agree that it *is* an example of a transitional form.

Archeopateryx is a classic intermediate; it is a reptile-bird that bridges the transformation from the reptile to the bird[11]. Seven examples of this 150 million year old species are known to exist. Why is it not simply a bird, as creationists claim? There are few differences in the morphology of living birds and reptiles—including dinosaurs—of the Mesozoic Era. Birds are distinct in that they have feathers, four-chambered hearts, horny bills, unique wings, a pronounced breastbone and no teeth. *Archeopateryx* had feathers, wings, and a bill, too, just like a contemporary bird, but it was remarkably reptile-like because it had teeth, dinosaur-like feet, a bony tail, but no keeled breastbone.

A sequence of three evolutionary intermediates linking land animals to the whale has been discovered in the last two decades[12, 13]. Carl Zimmer provides a comprehensive overview of eight intermediates in the tree of life starting 64 million years ago with coyote-like mammals called mesonychids and ending up with the fully marine *Mysticetes* and *Odontocetes* species that originated 40 million years ago and continue until today[14]. A few of the more famous entries include *Ambulocetus*, the walking whale which is the near-perfect intermediate in the middle of this sequence. It had large rear legs along with front legs that would have enabled it to be mobile on the land or in the waters. *Basilosaurus*, which followed, had tiny, "leftover" hind legs but was a fully marine animal, incapable of crawling about on land. Zimmer plainly informs the reader that intermediate nature of these creatures is undeniable, even though the relationships between these intermediates are not a certainty.

How about a nicely branching family tree of elephant evolution dating back 50 million years to a runty little critter with barely a snout? Dozens of species litter this family tree, and the relationship between today's species and these predecessors is obvious[15].

The evolution of mammals from mammal-like reptiles is clearly documented in the fossil record, beginning with animals having undifferentiated teeth a single, middle-ear bone, and ending with mammal-like animals with rows of differentiated teeth (incisors, molars, canines) and three middle-ear bones[16].

The human fossil record is one of the very best examples of macro-evolutionary changes[17, 18].

Finally, a very recent find[19] revealed what creationists had always dared scientists to find; a 375 million year old fossil of a "fishapod", an animal in the transition between fish and four-legged land animal (tetrapod). This creature, called *Tiktaalik roseae* was fish-like in that if exhibited fins and scales. It also contained evidence of primitive limbs in the forward fins, however, such as "digits, proto-wrists, elbows and shoulders"[19].

The first amphibians looked like fish more than any other amphibians over the last 380,000,000 years.

The fossil record indicates that fish preceded amphibians. One would therefore expect that the gradual changes involved in this transition would result in the earliest amphibians sharing more attributes with fish than later amphibians. Such is the case, and it holds for other major transitions. This pattern is repeated for several others major transitions in the fossil record. For example, *the first reptiles were more amphibian-like than the reptiles that followed*[20], *the first mammals shared more attributes with reptiles than the mammals that followed*[21,22], *and the first birds were more similar to dinosaurs than the birds that followed*[23].

There are animals alive today that are in a transitory state.

The whale fossil record clearly demonstrates an extinct intermediate, *Ambulocetus*, that was seemingly well suited for life on land or in the sea millions of years ago. But what of contemporary life? You can visit you local zoo to see a living animal thriving in the land-to-sea transition; the seal[24].

There are animals alive today on the "branch point" of the tree of life, ready to split into new species.

The tree of life is characterized by branch points; positions where a branch splits into two, representative of one species giving rise to a new species. Living animals that exhibit so many living intermediates that the extremes of variation are clearly two species, are referred to as "ring species" or "insipient species", such as salamanders in California and gulls in the polar latitudes[25,26]. North America, for example, is home to the herring gull. An examination of the herring gull's characteristics as we move westward from Alaska to Siberia shows a series of intermediates. Most notable is the change in color as herring gull becomes darker, ultimately being classified as the lesser black-backed gull. Both the herring gull and lesser black-backed gull inhabit Northern Europe. Are these simply two colors of the same bird? No, they are two separate species! In addition to the different colors, they have different markings on their legs, they nest in different sites, and they do not interbreed—yet they are connected by a series of intermediates. What would make the divergence complete between these two species? The extinction or isolation of the intermediates by an adverse phenomenon such a climate change or natural disaster could do the trick.

Evolution can account for the "sudden origin" of species.

The vast majority of the fossil record is packed with species that appear stable for long periods of time and are suddenly followed by other species. "Suddenly" does not mean "instantly", however, and "other" does not mean "completely unrelated". Most scientists have concluded that the period of time associated with the appearance of new species is attributable to ecological changes in the habitat. These changes, whether attributable to fires, earthquakes, climate changes, attacks by predators, meteorite impacts that occur rapidly with respect to the deposition of fossil layers. For example, geographical isolation can prompt the forces of natural selection to produce new species similar to its predecessors within thousands to tens of thousands of years, a flash of time that can slip through the fossil record undetected[27]. Have all of the genetic changes directly responsible for new species been clearly identified? No, but genetic phenomena that can cause new species to suddenly appear have been outlined by several authors. Jeffrey Schwartz, for example, explains that although the eventual pairing of recessive genes responsible for novel physical features emerge slowly, once they are in place there will be a sudden and dramatic change in the attributes of the organism and the potential for the recessive gene for a mutation to then become dominant[28, 29]. May it take another century to clarify the exact steps that yield new species? Perhaps. But the general principles have been laid down, and the refining processes of natural selection, especially in a time of ecological disruption, can account for new species.

Several "drivers" of evolution have been proposed.

Richard Dawkin's, in his book *The Selfish Gene*[30], asserts that evolution is motivated by the struggle between genes to have accurate copies of themselves passed on to successive generations. Niles Eldredge argues that while such competition is important, it is insufficient to account for the dominant patterns of evolution in the fossil record. Eldredge identifies the primary driver of evolution to be the physical environment that disturbs ecosystems and species[31]. It is not clear that an either-or option is the only reasonable reconciliation between these two viewpoints; many are comfortable with both causes affecting evolution at different scales.

Evolution can be observed in "real time".

Evolution happens. Darwin reasoned that it did based on the evidence he collected, but he did not observe it occurring. Scientists have looked for evidence of the process of evolution, and they have found that Darwin was right. Mutations lead to very slight variations in organisms that are then subjected to the pressures of natural selection, which sorts out the winners from the losers. This repeating cycle from generation to generation is the engine of evolution. One can actually observe life evolve if the organism reproduces rapidly[32]. For example, you are undoubtedly familiar with bacteria that "develop a resistance" against antibiotics. Did you ever stop and wonder how those little guys did that? Did they go to a drug rehab program for small-scale scum? No! Mutations during reproduction led to variations that were subjected to a strong environmental pressure of antibiotics. Some of these variations produced organisms capable of surviving in the presence of the antibiotics. These "mutant" bacteria have benefited from evolution (much to our displeasure) because they are now able to survive in the presence of antibiotics that their ancestors had difficulty dealing with. Even viruses, such as HIV, evolve, making the cure somewhat elusive because the disease itself is a moving target. It's not just the little buggers that can evolve before our eyes. Jonathan Weiner's Pulitzer Prize-winning account of Peter and Rosemary Grant's 20 year study of the finches—all of them—isolated on one of the Galapagos Islands is a testament to the remarkable changes wrought by natural selection[33]. Endler's observations of the changing spots of guppies in the streams and ponds of their South American habitat are another vivid display of measurable evolution[34].

The rate of evolutionary change of wildlife can be measured.

Not only can evolution be observed by scientists, the rate at which it occurs has been measured[35, 36]. The rate at which changes in a measurable characteristic occur are measured in terms of "darwins", where one darwin means that the average measurable value of the trait (such as the length of a bone or a beak) has increased or decreased by a factor of 2.718 (that value is equal to e, for you mathematicians) during a million years, or 0.000002718 during one year. In a study of guppies that were transplanted from a waterfall pool to an upstream pool that did not contain the guppie-munching chiclid fish, changes in guppie morphology occurred rapidly. The size of the guppies at maturity increased, as did the age at which they reached sexual maturity. In their incredibly well-documented study of the finches on the Galapagos, the Grants measured rates of change equal to 25,000 darwins during a drought and 6,000 darwins after an incredibly wet season[37].

The rate of change of evolution is fast enough to explain even the most dramatic changes in the fossil record.

The rates of change noted in studies of guppies, finches, lizards and sparrows indicate that the rates of evolution observed in nature are hundreds to millions of times faster than that noted in the fossil record, even during the rapid bursts of evolution. Darwin's mechanism is more than adequate to account for these changes. But if the rates of observable evolution are so fast, why are the changes in the fossil record so slow? Why isn't the evolution in the fossil record hundreds or millions of times more dramatic than it is? Evolution can take a rapid turn, but then slow down for a long period of time—yielding a slow average. Evolution can even make a U-turn, resulting in a changes that are dramatic in the short-term, but more modest in the long run. For example, a Galapagos Islands drought in 1976 depleted and altered the food supply, and the biggest birds with the deepest beaks had the advantage—differences as small as ½ millimeter made the difference between life and death[38]! The finches on one of the Galapagos Islands got bigger by natural selection in 1977, and in the following year, the female finches' romantic attraction for large males resulted in sexual selection that favored an increase in size of the subsequent generation. In the following four years, bigger remained better. Well, if finches have been around for a long, long time, why aren't they gigantic, rather than small as sparrows? An extremely wet 1982–1983 on this desert island provided the answer. The changes in the food supply wrought by this flood resulted in the natural selection of smaller finches, reversing the previous trend[39]. Therefore the rapid evolutionary "wobble" alternating between the natural selection of big and small could average out to a modest change over the course of longer time periods.

Evolution can account for complexity.

Richard Dawkins' book *The Blind Watchmaker* makes a case for the apparent design of nature through mutations and natural selection[40]. The marginal benefit of a minor change induced by a mutation over a short period of time can yield complexity if a long period time is available for a sequence of subtle changes. Eons are needed for evolution to evoke complexity, and a trillion days have elapsed since the inception of life. Dawkins' explains the general process through which evolution can evoke complexity through a series of modest improvements of imperfect yet functional organs.

The mechanism of inheritance of traits has been established.

Although his explanation of natural selection was on the mark, Darwin remained clueless concerning the mechanisms of inheritance and mutations. He conjectured that parental characteristics blended when they were passed to the next generation. Gregor Mendel, a brilliant Austrian monk whose work was not appreciated until after his death, pioneered the systematic study of the inheritance of features[41]. Mendel showed that the information concerning a trait of each parent was transmitted intact to the children in a predictable manner. Rather than blending, these characteristics were inherited from either parent.

The mechanism of mutations has been identified.

The methods by which mutations occur have been identified[42]. The molecular processes associated with the reproduction of strands of DNA that compose genes have a level of variability. If you read Appendix L, you will find that the organic base T matches up with A while G pairs with C to form the rungs of the DNA ladder. The "wrong" letter can be matched up (T-G rather than T-A, for example). Other errors include the deletion of a segment of DNA or the "insertion" of a segment of DNA. Mutations can be of little consequence, detrimental or beneficial. Although these changes are commonly considered errors, they also represent opportunities for development of life and the origin of species.

Evolution can account for an increase in genetic information and the genome length.

The human genome contains about three billion base pairs (rungs of the DNA ladder) in which some 32,000 genes are imbedded[43]. The bacterium *E. coli* has only about 4.6 million base pairs which encode about 4300 genes[44]. Our single-celled common ancestor that lived nearly four billion years ago probably had even smaller genomes than today's bacteria. If life did evolve from a relatively simple, single-celled creature, how did such a tremendous increase in the length of DNA occur along with the smaller, yet still substantial, increase in the number of genes? Mutations during DNA replication can result in the addition of base pairs[45]. Most frequently, though, new genes emerge from the doubling of an existing gene and its insertion in the chromosome in tandem next to the parental gene[46]. Double genomes can also result from the combination of the DNA complement from each parent gene. Mobile genes can multiply and insert themselves within the genome at several sites. Computer simulations of the information gain of a protein have indicated that increases in information can occur in conjunction with punctuated equilibrium without violating any laws[47]. Once these gains in the genome have been achieved, the pressures of natural selection sort out the changes that lead to improved morphology for the environment from those that are detrimental.

DNA contains evolutionary history.

The genomes of organisms are a testament to their common ancestry and the nearness of their relationship on the tree of life. The great apes bear the greatest genetic similarity with humans, which is not surprising in that their ancestry and ours parted ways only about 7 million years ago[48]. The DNA of a chimpanzee is about 98% identical to human DNA. While this hardly means that chimps are

98% human, it confirms that those creatures who bear some resemblance to humans and diverged from our ancestors most recently are most like us in genetic composition[49]. Creatures that parted ways tens of millions or hundreds of millions of years ago share a multitude of genes that date back to their common ancestry. About 46% of the proteins found in yeast are found in humans[50]. There are relationships between all genomes and their patterns are consistent with the tree of life described by evolution[51-53].

Evolution explains why embryos have similar features.[54]

In was first observed in the eighteenth century that the young embryos of animals are remarkably similar in form. For example, the human embryo is very similar to the embryos of the rabbit, cow, pig, chicken, tortoise, salamander and fish. The older the embryos are, the more obvious the differences become. Although one could argue, as creationists do, that small young embryos must be simpler and therefore more similar than the more developed embryos, these embryos always have traits that are peculiar to their ancestral lineage. (Creationists correctly point out that Haeckel's famous 1870 drawings of embryonic similarities of these animals contained the fraudulent insertion of dog embryos labeled as human embryos, nonetheless the subsequent inspection of human embryos only confirmed the similarities. Haeckel's fraud no more invalidates the remarkable embryonic similarities of species than the antics of modern-day TV faith healers invalidate Christianity.)

Evolution explains why developing embryos temporarily exhibit traits of other animals.[55]

Those who studied ontogeny, the origin and development of an individual organism from embryo to adult, not only wondered at the similarities of young embryos, but the remarkable changes they underwent as they developed. Recapitulation is the study of the embryonic emergence and subsequent loss of various characters or structures that appeared during the evolutionary history of a species. For example, the fossil record shows that whales developed from land animals with teeth, and the embryos of baleen whale embryos develop teeth that are reabsorbed and lost. Dolphins also evolved from land animals, and both the whale and the dolphin embryos exhibit four tiny leg-like structures, the ones in back disappear before birth while the front two develop into flippers. Birds, mammals and fish develop gill slits in the neck region, yet they disappear as the birds and mammal embryos develop. Creationists try to invalidate these observations by correctly pointing out that Haeckel erroneously said that "Ontogeny is the recapitulation of phylogeny." In other words, Haeckel went too far by implying that the developing embryo morphed through its *complete evolutionary history* as it developed. This is obviously untrue because the developing human embryo never displays the complete appearance of an adult fish or adult reptile or adult ape. Even though Haeckel's exaggeration was false, it remains true that the developing human embryo temporarily exhibits a few animal-like characteristics associated with its ancestry that are completely absent from newborn humans, such as tails, gill slits, fish-like heart structures, ape-like coats of hair that are shed, and divergent big toes that eventually line up with the other four toes.

Evolution explains why animals have useless body parts.[56]

Although many features that point to an evolutionary past are resorbed by the developing embryo, some hang around long enough to make it through the birth process and hang out throughout adulthood. These organs, termed as "vestigial structures", are either not functional, marginally functional or not fully functional, and may otherwise be thought of as useless of nearly useless body features. Every animal has them; you have a bunch of them hiding inside that sack of flab you're sitting in. Go ahead, think about the importance of the appendix, the tailbone, the sinuses, our pathetic amount of body hair, goosebumps, ear-wiggling muscles that can barely move our ears, the vomeronasal organ (a small divot in the nose lined with nonfunctioning chemoreceptors), and wisdom teeth. An examination of our evolutionary past brings the original purpose of these organs into clear view. For example, the appendix helped the digestion of our ancestors' cellulose-rich diet. The tailbone helped to support the tail! Sinuses may help to moisten the air we breathe a bit, but in animals with an acute sense of smell, the sinuses are lined with olfactory tissues that provided a far more acute sense of smell; our DNA apparently contains broken genes for additional odor receptors. Because early humans had to chew a lot of plants to get enough calories to survive, they wore out a lot of teeth and the wisdom teeth replaced the teeth lost to wear. Creationists have no trouble with vestigial organs; they simply find any possible use they may have and present it as the sole reason that the organ was designed by God. For example, wisdom teeth help you to chew food, and muscle and ligament tissue is attached to your tailbone. Otherwise they simply assert that vestigial organs have an important and mysterious role to play, even if they do not know what that role is and even if the organ can be removed without detriment (and often to the benefit) to the animal that possesses it.

Organisms are rugged survivors, not perfect life forms.

Natural selection may sort winners from losers, but it cannot shape the perfect. Success requires being rugged enough to survive rather than perfection. Perfection is neither required nor possible. Marginally functional organs, useless body parts, extinctions, design flaws and jury-rigged morphologies are confirmations of evolutionary process subjected to random mutations and unpredictable environmental disturbances. Natural selection promotes the successful candidates, but cannot produce an invincible, flawless creature. Impeccable design remains the unrealized dream of Intelligent Design. The closest thing to a perfect species is that slimy alien that keeps on trying to devour Sigourney Weaver in the Alien movies.

Four billion years is a long, long time.

The evolution of life needed time to succeed, and four billion years is quite a long time. The time available for the process of evolution to work its wonders in the transformation of life on Earth is almost unimaginable. It is difficult for us to conceive of the biological changes that could have occurred during this time or how brief our own existence is compared with the history of life on Earth. For example, let's correlate the last 3.65 billion years of evolutionary history with the last 100 years—that's about the longest period of time that most of us can easily appreciate. Every day during this century would correspond to 100,000 years, each minute would correspond to about 70 years, and each second would correspond to slightly more than a year. In this frame of reference, life began on January 1, 1901, and today would correspond to midnight on Dec. 31, 2000. Microscopic life would have been the main actor between 1900 and 1985. The Cambrian Explosion would have happened in 1985, the dinosaurs would have died off in February 1999, the first animals that looked anything like humans would have showed up in November 2000, and *Homo sapiens* would have been first spotted on December 30, 2000. Modern human civilization would have begun roughly at 9:30 PM on December 31, 2000, Jesus would have been born around 11:30 PM and crucified a half-minute later, and the Declaration of Independence would have been signed just moments before 11:57 PM. Your favorite 70 year-old relative would have been born just one minute before midnight, and your favorite teen would have showed up about a fraction of minute before midnight.

Evolution is not random.

Many of us, especially people of faith, struggle with the notion that that life is the result of a random, natural process. Although the mutations that cause variations may be random, natural selection is anything but random. Natural selection is a distinctly non-random means of advancing life most suited to thrive in its local environment. Natural selection is a rigorous test that many have failed because their characteristics do not serve them well. The winners are rewarded with the grand prize, the opportunity to reproduce and pass their traits on to their offspring, and the inheritance of these favored features enhanced the chances of survival for the progeny. Darwin called this process "descent with modification" and it has been going on for nearly four billion years since life began and more than a half billion years since the Cambrian Explosion. Given very long periods of time, the repeating cycle of mutation, variation, and natural selection has resulted in the variations within species and the origin of new species.

Evolution does not violate any of the laws and theories of science, including the Second Law of Thermodynamics.

Evolutionary theory does not require an exemption from any other branch of science or law of nature. Life continues to evolve today at observable rates, and the Second Law of Thermodynamics no more prohibits the evolution of life in the past than it does in the present. The Second Law of Thermodynamics requires that the chemical and molecular disorder of processes—even biological ones—always increase. Therefore any system that is free of external influences will become more disordered. Although the Second Law cannot tell how fast such a change will occur, it can tell us what the ultimate change would be. It is easy to see why evolution appears to violate the Second Law; life has progressed from some primitive unknown early life form into bacteria and then into millions of species of complex organisms!

The Second Law applies to the whole process, though, which includes *the system and its surroundings*. As a result, the increased order of any living organism will be more than compensated for by the decreased disorder associated with its interactions with the environment. Therefore the total change in entropy ends up being a net increase and all is well with the Second Law of Thermodynamics! Can the Second Law of Thermodynamics ever be applied only to an organism and not to its surroundings? Yes, but only if the organism is completely isolated from the sun, air, food and water. In this case, there would be no change in the disorder of the surroundings and the total change of entropy would be manifest in the animal alone. For example, the Second Law of Thermodynamics would demand that a duck would tend toward disorder if it were blindfolded, gagged, stuck in a Zip Lock bag, and wrapped in insulation. This duck would die before it even thought of evolving. Life was hardly constrained in this manner during the past four billion years, though. Living organisms are still free to interact with their environment as they are subjected to the forces of natural selection. They can take in the sun, fresh air, clean water and good meals can expel their heat, spit, breath and waste. When the total change in entropy associated with a living organism and its surroundings are considered, the net change is a decrease in accordance with the Second Law of Thermodynamics.

Most people recognize that the creationist appeal to ever-increasing disorder in life doesn't quite make sense. A tiny seed becomes a huge complex tree in a few years. Nine months after a woman's single-celled egg is fertilized, an incredibly complex trillion cell baby is born. Creationists point out that such increases in complexity are only possible because an Intelligent Designer has programmed all of the necessary *information* needed for the development of a human into our genes. Entropy can indeed be described in terms of information theory, where statistical entropy is a probabilistic measure of uncertainty, and information is a measure of a reduction in entropy. For example, the information content of the human genome is much greater than that of our ancient single-celled common ancestor. So where did the new information that directs the development of humans originate? And how could such information appear without violating the Second Law of Thermodynamics? We have already reviewed the means by which evolution can increase the content of a genome[57]. Natural selection then acts on these changes as they are expressed.

A complete mathematical derivation of the laws of thermodynamics are available in many texts, but their application to biological systems and answers to common creationist objections are concisely summarized in many books, such as *Biological Thermodynamics*[58].

References
1. Niles Eldredge; The Triumph of Evolution and the Failure of Creationism; Henry Holt and Company; 2000; New York, NY, 36
2. Niles Eldredge; The Triumph of Evolution and the Failure of Creationism; Henry Holt and Company; 2000; New York, NY, 29
3. Niles Eldredge; The Triumph of Evolution and the Failure of Creationism; Henry Holt and Company; 2000; New York, NY, 32-34
4. Jonathan Weiner; The Beak of the Finch, Vintage Books, New York, 1994, 113-156
5. Ernst Mayr; What Evolution Is, Basic Books, New York, NY, 2001, 40-69
6. Niles Eldredge; The Triumph of Evolution and the Failure of Creationism; Henry Holt and Company; 2000; New York, NY, 26-31] [Ernst Mayr, What Evolution Is, Basic Books, New York, NY, 2001, 19-27
7. Kenneth Miller; Finding Darwin's God—A Scientist's Search for Common Ground Between God and Evolution; 1999, Cliff Street Books, Harper Collins; New York, NY, 93-94
8. Kenneth Miller; Finding Darwin's God—A Scientist's Search for Common Ground Between God and Evolution; 1999, Cliff Street Books, Harper Collins; New York, NY, 41-43
9. Ernst Mayr; What Evolution Is, Basic Books, New York, NY, 2001, 16,18
10. Niles Eldredge; The Triumph of Evolution and the Failure of Creationism; Henry Holt and Company; 2000; New York, NY, 129-134
11. Niles Eldredge; The Triumph of Evolution and the Failure of Creationism; Henry Holt and Company; 2000; New York, NY, 124-126
12. Peter Andrews, John Barber, Michael Benton, Marianne Collins, Christine Janis, Ely Kish, Akio Morishima, J. John Sepkoski, Jr., Christopher Stringer, Jean-Paul Tibbles; The Book of Life—An Illustrated History of the Evolution of Life on Earth, general editor Stephen Jay Gould, W.W. Norton and Co., New York, NY, 2001, Introduction by Stephen Jay Gould, 2-3, 186
13. Kenneth Miller; Finding Darwin's God—A Scientist's Search for Common Ground Between God and Evolution; 1999, Cliff Street Books, Harper Collins; New York, NY, 264-265
14. Carl Zimmer; Evolution—The Triumph of an Idea, HarperCollins Publishers, 2001, 135-141
15. Kenneth Miller; Finding Darwin's God—A Scientist's Search for Common Ground Between God and Evolution; 1999, Cliff Street Books, Harper Collins; New York, NY, 94-97
16. Niles Eldredge; The Triumph of Evolution and the Failure of Creationism; Henry Holt and Company; 2000; New York, NY, 54
17. Niles Eldredge; The Triumph of Evolution and the Failure of Creationism; Henry Holt and Company; 2000; New York, NY, 56-60,126-129
18. I. Tattersall, J. Schwartz; Extinct Humans; Westview Press; Boulder Colorado; 2001
19. John Noble Wilford's article in the Thursday April 6, 2005, entitled Fossil Called Missing Link From Sea to Land Animals—A Giant Fish's Forward Fins are Viewed as Limbs in the Making, describing the publications of a team led by Neil H. Shubin in Nature: Daeschler E. B., Shubin N. H., Jenkins F. A. Jr, Nature, 440. 757—763 (2006); Shubin N. H. Daeschler E. B., Jenkins F. A. Jr, Nature, 440. 764—771 (2006).
20. Kenneth Miller; Finding Darwin's God—A Scientist's Search for Common Ground Between God and Evolution; 1999, Cliff Street Books, Harper Collins; New York, NY, 40
21. Kenneth Miller; Finding Darwin's God—A Scientist's Search for Common Ground Between God and Evolution; 1999, Cliff Street Books, Harper Collins; New York, NY, 40
22. Ernst Mayr; What Evolution Is, Basic Books, New York, NY, 2001, 14-16
23. Kenneth Miller; Finding Darwin's God—A Scientist's Search for Common Ground Between God and Evolution; 1999, Cliff Street Books, Harper Collins; New York, NY, 40
24. Peter Andrews, John Barber, Michael Benton, Marianne Collins, Christine Janis, Ely Kish, Akio Morishima, J. John Sepkoski, Jr., Christopher Stringer, Jean-Paul Tibbles; The Book of Life—An Illustrated History of the Evolution of Life on Earth, general editor Stephen Jay Gould, W.W. Norton and Co., New York, NY,2001, Introduction by Stephen Jay Gould, 3
25. Kenneth Miller; Finding Darwin's God—A Scientist's Search for Common Ground Between God and Evolution; 1999, Cliff Street Books, Harper Collins; New York, NY, 47-48
26. Richard Dawkins; A Devil's Chaplain—Reflections on Hope, Lies, Science and Love, Houghton Mifflin, 2003, 20-22
27. Niles Eldredge; The Triumph of Evolution and the Failure of Creationism; Henry Holt and Company; 2000; New York, NY, 56-60, 71-86
28. Jeffrey H. Schwartz; Sudden Origins—Fossils, Genes and the Emergence of Species, John Wiley and Sons, New York, NY, 1999
29. I. Tattersall, J. Schwartz; Extinct Humans; Westview Press; Boulder Colorado; 2001
30. Richard Dawkin;, The Selfish Gene, Oxford University Press edition, Oxford, 1989 (first printing 1976)
31. Niles Eldredge; The Triumph of Evolution and the Failure of Creationism; Henry Holt and Company; 2000; New York, NY, 86
32. Kenneth Miller; Finding Darwin's God—A Scientist's Search for Common Ground Between God and Evolution; 1999, Cliff Street Books, Harper Collins; New York, NY, 48-51,103-107
33. Jonathan Weiner; The Beak of the Finch, Vintage Books, New York, 1994

34. Jonathan Weiner; The Beak of the Finch, Vintage Books, New York, 1994,89-96
35. Kenneth Miller; Finding Darwin's God—A Scientist's Search for Common Ground Between God and Evolution; 1999, Cliff Street Books, Harper Collins; New York, NY, 108-111
36. Jonathan Weiner; The Beak of the Finch, Vintage Books, New York, 1994,89-96
37. Jonathan Weiner; The Beak of the Finch, Vintage Books, New York, 1994,110
38. Jonathan Weiner; The Beak of the Finch, Vintage Books, New York, 1994,70-82
39. Jonathan Weiner; The Beak of the Finch, Vintage Books, New York, 1994,110
40. Richard Dawkins; The Blind Watchmaker—Why the Evidence of Evolution Reveals a Universe without Design, W W Norton and Company, New York, 1996
41. Carl Zimmer; Evolution—The Triumph of an Idea, HarperCollins Publishers, 2001, 74-78
42. Lynn Helena Caparole; Darwin in the Genome—Molecular Strategies in Biological Evolution, McGraw-Hill, New York, 2003, 19-25
43. Jeremy Cherfas; The Human Genome—A Beginner's Guide to the Code of Life, Doring Kindersly, London, 2002, 47-49
44. Blattner et al.; The Complete Genome of E. coli, Science 277 (Sept. 1997), 1453-1462
45. James D. Watson with Andrew Berry; DNA—The Secret of Life, Alfred A. Knopf, New York, 2003, 202-211
46. Ernst Mayr; What Evolution Is, Basic Books, New York, NY, 2001, 38-39
47. Thomas D. Schneider; Evolution of Biological Information, Nucleic Acids Research 2000, 28(14) 2794-2799
48. Jonathan Marks; What It Means to be 98% Chimpanzee,—Apes, People and Their Genes, University of California Press, Berkeley, CA, 2002, 9-10
49. Jonathan Marks; What It Means to be 98% Chimpanzee,—Apes, People and Their Genes, University of California Press, Berkeley, CA, 2002, 7-31
50. James D. Watson with Andrew Berry; DNA—The Secret of Life, Alfred A. Knopf, New York, 2003, 215
51. Jeremy Cherfas; The Human Genome—A Beginner's Guide to the Code of Life, Doring Kindersly, London, 2002, 47-53
52. Peter Andrews, John Barber, Michael Benton, Marianne Collins, Christine Janis, Ely Kish, Akio Morishima, J. John Sepkoski, Jr., Christopher Stringer, Jean-Paul Tibbles; The Book of Life—An Illustrated History of the Evolution of Life on Earth, general editor Stephen Jay Gould, W.W. Norton and Co., New York, NY,2001, 32-33
53. James D. Watson with Andrew Berry; DNA—The Secret of Life, Alfred A. Knopf, New York, 2003, 213-215
54. Ernst Mayr; What Evolution Is, Basic Books, New York, NY, 2001, 12-39
55. Ernst Mayr; What Evolution Is, Basic Books, New York, NY, 2001, 12-39
56. Ernst Mayr; What Evolution Is, Basic Books, New York, NY, 2001, 12-39
57. James D. Watson with Andrew Berry; DNA—The Secret of Life, Alfred A. Knopf, New York, 2003, 202-207
58. Donald T. Haynie; Biological Thermodynamics, Cambridge University press, Cambridge, UK, 50-72, 293-329

Appendix R.
Is God an Evolutionist?

Let's summarize our findings on the relationship between God and evolution.

Evolution as History—No Problem!

There has been a three and a half billion year fossil record of life on this planet, with chemical evidence of primitive life stretching back nearly four billion years. Although these traces of ancient life are fragmentary, God's knowledge of these events is complete. And no matter how many drawings you see that depict God as an old white guy making some young white guy in His image, there is no biblical reason to believe that *Homo sapiens* were the inevitable end product of evolution. God simply let the natural forces unfold in an uninhibited manner on Earth, yielding a species that was suitable to receive an eternal spirit. God let nature take its course and humans happened to happen, but we became man made in His image only when He took a keenly personal interest in us and gave us a spirit. *Therefore, God is an evolutionist with respect to the history of life. Further, the history of life on Earth shows no signs of being supernaturally constrained or guided to produce animals with a human form.* This perspective is offensive to those who believe that God had our specific bodily form in mind before time began based on verses like this. *Ephesians 1:3-6 Praise be to the God and Father of our Lord Jesus Christ, who has blessed us in the heavenly realms with every spiritual blessing in Christ. For he chose us in him before the creation of the world to be holy and blameless in his sight. In love he predestined us to be adopted as his sons through Jesus Christ, in accordance with his pleasure and will—to the praise of his glorious grace, which he has freely given us in the One he loves.* Do these verses imply predestination of the human body form or the supernatural meddling with the evolutionary process to produce animals like us? I doubt it. It certainly speaks of our spiritual union with Christ that was ordained before the foundations of the Earth were laid.

Evolution as Process—No Problem!

Evolution is the best scientific model for describing how the changes in the nature of life on Earth occurred. The mechanism of evolution poses no threat to our faith or our God because the Bible is silent concerning how God made anything. The Bible does not endorse or prohibit any process associated with the changes in the architecture of life. What makes us presume that God must incessantly and miraculously tinker with the universe in order to have an intimate interest in our lives, other than our presumptions about how God "should" behave Himself? The ability to create a universe in which life—including one particular species so remarkable that it still merits God's personal interest—could evolve on a small blue planet via natural processes should be considered as one of God's most brilliant achievements. *God has never revealed how He created life on Earth; therefore there is no biblical reason to believe that God did not let species appear via evolution.* He did not have to supernaturally tinker with this mechanism to ensure that evolution was moving along in the appropriate direction. And there's no need to add the silly disclaimer that God "guided" the process, which is no more than a final attempt to add a touch of the supernatural to an elegant natural process just to make you feel more secure. The ability of life to evolve is amazing; the God who created a universe in which it could happen is ingenious.

Philosophies That Some Folks Associate with Evolution Are a Problem

The naturalistic philosophies that some promote based on evolutionary science contradict the teachings of the Bible. God is not a malleable set of moral codes that can be used to validate a lifestyle. *I think that God does not subscribe to the amoral dogma of evolutionary philosophies that ride the coattails of evolutionary science.*

Theologies That Some Folks Link with Evolution Are an Even Bigger Problem

Worshipping the planet or anything on it is idolatry. Denying the existence of God is foolish. Attributing the Christian faith to the evolution of an over-imaginative brain is a clear denial of the empty tomb of Christ. The revelation of His Word and the mission of His Son cannot be summarily dismissed as legends simply because the atheistic scientists do not believe in God. *Perhaps God considers atheism that some associate with evolution to be symptomatic of a rejection of spiritual truth imparted to man, rather than a rigorous scientific finding.*

Appendix S. Golden Rules

Church Rules

Do not pretend that creationism is science.

Creationism should not be taught *as science* in home schools, private schools or public schools because it is not science. Although the different brands of creationism are perfectly viable *theologies* to discuss in churches or Sunday schools or Bible studies if one uses only the Bible to *deduce* our origins, they are not science. They do not offer a hypothesis that can be tested, they do not present reproducible data, and they offer no solid proof that well-documented scientific explanations of our origins—from the Big Bang to the age of the Earth to human evolution—are wrong.

Recognize that "teaching the controversy" in science class is a dishonest approach.

Intelligent Design proponents know that they cannot disprove Darwin's great idea, so their tactics have evolved (pardon the pun). Their new strategy that is alluring but deceitful; appeal to the American sense of fairness. Here's their ploy; let kids hear both sides of the Intelligent Design vs. Evolution battle in the science class of public schools and let them decide for themselves! It sounds great, but they fail to point out that *there is no controversy concerning the general principles of the evolution of life in the scientific community.* Although numerous details of the evolutionary process have yet to be ironed out, there is certainly a consensus in science that life evolved. This consensus is built on decades of evidence, not theology. The theory of evolution stands alongside the greatest scientific achievements of all time. So if you want to present the "controversy" concerning the religious, political, and social battles of evolutionist and creationists, present it where it belongs; a political science class, an American history class, a philosophy class, a religion class, or a Jerry Springer show. Save science class for science.

Hammer home the indisputable teachings of the Bible concerning creation that all Christians agree on.

No one, except cult leaders, can read the Bible and deny that God is the Creator, that it was His will to create everything, that creation declares His glory, that He is keenly aware of all life, that God's creation was very good, and that man was made in His image. You can teach all of this to even the youngest children without cluttering your lessons with half-baked pseudoscience.

Do not refute science in Sunday School.

The Bible is really thick and hardly anyone I know is familiar with its entire contents. Perhaps we, as Christians, should devote ourselves to the clear teachings of the Word of God rather than polluting Christian education with impotent refutations of complex biological, geologic, and cosmological processes.

Accept that acts of God can be natural.

The church should recognize that God has always had the authority to work through natural or supernatural means. There is no scriptural command for us to assume any mysterious event is supernatural, neither is there any reason to believe that God's universe cannot include random events, unguided phenomena, nasty bodily functions, chaos, mutations, or vicious animal behavior. It is a foolish mistake to take what may very well be the most wondrous expression of God's intelligence—that ability to create a universe with the innate ability to yield life on a planet like Earth—and to declare that only a disengaged god would dare to use such a slow and laborious technique. You are not as smart as God and He did not reveal the mechanisms of creation in the Bible; you have no business telling Him or anyone what types of physics He was "allowed" to use when He made stuff.

Do not concede the inspiration or accuracy of the scriptures to appease evolutionists.

Although you cannot extract scientific principles from the Bible, you shouldn't assume that it is completely barren of any divine revelation concerning our origins. You need not concede that the entirety of the first eleven chapters of Genesis, stretching from Adam to Abraham, is pure mythology that has no divine inspiration behind it. This book has made the case that even if one accepts all of the findings of science concerning our origins, one can still hold fast to the inspiration of scriptures and the actual existence of folks like Adam, Eve, Noah and Abraham.

Refute the spiritual errors of specific scientists rather than trying to reinvent science.

Although the church's pseudoscience misses the mark, there is a perfectly appropriate spiritual target to attack. There are truckloads of scientists who resent any and all things related to an intelligence higher than theirs, and your kids should be aware of it. Nevertheless, this does not mean that their scientific findings are wrong—just their spiritual insights. Scientists who overplay their hand and pontificate on the spiritual realm are fair game for a thorough repudiation. It is appropriate, necessary and easy to refute the atheistic and anti-Christian propaganda espoused by scientists, regardless of how brilliant they. Christians should be ready at all times to defend the faith against such attacks from any opponent.

School Rules

Do not attack faith in a science class.

Science can make its case about our origins without resorting to condescending remarks about faith, attacks on the integrity of the Bible, and attempts to invalidate the atoning work of Christ. When your children hear patronizing remarks about the sincerely stupid teachings of the Bible, exhort them to defend their faith. When your children hear patronizing remarks about the sincerely stupid teachings of the creationists, advise them that one need not defend unsubstantiated creationism in order to defend their faith.

Evolutionary history and the evolutionary process of change should be taught in science classes.

Evolution represents the state-of-the-art understanding of biology. You should have no reservation about your children learning about the different plants and animals that have inhabited out planet or how species have emerged or became extinct.

Creationist pseudo-science is a legitimate topic for classes discussing the historic viewpoints of our origins.

Creationism is a fair target in classes that survey our historical attempts to understand our origins. Students should be told, however, that throughout church history many Bible-believing Christians have not endorsed the literal interpretations of Genesis promoted by modern creationists. The conquest of creationism should be presented as proof that creationists, not the scriptures, are wrong.

Atheistic philosophies and religious convictions held by some proponents of evolution should not be presented as science.

Students should be told that not all scientists are ultra-liberal atheists, even though some very famous evolutionists are proud to hold such a title. The political, social, philosophical and religious convictions of scientists should not even be presented in science courses, let alone be touted as the only reasonable positions that an intelligent person can hold.

Talk is Cheap

Rather than try to sort these issues out, you may decide to keep your children in an evolution-free zone at school, home and church. Watch out; you may be inadvertently setting them up for failure. In my experience, it isn't the history or process of evolution that sends some Christian kids reeling in high school or college. The crisis occurs upon their sudden realization that so many so-called creationist facts that they have believed all of their lives are so demonstrably wrong and their understanding of science is so incredibly weak. This shouldn't be the case. There are many readily accessible books to help you understand science[1]; you should read some of them. If you don't have the time or the resources to do so, just talk with your kids about this stuff!

References
1. Appendix T

Appendix T.
Suggested Reading

Here are my favorite books that provide an understanding of the origins of the universe, life and man. There are some offensive remarks about faith in some of the science books, but if you have enough discernment to separate carrots from corn, then you should have no difficulty identifying and ignoring (or refuting) such comments.

1. The NIV Bible[1]

God's Word is the key to understanding God's nature, His role in creating the universe, and the spiritual nature of man.

2. Finding Darwin's God[2]

Kenneth Miller carefully refutes popular creationism, exposes the atheistic worldview that permeates some scientific literature, and presents an impassioned argument for the compatibility of the history and process of evolution with Christianity. Liberal theistic evolution at its finest!

3. The Meaning of Creation[3]

Conrad Myers outlines a persuasive theological argument for recognizing the literary patterns, rather than scientific or historical content, of Genesis One.

4. The Inflationary Universe [4]

Alan Guth provides an insightful first-hand account of understanding the inflationary expansion of the universe and the Big Bang event.

5. Rare Earth [5]

This book provides a magnificent overview of just how rare our planet and its animal life may be in the universe, even though microbial life may be very common.

6. The Book of Life [6]

This book is a magnificent illustrated overview of the evolution of life on Earth during the past four billion years presented by an impressive group of scientists.

7. DNA, The Secret of Life [7]

This golden anniversary review of the most famous molecule of heredity is presented by James Watson, one of the discoverers of its double-helical shape.

8. Unintelligent Design [8]

Mark Perakh methodically and patiently unravels and exposes the errors, illogical arguments, and questionable interpretations of Hebrew that underlie Intelligent Design. If you think that Intelligent Design is a great idea that is compatible and competitive with modern science, this book will be a real eye-opener!

9. Extinct Humans [9]

Tattersall and Schwartz present a compelling summary of the evolution of human species as reflected in the fossil record that includes a multitude of photographic images of human fossils.

10. The Seven Daughters of Eve [10]

Sykes provides a fascinating account of the genetic evidence of the living that points to our common ancestry in the past.

11. The Ancestor's Tale [11]

This is a great book, an adventure that begins with a search for the most recent common ancestor of living humans and races back over three billion years in search of the common ancestor of all life on Earth. Along the way we meet our closest and most recent ancestors, all of whom join us in the pursuit.

12. The Beak of the Finch [12]

Jonathan Weiner's Pulitzer Prize-wining account Peter and Mary Brant's study of the measurable evolution of finches in the wild over several decades illuminates the power of evolution, even in the short term.

13. The Triumph of Evolution and the Failure of Creationism [13]

An explanation of why evolution passes as science while creationism does not, as explained by Niles Eldredge, who (along with Stephen Jay Gould) proposed that bursts of evolution are followed by long periods of stability.

14. The Blind Watchmaker [14]

Skip over Richard Dawkins scathing remarks concerning faith and enjoy an excellent account of how evolution can produce the appearance of design.

15. Life's Origin [15]

J. William Schopf serves as the editor of this compilation of essays that explore avenues that may lead to an understanding of life's starting point.

16. The Story of the Solar System [16]

Mark Garlick has authored this concise and beautifully illustrated description of the Solar System and explanation of its origin.

17. Darwin in the Genome [17]

Lynn Helena Caprole presents a very readable account of how molecular-level genetic mutations fuel the fires of evolution.

18. Evolution, The Triumph of an Idea [18]

Carl Zimmer's thorough history of Darwin and Darwin's great idea is the companion volume to the PBS documentary on this topic, and Zimmer overtly separates his conclusions from spiritual convictions.

19. Darwin's Black Box [19]

No book makes a better case for Intelligent Design than this one.

It captured the complexity of life at the cellular level, and it also garnered the attention of both believers and scientists, who immediately began to embrace and refute it, respectively.

20. Tower of Babel [20]

Robert Pennock presents an incredibly well documented assessment of creationist history, agenda and teachings.

21. How Humans Evolved [21]

Boyd and Silk have drawn upon many fields of science to outline the evolution of human species in this comprehensive and well illustrated text.

22. When Science Meets Religion [22]

Need a break from the well-publicized antagonism between creationists and scientists? Ian Barbour's book tells scientists and believers how to get along without acting like the Hatfield's and McCoy's.

23. Mapping Human History [23]

This is a fascinating book that touches on our ancient ancestry and then plots the course of our ancestors' migrations during the last 100,000 years.

24. The Third Chimpanzee [24]

Jared Diamond presents a Pulitzer Prize-winning account of the evolution of the human animal, the similarities and distinctions we have with our closest relatives in the animal kingdom, and the means by which we rapidly changed from a big mammal to a world conqueror.

25. The Origin of Species [25]

Although this book is not exciting to read, it is historic and serves as a vivid testament to the genius and thoroughness of Darwin, and the power of his idea.

26. The Human Fossil Record, Volumes 1, 2 and 3 [26]

These three volumes are meant for the serious anthropologist, but I have found them to be a remarkable, and remarkably convincing, collection of descriptions of the major fossil finds in Africa, Europe and Asia that unveil the evolution of humans. They are also appropriate for dropping on the heads of those that insist there is no fossil evidence that humans evolved.

27. Evolution, The Remarkable History of a Scientific Theory [27]

This an extremely well written tale of the history of evolution from its inception until the present day, including the tumult it caused within science and religion.

28. The Elegant Universe, Superstrings, Hidden Dimensions and the Quest for the Ultimate Theory [28]

Brian Greene holds your hands as he walks you through special relativity, general relativity, quantum mechanics, and then string theory.

29. The Fabric of the Cosmos, Space, Time and the Texture of Reality [29]

Just when you thought you understood the universe from re-reading his prior book for four years, Brian Greene shows up again to guide you through time itself, a discussion of reality, and a look at what banged when the Big Bang banged.

30. A Short History of Nearly Everything [30]

What a nice book. Bill Bryson takes a stroll through the origin of the universe, Earth, life, humans, and civilization. This is a great book for reviewing our understanding of the origins of...nearly everything!

31. The Cosmic Landscape, String Theory and the Illusion of Intelligent Design [31]

A great book on recent advances in String Theory that show how the fine-tuning of our hospitable universe may be more mundane than miraculous! Our universe may be just one of an incredibly large number of universes that inhabit a vast multiverse, and we happen to be in one of the rare universes that has the attributes required for life to form and evolve.

References
1. The HOLY BIBLE, NEW INTERNATIONAL VERSION. Copyright © 1973, 1978, 1984 International Bible Society
2. Kenneth Miller; Finding Darwin's God—A Scientist's Search for Common Ground Between God and Evolution; 1999, Cliff Street Books, Harper Collins; New York, NY
3. Conrad Myers, The Meaning of Creation—Genesis and Modern Science, John Know Press, Atlanta, Georgia, 1984
4. Alan H. Guth, The Inflationary Universe—The Quest for a New Theory of Cosmic Origins, Helix Books, Perseus Books, Addison-Wesly, Reading MA, 1997
5. Peter D. Ward, Donald Brownlee, Rare Earth—Why Complex Life Is Uncommon in the Universe, Copernicus, Springer-Verlag New York, Inc., New York, NY, 2000
6. Peter Andrews, John Barber, Michael Benton, Marianne Collins, Christine Janis, Ely Kish, Akio Morishima, J. John Sepkoski, Jr., Christopher Stringer, Jean-Paul Tibbles, The Book of Life—An Illustrated History of the Evolution of Life on Earth, general editor Stephen Jay Gould, W.W. Norton and Co., New York, NY, 2001
7. James D. Watson with Andrew Berry, DNA—The Secret of Life, Alfred A. Knopf, New York, 2003
8. Mark Perakh, Unintelligent Design, Prometheus Books, Amherst New York, 2004
9. I. Tattersall, J. Schwartz; Extinct Humans; Westview Press; Boulder Colorado; 2001
10. B. Sykes; The Seven Daughters of Eve—The Science That Reveals Our Genetic History; Norton; New York, NY, 2002
11. Richard Dawkins, The Ancestor's Tale—A Pilgrimage to the Dawn of Evolution, Houghton Mifflin Company, Boston, MA, 2004
12. Jonathan Weiner, The Beak of the Finch, Vintage Books, New York, 1994
13. Niles Eldredge; The Triumph of Evolution and the Failure of Creationism; Henry Holt and Company; New York, NY, 2000
14. Richard Dawkins, The Blind Watchmaker—Why the Evidence of Evolution Reveals a Universe without Design, W W Norton and Company, New York, 1996
15. Life's Origin—The Beginnings of Biological Evolution, edited by J. William Schopf, University of California Press, Berkeley, California, 2002
16. Mark A. Garlick, The Story of the Solar System, Cambridge University Press, New York, 2002
17. Lynn Helena Caparole, Darwin in the Genome—Molecular Strategies in Biological Evolution, McGraw-Hill, New York, 2003
18. Carl Zimmer, Evolution—The Triumph of an Idea, HarperCollins Publishers, 2001
19. Michael J. Behe; Darwin's Black Box—The Biochemical Challenge to Evolution; Touchstone, New York, NY, 1996
20. Robert T. Pennock, Tower of Babel—The Evidence Against the New Creationism, MIT Press, Massachusetts Institute of Technology, 2000
21. Robert Boyd, Joan B. Silk, How Humans Evolved, 2nd Edition, W.W. Norton & Company, New York, 2000
22. I. Barbour; When Science Meets Religion, Enemies, Strangers or Partners; Harper Collins, 2000
23. Steve Olsen, Mapping Human History—Genes, Race and Our Common Origin, A Mariner Book, Houghton Miller, Boston, MA, 2002
24. Jared Diamond, The Third Chimpanzee—The Evolution and Future of the Human Animal, HarperPerennial, New York, NY, 1993
25. Charles Darwin; The Origin of Species—Complete and Fully Illustrated; Gramercy Books; New York, NY; 1998
26a. Jeffrey H. Schwartz, Ian Tattersall, The Human Fossil Record, Volume 1, Terminology and Craniodental Morphology of Genus Homo (Europe), Wiley-Liss, New York, NY, 2002; 26b. Jeffrey H. Schwartz, Ian Tattersall, The Human Fossil Record, Volume 2, Craniodental Morphology of Genus Homo (Africa and Asia), Wiley-Liss, New York, NY, 2003; 26c. Ralph L. Holloway, Douglas C. Broadfield, Michael S. Yuan, Jeffrey H. Schwartz, The Human Fossil Record, Volume 3, Brain Endocasts: The Paleoneurological Evidence, Wiley-Liss, New York, NY, 2004
27. Edward J. Larson, Evolution—The Remarkable History of a Scientific Theory, Modern Library, Random House Publishing, New York, 2004
28. Brian Greene, The Elegant Universe; Superstrings, Hidden Dimensions and the Quest for the Ultimate Theory, Vintage Books, New York, NY, March 2000
29. Brian Greene, The Fabric of the Cosmos—Space, Time and the Texture of Reality, Vintage Books, New York, NY, 2004
30. Bill Bryson, A Short History of Nearly Everything, Broadway Books, New York, NY, 2003
31. Leonard Susskind, The Cosmic Landscape—String Theory and the Illusion of Intelligent Design, Little, Brown and Company, New York, NY, 2006